W9-AXD-142

# Critical Issues in Fund Raising

## The NSFRE/Wiley Fund Development Series

*Beyond Fund Raising: New Strategies for Nonprofit Innovation and Investment*
by Kay Sprinkel Grace

*Critical Issues in Fund Raising* edited by Dwight F. Burlingame

*The Nonprofit Handbook, Second Edition: Fund Raising* by Tracy Connors

*Fund-Raising Cost Effectiveness: A Self-Assessment Workbook*
by James M. Greenfield

*The NSFRE Fund-Raising Dictionary* by National Society
of Fund Raising Executives

# CRITICAL ISSUES IN FUND RAISING

Edited by

**Dwight F. Burlingame, PhD, CFRE**

**JOHN WILEY & SONS, INC.**
New York • Chichester • Brisbane • Toronto • Singapore • Weinheim

This text is printed on acid-free paper.

Copyright © 1997 by John Wiley & Sons, Inc.

All rights reserved. Published simultaneously in Canada.

Reproduction or translation of any part of this work beyond
that permitted by Section 107 or 108 of the 1976 United
States Copyright Act without the permission of the copyright
owner is unlawful. Requests for permission or further
information should be addressed to the Permissions Department,
John Wiley & Sons, Inc., 605 Third Avenue, New York,
NY 10158-0012.

This publication is designed to provide accurate and authoritative
information in regard to the subject matter covered. It is sold
with the understanding that the publisher is not engaged in
rendering legal, accounting, or other professional services. If
legal advice or other expert assistance is required, the services
of a competent professional person should be sought.

*Library of Congress Cataloging-in-Publication Data:*

Critical issues in fund raising / edited by Dwight F. Burlingame.
     p.   cm. — (NSFRE/Wiley fund development series)
   Includes index.
   ISBN 0-471-17465-3 (cloth : alk. paper)
   1. Fund raising.   2. Nonprofit organizations—Finance.
I. Burlingame, Dwight.   II. Series.
HG177.C75   1997
658.15´224—dc21                    96-39628

Printed in the United States of America

10 9 8 7 6 5 4 3 2 1

## About the NSFRE/Wiley Fund Development Series

The NSFRE/Wiley Fund Development Series is intended to provide fund development professionals (and others interested in the not-for-profit sector) with top-quality publications that help advance philanthropy as voluntary action for the public good. Our goal is to provide practical, timely guidance and information on fund raising, charitable giving, and related subjects. NSFRE and Wiley each bring to this innovative collaboration unique and important resources that result in a whole greater than the sum of its parts.

## About the National Society of Fund Raising Executives

The NSFRE is a professional association of fund raising executives that advances philanthropy through its more than 16,000 members in 138 chapters throughout the United States, Canada, and Mexico. Through its advocacy, research, education, and certification programs, the Society fosters development and growth of fund raising professionals, works to advance philanthropy and volunteerism, and promotes high ethical standards in the fund raising profession.

## 1995–1996 NSFRE Publishing Advisory Council

B. Jeanne Williams, ACFRE, Chair
President, Forbes Health Foundation

Linda Chew, CFRE
President, Chew & Associates

Suzanne Hittman, CFRE
Seattle, WA

James A. Reid, CFRE
Principal Consultant, Philanthropic Resources Associates

G. Patrick Williams, ACFRE
President/CEO, Lourdes College Foundation

Patricia F. Lewis, CFRE
President/CEO, National Society of Fund Raising Executives

Marie A. Reed, EdD, CNAA
Vice President, Professional Advancement, National Society of Fund Raising Executives

# About the Editor

Dwight Burlingame is Director of Academic Programs and Research at the Indiana University Center on Philanthropy, Professor in the Graduate School, and Adjunct Professor of Philanthropic Studies and of Public and Environmental Affairs at Indiana University. Among the books he has written and edited are *Corporate Philanthropy at the Crossroads, The Responsibilities of Wealth,* and *Taking Fund Raising Seriously.*

# About the Contributors

**Helmut K. Anheier** is Associate Professor in the Department of Sociology at Rutgers University, Senior Research Associate at the Johns Hopkins University Institute for Policy Studies, and Visiting Associate Professor in Sociology at Johns Hopkins University. He is author of *The Third Sector: Comparative Studies of Nonprofit Organizations* and *The Emerging Sector*, and Editor of *Voluntas*.

**Margaret A. Duronio** is Director of Administrative Services in the Office of the Vice President of University Relations and Development at the University of Pittsburgh. Her most recent publication, co-authored with Eugene R. Tempel, is *Fund Raisers: Their Careers, Stories, Concerns, and Accomplishments.*

**Marilyn Fischer** is Assistant Professor in the Department of Philosophy at the University of Dayton and a member of NSFRE. Her most recent publication is "Philanthropy Injustice in Mill and Addams" in *Nonprofit and Voluntary Sector Quarterly*, 1995.

**James M. Greenfield** is a veteran fund-raising professional with 34 years experience as a development officer at three universities and five hospitals on both the east and west coasts and in between. Jim is author of three books and several articles on fund-raising practice, including *Fund-Raising Cost Effectiveness: A Self-Assessment Workbook.*

**Bruce R. Hopkins** is an attorney with Polsinelli, White, Vardeman, & Shalton in Kansas City. He is the series editor of *Wiley's Nonprofit Law, Finance, and Management Series*. A prolific writer on legal issues of nonprofits, fund raising and advocacy, among his most recent works is *The Legal Answer Book for Nonprofit Organizations.*

**Kathleen S. Kelly** is the Hurbert J. Bourgeois Research Professor in Communication and coordinator of the public relations sequence at the University of Southwestern Louisiana, Lafayette. She is the author of *Fund Raising and Public Relations: A Critical Analysis* (1991) and *Effective Fund-Raising Management* (1996).

**Michael O'Neill** is Director of the Institute for Nonprofit Organization Management and the Public Management Program at the University of San Francisco, where he also teaches. He is the author of several books and numerous articles on education and management topics including *The Third America.*

**Jon Pratt** is Executive Director and founder of the Minnesota Council of Nonprofits. He has written extensively on nonprofit issues, and among his more recent works is *Minnesota's Nonprofit Economy* (1995).

**Paul Pribbenow,** Dean for College Advancement at Wabash College, is currently working on a book about the moral meaning of professions in America. One of his most recent works is "Fund raising as Public Service: Renewing the Moral Meaning of the Profession" in *New Directions for Philanthropic Fundraising* (Winter, 1994).

**Paul G. Schervish** is Professor of Sociology and Director of the Social Welfare Research Institute at Boston College. A prolific writer, among his most recent works are *The Gospels of Wealth* and *The Modern Medicis*.

**Richard Steinberg** is Professor of Economics, Philanthropic Studies and Public Affairs at Indiana University/Purdue University at Indianapolis and a Visiting Scholar at Northwestern University. Dr. Steinberg co-authored *Economics for Nonprofit Managers* with Dennis R. Young (1995).

**Stefan Toepler** holds a graduate degree in business administration from the Department of Economics and Administrative Studies at the Free University Berlin in Germany, where he has also recently finished his doctoral dissertation on a comparative analysis of the U.S. and German foundation sectors.

**Lilya Wagner** is a Senior Fellow at the Indiana University Center on Philanthropy and former Vice President for Development and Corporate Membership at the National Association for Community Leadership. She is an author of several books and numerous articles on fund raising.

**Marjorie A. Winkler** is the Field Services Officer for Neighborhood Reinvestment Corporation and a longtime fund raiser and active member of NSFRE.

**Julian Wolpert** is the Henry G. Bryant Professor of Geography, Public Affairs and Urban Planning at the Woodrow Wilson School of Public and International Affairs, Princeton University, and is director of the Program in Urban and Regional Planning. He is the author of numerous articles on philanthropy, regional economies, and the nonprofit sector, including *Patterns of Generosity in America: Who's Holding the Safety Net?*.

**Dennis R. Young** is the former Governing Director of the Mandel Center for Nonprofit Organizations and Mandel Professor of Nonprofit Management at Case Western Reserve University. He is editor of the journal *Nonprofit Management and Leadership*, and author and editor of several books, including *Economics for Nonprofit Managers* (with Richard Steinberg) and *Corporate Philanthropy at the Crossroads* (with Dwight Burlingame).

# Contents

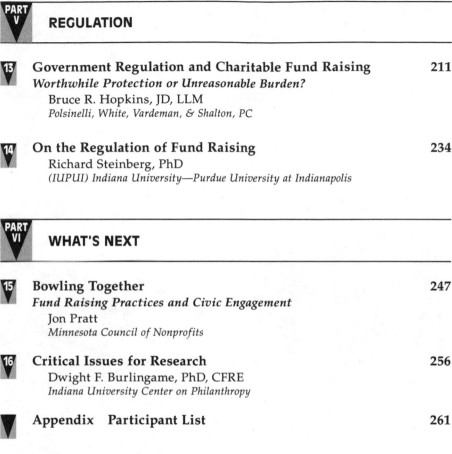

# Foreword

Is public policy a critical issue for a fund raiser? Yes, and I think of this from two perspectives: that of a fund raising practitioner and that of an advocate for the profession of fund raising.

First, the practitioner's perspective:

- "My board wants to raise $5 million for a new building. We're up to our ears in the annual campaign—designing the appeal letters, getting volunteers on board, planning the annual recognition dinner. My staff and funds have been cut. I have very little time or energy to devote to learning about what new laws or regulations are being considered."
- "What do you mean we have to state the fair market value of the event/item in our fund raising appeals . . . count pledges as revenue in the year the pledge is received . . . register with the state charity office in every state in which my organization solicits funds? How can we keep track of these new rules, let alone comply with them? We're already operating on a shoestring."
- "I see fund raising practices that seem to me to be unethical, if not unlawful. What can I do to assure my donors and perspective donors that my organization's fund raising practices are ethical? Is there any avenue that allows me to address the unethical practices of others?"
- "My not-for-profit is just getting started. We need to develop a donor base and/or seek grants or contracts to meet our operating expenses. Our costs are likely to be higher than normal during these start-up months/years, and our reported fund raising costs will be relatively high in proportion to programmatic expenditures. Will that affect our ability to raise funds?"

This is the reality. Fund raising executives are overworked, underinformed, and worried about whether they are in compliance with the myriad laws and regulations that affect their practice.

What can national organizations such as NSFRE do to assure that fund raisers are informed about public policies with which they must comply? Is it appropriate to require that our members take certain courses or pass certain tests to maintain their membership? Can we do anything to ensure that fund raisers who are not members of our association stay informed and act in compliance with relevant laws and regulations? Can the profession adequately regulate itself? Is licensing of fund raisers a good idea? If so, what group should be responsible for licensing—a governmental entity, a quasi-governmental entity, an elected or appointed body of practitioners?

What can we, academicians and practitioners, do to inform lawmakers and regulators about the implications of the policies they propose and enact? Is it appropriate for those of us who have a deep interest in the not-for-profit sector to try to develop consensus on policy issues and lobby for laws and regulations that benefit the sector? Is it wishful thinking to hope for such consensus when the sector represents such disparate interests and goals? These questions deserve attention and research to provide a statistical, objective basis for fair debate.

There is a very real need for comprehensive education and training programs to help develop basic understandings and a common language that fund raisers can use to communicate with each other—and with donors, policy makers, and the public. All who work as employees or volunteers in the not-for-profit sector should understand the rationale for the sector and have a basic knowledge of its history, as well as current laws and regulations that affect the sector. There should be commonly known and accepted standards of ethical professional practice. And there should be a common understanding of the meaning of these terms that define our practice: "Professional fund raiser" and "solicitor," for example, have different meanings in different state laws—a source of great confusion for those who must register to solicit funds in more than one state.

It also is imperative for not-for-profit organizations to work collaboratively to bring about effective public policies. Although some regulatory activity is appropriate to protect the public interest (e.g., disclosure and accountability requirements for not-for-profit fund raising), other regulatory requirements seem to be "paper tigers," increasing the paperwork burden for legitimate not-for-profits but having no effect on the fraudulent practices they were designed to curb. The not-for-profit community should help policy makers sort out the "good" policies from the "bad"—by providing information on the effects those policies have on giving behavior, fund raising costs, and service delivery.

It is probably wishful thinking to hope that the not-for-profit community could speak with one voice; but we can work to identify our common interests and build coalitions to inform and lobby policy makers to advance those interests. There is immense power and influence within the not-for-profit sector, and tremendous potential to have an impact on public policy—if we act together.

In the current political climate, funding cutbacks and increasing regulatory activity are the order of the day. There will be increasing competition for government and private dollars, and painful choices to make. Central to the debates that are occurring now, and will continue to occur, is the need for informed advocacy and decision making. Research—both basic and applied—will form the basis for these debates.

We need solid information on the impact of the not-for-profit sector on the economies of communities, states, and the nation. We need to know what effect the quid pro quo disclosure rules have on individual giving. We need facts about what it costs not-for-profits to comply with reporting requirements of the Internal Revenue Service such as IRS Form 990. It would be interesting to see an analysis of the potential impact of requiring all not-for-profit organizations to complete the 990; can research tell us whether requiring religious organizations to comply with IRS reporting requirements is an abrogation of the constitutional provision for separation of church and state? We need information about not-for-profits unrelated business income. How extensively do not-for-profits use unrelated business activities to produce revenue? Does this activity represent unfair competition with for-profits? What effect will payment in lieu of taxes (PILOT) programs have on exempt organizations? Are such programs taxes in disguise? We need a cost-benefit analysis of state charitable solicitation registration and reporting requirements. Do these requirements actually reduce fraudulent activity? At what cost to legitimate not-for-profit organizations?

We have a strong tradition of partnership between the not-for-profit sector and government in meeting societal needs. The sector, though small compared with government, contributes to our welfare by providing a wide variety of services and, perhaps more importantly, opportunities for innovation and reform. If we are to protect and enhance this important tradition, we must be able to validate the contributions the not-for-profit sector makes to society—as well as the limitations of this sector's capabilities. And we must be able to provide rationale for public policies such as the tax exemption for charitable organizations and income tax deductions for individuals' charitable donations.

If you are a researcher, I encourage you to consider studying the not-for-profit sector. If you are a practitioner, I urge you to discard preconceived notions and to investigate new findings about fund raising and the not-for-profit sector. And I charge all of us to provide policy makers with useful data to encourage informed decisions that will support and enhance our tradition of philanthropy and volunteerism.

This work addresses some of the issues the profession must discuss. It will help practitioners ask the right questions and, in some cases, begin to formulate the answers. The information in this book will assist the profession's leaders as they address issues related to regulation of the profession.

And of even greater importance, the book will help us all in our endeavor to increase donor trust—an essential ingredient in advancing philanthropy.

Patricia F. Lewis, CFRE
President and CEO
National Society of Fund Raising Executives

# Preface

The importance of fund raisers maintaining the trust of citizens as they raise money for charitable causes cannot be overemphasized. As the fund raising field continues to grow and particularly as the number of professional fund raisers grows to meet the needs of increased numbers of organizations seeking support for their missions, research to support and undergird the profession of fund raising is vital.

Research in fund raising has not kept pace with the explosive growth in practice. Thus, this work had its genesis in the recognition that a concerted effort was needed to begin to understand what has been done and what research is needed in the future.

The National Society of Fund Raising Executives (NSFRE) and in particular the Research Council of NSFRE and the Indiana University Center on Philanthropy took the lead with the participation of other professional associations, educational programs and centers, and other interested parties to hold a think tank that would bring researchers and practitioners together to share many common concerns about fund raising theory, principles, and practice. From their ideas, it is hoped that practitioners will find possibilities for enhancing their own work. It is hoped that researchers will find many additional questions that will compel them to action. And, it is fair to say that every participant at this think tank wanted to encourage practitioner/researcher iteration that would lead to accomplishing the premise that research needs to be informed by practice, and practice needs to be informed by research.

On June 1–3, 1995, the Think Tank on Fund-Raising Research was held at the Indiana University Center on Philanthropy in Indianapolis. In addition to NSFRE and the Indiana University Center on Philanthropy, the Council for Advancement and Support of Education (CASE) and the Association for Research on Nonprofit Organizations and Voluntary Action (ARNOVA) were cosponsors. Scholars and practitioners (see Appendix for a list of participants) presented papers and discussed the following issues:

Demographics of Giving
Financial and Management Issues
Factors Affecting Motivation of Donors
Impact of Government and Public Policy

Equity and Ethical Issues
International Fund Raising
The Fund-Raising Profession

At the end of the conference, many of the participants recognized that the often-cited gap between practitioner and researcher is misportrayed as a gulf. For in fact, most researchers in this field are themselves practitioners who have to seek funds, manage at least a small unit, and communicate with their constituents through reports, and the like. Practitioners for their part are almost always seeking and conducting some kind of informal data collection and research, engaging in reviewing research findings and reading the literature as they go about their practice.

The immediate challenges for raising more funds often leave practicing fund raisers with little time to ponder over serious questions about fund raising as a profession. However, such action is critical to the profession's growth and development. Research and the resultant findings are key ingredients in the lives of professional fund raisers. Thus, they must allocate time for reflection as they seek to address fundamental issues through the mission of the organization for which they raise funds.

## Overview

As was mentioned, the genesis of this work was a collection of papers commissioned for the Think Tank. The chapters build on the discussions held at the conference and represent a concerted effort to cover the critical issues facing fund raising today. Much progress has been made in the past decade, but each new research effort seems to create more uncharted scholarly territory. It is indeed an exciting time in the fund raising field.

The chapters in Part I focus on professionalization and management issues of fund raising. Paul Pribbenow introduces the notion of "professional formation" to the field of fund raising by pointing out that those who practice research in the field must be both teacher and "rhetor"—one who leads a public conversation—since both the conduct of and the study of fund raising are public practices and must be guided by moral principles as well as technical competence. In discussing the five contexts in which fund raisers operate—historical, organizational, social, professional, and personal—Pribbenow emphasizes the need for bringing honor, moral probity, and a sense of public responsibility to philanthropic fund raising.

Dennis Young examines research questions related to managing nonprofit resources from the perspective of the development of diverse types of support, strategic implications, and stewardship of economic resources. Helpful existing research is reviewed and new areas of research are suggested that will address current and future issues facing the field.

Part II provides an overview of the fund raising profession's social, ethical, and equity dimensions.

Margaret Duronio took an empirical approach to identifying the nature of fund raising and who practices it. Based on a random-selected sample survey of 1,748 members of major fund raising organizations and personal interviews of 82 respondents, Duronio provides a profile of the average fund raiser, including work history and longevity with his or her organization. The interviews provide background and attitudinal understandings about the fund raising profession. Duronio found the strong normative orientation that Pribbenow deems critical to the formation of the fund raising profession.

Noting that there is little if any research in the ethics of fund raising, Michael O'Neill suggests a number of research topics that will contribute to a theory of fund raising ethics. He cites the work of Carbone and Duronio as a beginning effort in this direction, but encourages further attention to the ethical dilemmas that fund raisers face and how they deal with them. Analysis and empirical research into such areas as the relationship of giving and culture, the perceptions of donors, codes of ethics, and ethical dimensions of potential donor research will further develop the fund raising profession.

Marilyn Fischer explores diversity and equity, first in a philosophical sense, and then as they relate to fund raising. She discusses research that implies that many ethnic groups appear less philanthropic than whites, if only formal donations and volunteering are considered. However, informal giving patterns may be the norm in many other cultures, and might be unseen if the researcher only focuses on the dominant culture definition of philanthropy. Perceptual inequities may exist in employment and pay in nonprofit organizations, while institutional inequities are often perpetuated by using personal connections for choosing volunteers and board members, and in hiring staff. Fischer urges the reader to reject the notion that some of us are diverse, while others are "normal"; she suggests that we must understand that all people are diverse in order to make progress on issues of inequity.

Part III examines the distribution of giving both in the United States and in Europe as well as what we know about donor motivation.

While INDEPENDENT SECTOR reports have provided insight into demographic profiles of those who give and volunteer, Wolpert asserts that relying solely on such data does not give a complete picture of donors. Cognitive and emotional factors and social context of solicitation also play a role that is not yet clearly defined. Wolpert suggests community studies as one way to complement demographic profiles, since donors with similar demographic characteristics do not give uniformly in different geographic locations.

Helmut Anheier and Stefan Toepler offer a broad look at the fundraising activity in several Western European countries. By comparing and contrasting American charitable giving practices to those in Germany, Great Britain, and France, the authors conclude that charitable giving traditions have existed in these countries for a long time. The practice of "fund raising" on the other hand has been quite different than in the United States. Government, religion, and other cultural factors play significantly different roles in raising money for charity. However, many U.S. fund raising strategies are being adapted for local European use.

Paul Schervish introduces the "identification" model rather than the "altruism" model as a more productive and logical way to understand why donors give to various causes. After reviewing what we have learned from the fund raising research to date, he presents the results of his empirical studies of donor motivation utilizing multivariate analysis. Studies of wealthy donors produced eight variables that affect motivation to donate; Schervish suggests these variables provide a conceptual framework to understand all giving. After a review of these factors, further studies are suggested that will advance the understanding of donor motivation.

According to Kathleen Kelly, it is important to recognize the differences between philanthropy and fund raising. Using theories of asymmetrical and symmetrical presuppositions in fund raising, Kelly asserts that symmetrical presuppositions assume that donors give for a complex mix of reasons—including the common good and self-interest. She concludes that fund raisers don't convince donors to give, but rather influence where they give their charitable gifts. Kelly urges researchers to adopt the notion that giving behavior is a social exchange and therefore must be studied in the context of two-way relationship, and not just from the donor's perspective.

Part IV explores models and measures of determining successful fund raising management.

Fund raising costs and their relationship to performance have been and continue to be significant issues facing the profession. James Greenfield notes that the current inconsistencies in reporting results of fund raising activities simply lead to confusion. He advocates applying specific performance measurements to each fund raising endeavor and suggests that over time the organizational history based on consistent performance criteria will be the best guide for future budget planning for fund raising. Greenfield's model employs nine specific performance measures that can be applied to each solicitation activity. Over time, the performance data become more mature, which increases the reliability in predicting continued gift support.

A classic guideline in fund raising has been the hierarchy of giving, which defines that the typical organization will raise 60 to 90 percent of its funds from 40 to 10 percent of the donors. Marjorie Winkler reviews the application of the classic fund raising formula to new and grassroots organizations and finds that it does not necessarily work. She cites differences between formula and nonformula organizations in many areas: environmental factors such as prosperity of geographic area, size of population, corporate and foundation funding bases, cultural diversity, ethnic values, and character of donor/client base. Her results from an eight-year study of nonformula organizations' fund raising efforts give practitioners and research much to debate and test in the field.

Lilya Wagner advises American fund raisers to be aware of cultural context when sharing fund raising expertise abroad. It seems almost trite to caution against making generalizations across cultures and national lines but the continued failure of heeding such advice is evident. History, language, heterogeneity of population, economic conditions, and religious beliefs all have powerful influences on attitudes toward philanthropy. Wagner explores common global themes and offers specific recommendations to those who counsel would-be fund raisers in international cultures.

Part V explores the much debated fund raising regulation by government. In his chapter, Bruce Hopkins criticizes the proliferation of state regulations on charitable fund raising by noting that evidence does not suggest the need for such increased control. Further, he sees little proof that regulation deters fund raising fraud and abuse, but rather puts undue financial burdens on the vast majority of legitimate charities. Hopkins suggests that both federal and state regulatory activity will continue to increase in the current political climate. Two pressing research priorities are evident: quantification of the extent of fraud and other abuse in fund raising; and identification and development of ways to measure the effectiveness of laws and regulations in deterring such practices.

Richard Steinberg asserts that the use of fund raising-cost ratios to measure efficacy of nonprofit organizations is not useful, and may, in fact, be harmful to some nonprofits. Regulation predicated on these ratios is often based on the notion that they will separate the "good" from the "bad" nonprofit organization, according to how great a percentage of the funds raised is spent on the costs of fund raising. The idea is to prevent fraud and abuse. Steinberg argues, however, that many worthwhile groups may have high cost ratios for a variety of other legitimate reasons. Problems with fraudulent activities may be best curbed in large part through enforcement of existing laws as well as donor education about the mission of the nonprofit.

Part VI concludes this book with a brief look at civic participation and how it translates into more support. It also includes a list of research questions generated by the participants of the conference through their discourse.

Playing off of Robert Putnam's article "Bowling Alone" and others who have joined in the debate about the decline in public life, Jon Pratt laments the increasing lack of personal involvement in nonprofit fund raising. Direct mail and telemarketing techniques have infused needed funds into some organizations, but in many cases the costs in lost personal contact with nonprofit organizations outweigh the benefits gained. Pratt argues for organizations actively encouraging public meetings, open board meetings, and cross-promotion of nonprofit events to help recreate engaged citizens who will volunteer, donate money, vote, and know their neighbors.

NSFRE has distributed a research agenda and policy on fund raising research since 1991. The critical issues concluding this work were used in revising and enhancing that agenda. It is hoped that they will also further discourse and research across the field by organizations, scholars, and practitioners.

DWIGHT F. BURLINGAME

*Indianapolis, Indiana*
*January 1997*

## Acknowledgments

Although too many people contributed to the success of this project to thank them all here, I want to convey special thanks to Joe Mixer and Cathlene Williams for all of their work on behalf of this effort; to Janet McIntyre for her assistance in editing; and to the funders—the National Society of Fund Raising Executives, the Council for Advancement and Support of Education, the Indiana University Center on Philanthropy, and an anonymous donor—for financial support. Finally, my thanks to Audrey Burlingame who always supports me in the extra hours it takes to get such projects completed.

# Professions and Nonprofits

# And We Will Teach Them How

## Professional Formation and Public Accountability

PAUL PRIBBENOW, PhD, CFRE
*Wabash College*

> *Needs which lack a language adequate to their expression do not simply pass out of speech: they may cease to be felt.*
> —Michael Ignatieff, *The Needs of Strangers*

> *So guide us in the work that we do, that we may not do it for self alone, but for the common good . . .*
> —*The Book of Common Prayer*

> *What we have loved, Others will love, and we will teach them how.*
> —William Wordsworth, *The Prelude*

The gathering of scholars and practitioners at the Indiana University Center on Philanthropy to explore the landscape of research in philanthropy and philanthropic fund raising has led to a deeper understanding of the rich complexities at the intersection between theory and practice. These complexities need to be viewed in the context of the "ambiguous ends" (Payton, 1988) of philanthropy in our society. This important perspective is a reminder that our work as scholars and practitioners in this field must not be viewed as the pursuit of some objective body of knowledge, to be posited once and for all. Rather, we are participants in the common work of encouraging imaginative and responsible reflection and discourse among scholars, practitioners, and citizens, about the social and moral ecology that characterizes the philanthropic sector in our democracy.

To promote such reflection and discourse, we must—as researchers in philanthropy and philanthropic fund raising—assume at least two crucial roles. First, we must accept the role of *teacher*. We must share the tenets of life-enabling education with professional colleagues and fellow citizens. Robert Bellah and associates have suggested that this life-enabling education would promote a "society with a healthy sense of the common good, with social morale and public spirit, and with a vivid memory of its own cultural past" (Bellah et al., 1991, p. 176).

Second, we must assume the role of *rhetor*. We must understand our responsibility, in the traditional sense of rhetor, as one who "leads a public conversation, appealing to traditional sources and contemporary inventions on behalf of shared purposes and goals" (Keifert, 1991, p. 131). As teachers and rhetors, we position ourselves in the places and contexts where public discourse and accountability must be promoted, challenged, nurtured—made a genuine part of our democracy.

In the context of these two important roles, the framework for this chapter will help make sense of two key, related objectives: (1) the need for all who are involved in philanthropic fund raising to seize the crucial role as teachers whose chief aim is to "form" professionals as persons who are reflective, responsible, skilled, and imaginative practitioners; and (2) our obligation as teachers and rhetors to position all professional work in the service of the public good; indeed, we have the responsibility to "form" professionals to be public servants, to be accountable to the needs, the goods, the processes that define a genuine and healthy participative democracy.

With those objectives in mind, this chapter is organized in three sections. First, I will consider professional formation, adapting a tradition of spiritual formation that is found in various religious communities. Second, I will argue that all genuine professions in our society arise in response to, and are accountable to, public practices that reflect values and commitments that our democracy has determined are central to its common life. Since philanthropy is one of those public practices, philanthropic fund raisers need to be formed and held accountable by the philanthropic values and traditions (in all of their complex and dynamic aspects) that have helped to define the American democracy. The final section focuses on five contexts or environments in which philanthropic fund raisers practice their craft, with suggestions for some concepts and tools that might be helpful in their work.

## Professional Formation and the Grace of Great Things

Parker Palmer, in a 1993 speech to the American Association for Higher Education, drew upon the German poet Rilke to propose that the community of knowing, teaching, and learning (of which we all are a part) is drawn and held together by "the grace of great things," by which he means not great as in "noble," but great as in "real" and "honest," great because "they reveal the world in its wonders and terrors and ordinariness . . ." (Palmer, 1993a, p. 6).

Palmer's vision of this community of learning is central to transforming professional education in our society. How will we ever move beyond what William F. May (1987) has called the "transactional" and ahistorical nature of professional work if we do not educate our professionals to see and live in a world that is not bounded by their own needs, by the limits of objective knowledge, by a culture focused on how to protect each individual's own interests rather than the wonder, the terror, even the ordinariness, of the human adventure?

In fact, one reason I have chosen to use the phrase "professional formation" instead of professional education is that professional education has come to be seen as such a limiting, technical, self-serving enterprise (Schön, 1983). Professional formation encompasses not just the technical expertise of the practitioner (as important as such expertise is to the responsibility we bear as professionals in society), but draws upon the "great things" that are available to professionals as they think about, offer perspectives, and take leadership roles as good citizens in the many contexts of practice.

Elsewhere, I have referred to this notion of professional formation as "vocational education," focusing attention on the motivations of, and a broader and deeper vision of the ends to be served in, professional work (Pribbenow, 1993). Here, I want to briefly develop some links between the tradition of spiritual formation and the demands of professional formation, which parallel the broader claims of vocational education for professionals.

In his *To Know as We Are Known: Education as a Spiritual Journey*, Parker Palmer (1993b) suggests that much of the educational process in our society is characterized by a deep separation between the knower and the known. This objectivist way of knowing is an integral (and he would say, unfortunate) part of the way professionals interact with clients, with each other, and with the wider society. We are taught that knowledge is out there to be grasped, that the rules are procedural, that our own perspectives and values should not encroach on the objects we are studying. In our professional work, we are responsible only to apply our expertise, to follow the rules, to get the job done.

Palmer argues that we must focus our attention instead on the normative, moral, and public aspects of knowledge and practice, and he would agree with Bruce Robbins (1993), when he says that good professional education is about the "business of producing individuals who hold ethical, epistemological, aesthetic and political beliefs, and whose attachment to their work is inextricable from those beliefs . . ." (p. 23). Palmer's (1993b) contention is that we will not achieve this more normative understanding of professional formation without helping to create the sort of discipline in professionals that readies them for a breakthrough of humility and faith. Reverence without idolatry, love, and grace can create an openness to understand and integrate the "grace of great things" into their professional knowledge and practice.

This discipline that Palmer suggests we adapt to help "form" members of the community of learning has four central aspects. First, it challenges us to be *imaginative and expansive* in our ways of learning about ourselves, about our work, and about our world. Professional education suffers because it exists fragmented from the liberal arts. We segment professional education, whether in the university or in other settings, from all the wonders, terrors, and ordinariness illustrated by other disciplines of thought and study, by other traditions of culture and religion, by other ways of practicing a profession.

How can we integrate this imaginative, expansive vision of life and human experience in the education of professionals? One way I have pursued this broader understanding of professional education is to use Maya Angelou's poem, *On the Pulse of the Morning* (1993), written for the inauguration of President Bill Clinton, as a pedagogical tool to set the broader cultural and historical context for practicing fund raising or management. At the beginning of my courses on philanthropy and ethics, Angelou's haunting words offer students an opportunity to reflect that:

> History, despite its wrenching pain,
> Cannot be unlived, but if faced
> With courage, need not be lived again. (p. 7)

I can imagine no more important lesson about the American society in which philanthropy has played such a remarkable role.

Second, the discipline of professional formation challenges us to understand the *need for silence and contemplation* as a way of freeing our weary minds to receive the humbling truths found in our everyday lives. In his wonderful book, *The Active Life* (1990), Palmer tells his own story of coming to grasp how activity and contemplation must be integrated in our lives if we are to be responsible practitioners of any craft in the world. We all know how difficult it is to be quiet, but without the silence, we will not know the voices of truth that come from unexpected places and persons.

How can we make silence a genuine part of forming professionals? I have recently adapted the Quaker communal understanding of clearness committees as a tool for helping staff members in the workplace seek answers to professional and management issues through a supportive process of inquiry and reflection (Farnham et al., 1991). These so-called management clearness committees are ways of modeling the role of silence in the workplace as they help individuals realize that answers and resolutions do not always come from someone else, imposed on or provided for us. Instead, the answers may be within, to be sought and discovered in a reflective process.

Third, the discipline of professional formation presents a challenge to understand the role of *solitude,* of being alone, detached from normal routines, reliances, and roles. As Palmer (1993b) says, "If silence gives us knowledge of the world, solitude gives us knowledge of ourselves" (p. 121). In solitude, we discover and can respond to the self-deception and distortion that are so much a part of life in our culture. We all have some sense of how easy it is to deceive ourselves with some notion of our personal power or knowledge or expertise.

How can we make the humility of solitude a part of how we form professionals? I am struck by how "retreats" have become mere extensions of the workplace, to be used as intensive time to get the planning done or to resolve big office problems. What would it mean to see retreats in the traditional sense of opportunities to be detached from routines and roles, to be apart from the normal so as to seek a clearer understanding of ourselves and our work? It certainly would mean making space for the pursuit of what Lee Bolman and Terry Deal (1995) have called the "ancient spiritual basics—reclaiming the enduring human capacity that gives our lives passion and purpose" (p. 6).

It is crucial that these challenges of silence and solitude not be seen as contradictory to the important role of community in learning and formation proposed earlier. It is a fascinating (and very difficult to grasp) paradox that only in silence and solitude do we learn the genuine nature of community. The monastics who first defined the notion of spiritual discipline understood this paradox so well, and the durable forms of religious community they formed stand as the best example of how professional communities might be strengthened and enhanced if this discipline were made a part of professional education and formation.

Finally, the discipline of professional formation also challenges us to *find a place in our lives for some form of prayer.* This final challenge might step over the boundary for some professionals. We certainly can grasp the imagination and expansion of knowing. We might even be intrigued by the importance of seeking silence and solitude as part of the professional experience. But prayer? This decidedly religious practice is not without its crucial role in the formation of professionals. We live, we practice our craft, we seek to know and to serve, in a world that is broken and fragmented. We have lost touch with the deeper meaning of our work, of relationships with one another, of our place in the social ecology that genuinely characterizes humankind (Bellah, et al., 1985). I know this from my own experience as a professional, and from my friends and colleagues who share its implications and consequences with me every day. For me, prayer is a metaphor for admitting that I do not understand all that is happening around me, for giving up the prideful knowledge, "with which we divide and conquer and destroy the world" (Palmer, 1993b, 125). Prayer is the form that knowledge takes when I have taken responsibility for the fact that I cannot solve every problem, I cannot understand every situation. Prayer signifies my reconnection in a faithful relationship with all of life, through which my service as a professional is focused on its true end— through which I profess faith in something larger and wiser than my own powers (Palmer, 1990).

The idea of "formation" has a long history in education for the ministry. It reflects the process of self-reflection and dialogue with colleagues and the wider community about the meaning of our work, our call to serve, our vocation. This notion of professional formation, and the disciplines that might help to inform it, is certainly alien to professional education in contemporary America. (In fact, even our theological seminaries do not necessarily spend much time on spiritual formation of future clergypersons.) The time seems right, however, to transform our understanding of professional education along these lines because professionals have such important work to do. Our society desperately needs role models and leaders, not just for applying technical expertise and knowledge to social problems, but even more so for patterning a way of knowing, seeing, and living in the world that illustrates what it means to participate in the humane, graceful adventure of our common life.

## The Public Practices That Define Professional Work

The importance of professional formation thus is linked to the crucial role professionals play in defining, serving, and negotiating our common life as a society. How shall we understand this link between the public good and the professions?

Robert Bellah and William Sullivan (1987) offer a helpful framework for thinking about how all professional work is genuinely a form of public service. The professions in modern society have come to be viewed primarily as a market commodity, part of the capitalist economy to be sold to the highest bidder. Professional knowledge, expertise, training, status, and so forth, all become part of the package in pursuit of greater income and prestige. In the early twentieth century, the traditional role of the inherited professions (medicine, law and the clergy), and their claims to particular moral and political expertise, became difficult to sustain, and to deal with this difficulty, the professions turned to an increasingly scientific and technological understanding of professional work (Bellah & Sullivan, 1987). The first professional fund raisers joined in this move as they sought to define their profession (Cutlip, 1965).

Bellah and Sullivan (1987) contend that to conceive the professions in relation to public purposes, we must be able to conceive society in relation to the "moral bonds of trust, loyalty and mutual concern without which contracts, laws, and even economic exchanges threaten to turn into covert piracy and warfare" (p. 11). To promote a model of professionals as servants of the public good, we must also promote an understanding of the public that believes (and acts as if) it has a good in common.

This link between the professions and responsible citizenship is the key to understanding how we can sustain the notion that professions are forms of public service. Bellah and Sullivan (1987) define the link between the professions and responsible citizenship through the concept of "public practices," by which they mean the activities that help a society to define itself, affirm its common end, and promote its life (p. 16). Public practices help to sustain health, justice, welfare, education, and other public goods that undergird our common life. These practices are good in and of themselves, and are not dependent on the external goods that accrue to them. For example, the promotion of public sanitation is a public practice. It is a good thing to do, most of us would say. Though someone who promotes public sanitation might well be paid for that work and might receive some acclaim for a job well done, those external rewards do not define the practice. It is recognized as good because it serves the common good.

Professions have evolved around public practices. Social work developed as a response to the needs of the poor and troubled. The medical profession seeks to promote health. The legal profession pursues justice. Teachers serve to educate our young people. Fund raisers help support the important work of voluntary associations in our society by nurturing and sustaining philanthropy. These important objectives remain a central part of the work of these professions. The obstacles that our society puts in the way of professions pursuing these public goals have certainly deterred them from these public practices, but they are still present in the history and contemporary unfolding of their work. In helping professions and professionals reclaim these public practices as central to their work, we also help them to be better, more effective, more responsible citizens of the national community. In their public service, the professions become "important agents in promoting citizenship as participation in the practices of common life" (Jennings et al., 1987, p. 10).

Here, the professions and individual professionals are challenged to give up their narrow claims to serve public interest, and instead, are urged to reclaim their historic and valuable role as servants of the public good. As professionals live out the public practices that define and give meaning to their work, they help to model an understanding of our common life that challenges the status quo and helps to create public frameworks for addressing and resolving public problems. Such work is the proper and responsible purpose of professions in the United States, and it is the purpose that we must form professionals to grasp and celebrate and live out in their work.

## Forming Fund Raisers to Promote the Public Practice of Philanthropy

To draw together the concepts of professional formation and public practices, I will illustrate some of the ways that we must form professional fund raisers if they are to serve the public practice of philanthropy in our democracy.

There are obvious differences between the fund raising profession and other more traditional professions in our culture regarding the formation of professionals. The fund raising profession does not have the systematized professional education through which other professions mandate a core curriculum, an accepted body of knowledge and skills, and the pursuit of professional formation. Though the number of graduate degree programs in philanthropy and fund raising have grown during the past decade, there is still little consensus about the value and utility of formal professional training for fund raisers (Buchanan, 1993). Professional socialization and formation are left to less structured and often less rigorous professional development programs (like those offered by the professional associations) and to the mentor relationships between senior fund raisers and those in their charge. The process by which "new" professionals are socialized into the profession—the means by which they acquire the values and attitudes, and learn the culture, of fund raising—is left to senior professionals, who have their own differing opinions about the motivations, priorities, and purposes of fund raising (Carbone, 1989).

The potential for genuine professional formation for fund raisers both concerns and excites me. My concerns are obvious. Without the widespread system of professional education leading through universities, what is to provide the standards, the processes, the momentum for progress in more substantial and responsible understandings of the practice of fund raising? How can we rely on senior professionals to both grasp and practice this obligation to "form" their junior colleagues? I am reminded nearly every day that my way of seeing my responsibilities to serve as a mentor and teacher to aspiring fund raising professionals is not widely shared among my senior colleagues. Despite the growing concern about research and education for the fund raising profession, as shown by the Indiana University conference, our short- and intermediate-term problems remain. We must rely on senior professionals, on less formal professional development programs, on the limited contexts for more formal professional education (degree and nondegree) to retain the focus on professional formation for fund raisers. And wherever possible, teachers and researchers must build in a challenge to senior professionals, to the professional associations, and to more and more educational institutions, to seize their role as teachers and mentors of a group of professionals who are crucial to the philanthropic well-being of our society.

On the other hand, because notions of professional education for fund raisers, are not yet reified, an extraordinary opportunity exists to shape that education for the normative, moral, and public roles fund raising professionals must play in our society, as well as for the process and substance of professional formation necessary to make such a vision of the profession real. I am motivated in my work by the possibility that my teaching (and that of my many colleagues who share this vision) might shape a generation of professionals who see themselves as public servants.

The following subsections illustrate how professional fund raisers can be formed to bring the perspective, the language, the metaphors, the technical and moral skills, needed to serve the public practice of philanthropy in five different contexts of our society—historical, social, organizational, professional, and personal.

## THE HISTORICAL CONTEXT

The *historical context of fund raisers' work* is a serious concern. Apart from the fact that most fund raisers have not read Kathleen McCarthy (1982) or Louise Knight (1992) or Scott Cutlip (1965) or Robert Bremner (1988), they simply do not think about how their work in the philanthropic community fits historically into a larger and longer and richer tradition of giving and receiving. In teaching, I focus on the trends and concepts we learn from the history of American philanthropy, and how much of what we do today reflects a historical trend. This is a liberating thought: I am not alone. I am part of the cloud of witnesses who have shaped and manipulated and celebrated and tainted and made real the wonder and terror and ordinariness of philanthropic activity in our democracy. I love the calendar of philanthropic events in Robert Bremner's *American Philanthropy*. I am struck by Louise Knight's exploration of Jane Addams's notion of "humane philanthropy." I revel in studying philanthropy at the turn of the twentieth century in Chicago, and in discovering what it teaches me about the themes and dynamics of my work in Chicago on the brink of the turn of the millennium. Mary Ann Glendon (1991), the Harvard law professor, reminds us of the "indigenous resources" that are part of our country's history, and how valuable they are in informing our ways of seeing and responding in the world today. How are practitioners promoting this historical context among young fund raisers? A quick look at the major books on fund raising over the past decade reveals little by way of an exploration of this history. How can fund raisers understand their place in this grand tradition if our emerging professionals to not learn to celebrate and know these valuable indigenous and common resources?

## THE SOCIOCULTURAL CONTEXT

The second environment fund raising professionals need to understand as central to their work is *the wider public or sociocultural* context. In addition to the need to see professional work as a form of public service, fund raisers have a special obligation to be aware of and active in the various dynamics of public life. Philanthropy is lived out, for better or for worse, in public, and the trends that have an impact on that public, including economic, political, cultural, and religious issues, are of great significance to our roles as good citizens and as effective, responsible professionals. One salient example will make my point. In my role as president of the National Society of Fund Raising Executives, Chicago Chapter, I have become more and more aware of the many governmental and legislative initiatives that affect the work I do and the public sector in which philanthropy is practiced (Bush, 1991). It is my good fortune to have several experienced and committed volunteers at work on governmental relations issues, who do a fine job of keeping me abreast of pressing issues and trends. At the same time, as I have been exposed to these tax and regulatory issues that bear on our work, I also have been struck by how otherwise talented and successful colleagues completely turn off when government relations issues come up for discussion. They don't understand, they're not interested in understanding, and there it stops.

This is a troubling situation. If even senior colleagues will not investigate and participate in advocacy about these crucial issues to society and our profession, what can be the likely response of the next generation of fund raisers who will not have been taught to "pay attention," as Robert Bellah and his associates describe it in *The Good Society* (1991). By allowing ourselves to be distracted, and to institutionalize that distraction in our profession and in our attitudes toward our role in society, we give up control over trends and actions that define the context in which we practice. As Bellah (1991) says, ". . . we bear a special responsibility to bring whatever insights we have to the common discussion of new problems, not because we have any superior wisdom but because we can be . . . ambassadors of trust in a fearful world" (p. 286). If we don't pay attention, we shirk this responsibility to participate in our common life and to be citizens who help others to trust that ours can be a good society.

## THE ORGANIZATIONAL ENVIRONMENT

The context of the *organizational environment in which fund raisers practice* is difficult and perplexing. On the one hand, fund raisers owe great allegiance to their organizations. The fund raiser is to believe in the organization's mission, work in its best interests, help to make it successful. The organization pays the fund raiser to do so—here is that wonderful rub between professions as callings to public service and professions as careers that enable practitioners to earn a living. At the same time, organizations can become very confining and limiting contexts for such work. We must teach emerging professionals to view the organizations in which they work as subcommunities of a larger moral community. They must see the educational or cultural or social service mission of their organizations as part of a wider social ecology that serves the public good. They practice their craft in that subcommunity, which is a crucial context for their work, but they serve a common good that transcends the work of their organization, that may even occasionally be in conflict with their organization's values and work (Camenisch, 1983). This is a tough lesson for some of my senior colleagues to integrate into their own practice. How are we to serve the public practice of philanthropy when we are held so accountable for the needs of our own organizations?

To broaden understanding of how the commitment to the public good serves us all, I often use the challenging notion of the distinction between a world marked by the metaphor of scarcity and one marked by the metaphor of abundance. We know the story. There is never enough money, enough time, enough people. This vision of scarcity has concrete implications for life in organization. It leads the participants to guard their territory, their lists, their people, their prospects, their good ideas. As an alternative to this scarcity vision, consider the notion that we are a people best marked by the metaphor of abundance. There are concrete ways to make our lives more abundant. Some of those ways simply involve better management skills: We can set better priorities; we can work together, collaborate; we can ask for help; we can pool our skills and imagination to look for new solutions; we can take risks. But more than these management techniques, this approach primarily involves a different way of looking at the world that we would do well to instill in our staffs, boards, colleagues in the profession, and fellow citizens, because it does not permit wallowing in the self-made scarcity of a world that we have hardly begun to know and trust.

## THE PROFESSIONAL COMMUNITY

The fourth context for philanthropic fund raisers is the *professional community* we belong to as a result of our commitment to the values and goods of philanthropy in our democracy. It says so right there in the NSFRE and CASE codes of professional ethics and standards of practice we agree to on the membership forms. I have great respect for the hard work and the rigorous process that underlie these codes, but in my work on the sociology of professions, I have been struck by the clash between ideal and real in these professional codes across the spectrum of professions in our culture.

The challenge the professional community presents to fund raisers is not about codes and self-regulation; it is about the responsibility we bear to recover and renew the public practice of philanthropy in our society. The philanthropic community is out of balance, and we must shoulder some considerable responsibility for that fact. We have allowed ourselves to be placed in the role of philanthropic expert in this society, and we have taken over more and more of the tasks and responsibilities that need to be shared among all participants in the philanthropic process and national community.

Think about the state of boards of directors and trustees, about the role of volunteers, about the relationships between foundations, corporations, and nonprofits, about the involvement of program staff in fund raising for our organizations, about the donors and their rights, about the recipients of philanthropic giving and their voice in the process. All of these players, along with the many citizens of the commonwealth who are seriously uninformed about the public practice of philanthropy, need leadership and service in pursuit of a healthy, vital, just philanthropic process. Our professional associations need to focus their attention on these various participants in the process, these other members of the community, and how we can help to make the philanthropic community a vital, healthy context in which all participants have a voice at the table. Our needs as professionals only make sense, only are responsibly met, when we have kept our eyes on the wider community we are here to serve.

## THE PERSONAL CONTEXT

One of my favorite exercises in teaching about the *personal context of* philanthropy is to ask fund raisers (and others) to reflect on the influences that shaped their own understanding of this profession. It is remarkable to see the links they are able to make, both for good and for not so good, in drawing these influences into their way of seeing their work. I recently asked myself this question—my answer provides a clue to why I am here, why I care about the things I do, and how I hope to continue to bring whatever ideas and practices and tools I can to this effort to "form" our profession and to define its role as a public service.

My earliest memories of philanthropic activity begin early on a Saturday morning some 23 or 24 years ago, when my father, a Lutheran minister, and I hopped into a borrowed pickup truck to commence a day of work on behalf of the Church World Service's CROP program. Though most of you probably know CROP today through its annual "walks," in rural areas 20 years ago, CROP sponsored a number of different programs, including the grain contribution effort we helped with that day.

For eight or nine hours that Saturday, my dad and I drove from farm to farm in our southern Wisconsin community gathering contributions of grain from generous farmers. When our pickup was full, we would drive to a local grain elevator to unload. At the end of the day, our various contributions were totaled by the grain elevator operator and the contributed grain was transported to a Church World Service barge or flatbed, ultimately ending up in Africa or Asia as part of U.S. efforts to alleviate world hunger.

On that Saturday, my dad and I were grain-gatherers. Along with the grain-givers (the farmers), the grain storers and counters (the grain elevator operator), the grain brokers (Church World Service), and the grain recipients (the hungry of the world), we participated in a philanthropic community where each member did his or her part, helping to relieve a need, building a healthier world.

It is a simple picture of a complex set of dynamics. It is, however, a picture that defines who I am and what I care about in my work. I was called to become a grain-gatherer. I live out that vocation every day in my professional life. From my early experience, however, I know well that my work makes no sense outside the community of grain-givers, brokers, and recipients, who share my commitment to a more humane and responsible world.

I have great trust in the philanthropic community, of which my work as a professional fund raiser is such an important part. I believe that I have a pressing responsibility to ensure that the philanthropic community, with all of its constituent parts, continues to reflect the best traditions and values of a democratic society.

The professions dominate our lives. They heal our bodies, measure our profits, save our souls, raise our money. At the same time, there is great ambiguity in our society about professionals. They often are viewed as elitists, using their expert knowledge to manipulate others and serve only their personal interests. The juxtaposition of the important role of professions and our ambiguous feelings about them corresponds to the ways in which professionals themselves have lost contact with the meaning of their work. The traditions of service, of stewardship, of being called to pursue some deeply held vision and commitment—traditions that are part of the American cultural heritage—have been lost.

These crises of professionalism—the ambiguous role of professions in society and the related issue of how professionals understand the moral and public nature of their work—need to be faced and addressed by the professions and by those of us who care deeply about the public practices those professions are formed to promote and serve. They need to be addressed by all of us, from our personal perspectives and as a community of learning that believes in the grace of great things.

What we have loved, others will love, and we will teach them how.

## Bibliography

Abbott, Andrew. *The System of Professions: An Essay on the Division of Expert Labor.* Chicago: University of Chicago Press, 1988.

Angelou, Maya. *On the Pulse of the Morning.* New York: Random House, 1993.

Bellah, Robert N., and Sullivan, William M. "The Professions and the Common Good: Vocation/Profession/Career." *Religion and Intellectual Life,* 1987, IV:3, 7–20.

Bellah, Robert N., Madsen, Richard, Sullivan, William M., Swidler, Ann, and Tipton, Stephen M. *Habits of the Heart: Individualism and Commitment in American Life.* Berkeley: University of California Press, 1985.

Bellah, Robert N., Madsen, Richard, Sullivan, William M., Swidler, Ann, and Tipton, Stephen M. *The Good Society.* New York: Alfred A. Knopf, 1991.

Block, Peter. *Stewardship: Choosing Service over Self-Interest.* San Francisco: Berrett-Koehler, 1993.

Bloland, Harland G., and Bornstein, Rita. "Fundraising in Transition: Strategies for Professionalization." In *Taking Fundraising Seriously.* Eds. D. Burlingame and L. Hulse. San Francisco: Jossey-Bass, 1991, 103–123.

Bolman, Lee G., and Deal, Terrence D. *Leading with Soul: An Uncommon Journey of the Spirit.* San Francisco: Jossey-Bass, 1995.

Bremner, Robert. *American Philanthropy.* 2nd ed. Chicago: University of Chicago Press, 1988.

Brint, Steven. *In an Age of Experts: The Changing Role of Professionals in Politics and Public Life.* Princeton, NJ: Princeton University Press, 1994.

Buchanan, Peter McE. "Educational Fundraising as a Profession." In *Educational Fundraising: Principles and Practices.* Ed. Michael J. Worth.

Phoenix, AZ: American Council on Education and The Oryx Press, 1993, 368–379.

Bush, Betsy Hills. "What Fund Raisers Should Know about the Law." In *Taking Fundraising Seriously*. Eds. D. Burlingame and L. Hulse. San Francisco: Jossey-Bass, 1991. 200–218.

Camenisch, Paul. *Grounding Professional Ethics in a Pluralistic Society*. New York: Haven, 1983.

Carbone, Robert. *Fundraising as a Profession*. College Park, MD: Clearinghouse for Research on Fundraising, 1989.

Cutlip, Scott M. *Fundraising in the United States: Its Role in America's Philanthropy*. New Brunswick, NJ: Rutgers University Press, 1965.

Cutlip, Scott M. "Fundraising in the United States." *Society*, March/April, 1990, 59–62.

Elshtain, Jean Bethke. *Democracy on Trial*. New York: Basic Books, 1995.

Farnham, Suzanne G., Gill, Joseph, McLean, R. Taylor, and Ward, Susan M. *Listening Hearts*. Rev. ed. Harrisburg, PA: Morehouse, 1991.

Freidson, Eliot. *Professional Powers: A Study of the Institutionalization of Formal Knowledge*. Chicago: University of Chicago Press, 1986.

Glendon, Mary Ann. *Rights Talk: The Impoverishment of Political Discourse*. New York: Free Press, 1991.

Gustafson, James M. "Professions as 'Callings.'" *Social Service Review*, 1982, 56, 503–515.

Hall, Douglas John. *The Steward: A Biblical Symbol Comes of Age*. 1st ed. New York: Friendship Press, 1982.

Hatch, Nathan, ed. *The Professions in American History*. Notre Dame: University of Notre Dame Press, 1988.

Howe, Elizabeth. "Public Professions and the Private Model of Professionalism." *Social Work*, 1980, 25, no. 5, 179–191.

Ignatieff, Michael. *The Needs of Strangers: An Essay on Solidarity and the Politics of Being Human*. New York: Penguin Press, 1986.

INDEPENDENT SECTOR. *Ethics and the Nation's Voluntary and Philanthropic Community: Obedience to the Unenforceable*. Washington, DC: INDEPENDENT SECTOR, 1991.

Jennings, Bruce, Callahan, Daniel, and Wolf, Susan M. "The Professions: Public Interest and Common Good." *The Hastings Center Report*. Feb. 1987, 3–10.

Josephson, Michael. *Ethics in Grantmaking and Grantseeking*. Marina del Rey, CA: Josephson Institute, 1992.

Keifert, Patrick R. *Welcoming the Stranger: A Public Theology of Worship and Evangelism*. Minneapolis: Fortress Press, 1991.

Knight, Louise W., "Jane Addams' Views on the Responsibilities of Wealth," In *The Responsibilities of Wealth*. Ed. D. Burlingame. Bloomington and Indianapolis, IN: Indiana University Press, 1992, 118–137.

Marty, Martin E. "Social Service: Godly and Godless." *Social Service Review*, Dec. 1980, 479–495.

May, William F. "Adversarialism in America and the Professions." *Soundings,* 69:1-2 (Spring-Summer), 1987, 79–98.

May, William F. "Code, Covenant, Contract, or Philanthropy." *The Hastings Center Report.* Dec. 1975, 29–38.

McCann, Dennis P. "The Good to Be Pursued in Common." In *The Common Good and U.S. Capitalism.* Eds. O. F. Williams and J. W. Houck. Lanham, MD: University Press. 158–178.

McCarthy, Kathleen D. *Noblesse Oblige: Charity and Cultural Philanthropy in Chicago, 1849–1929.* Chicago: University of Chicago Press, 1982.

McCollough, Thomas E. *The Moral Imagination and Public Life: Raising the Ethical Question.* Chatham, NJ: Chatham House, 1991.

National Society of Fundraising Executives (NSFRE). *Profile: 1992 Membership Survey.* Alexandria, VA: NSFRE, 1992.

Palmer, Parker J. "Remembering the Heart of Higher Education." Keynote Address to the American Association for Higher Education, 1993a.

Palmer, Parker J. *The Active Life: Wisdom for Work, Creativity and Caring.* San Francisco: HarperSanFrancisco, 1990.

Palmer, Parker J. *To Know as We Are Known: Education as a Spiritual Journey.* Paperback ed. with new foreword. San Francisco: HarperSanFrancisco, 1993b.

Payton, Robert. *Philanthropy: Voluntary Action for the Public Good.* New York: American Council on Education and Macmillan, 1988.

Payton, Robert L., Rosso, Henry A., and Tempel, Eugene R. "Taking Fundraising Seriously: An Agenda." In *Taking Fundraising Seriously.* Eds. D. Burlingame and L. Hulse. San Francisco: Jossey-Bass, 1991, 272–281.

Pribbenow, Paul P. "Public Service: Renewing the Moral Meaning of Professions in America." PhD diss., University of Chicago, 1993.

Robbins, Bruce. *Secular Vocations: Intellectualism, Professionalism, Culture.* London and New York: Verso, 1993.

Rosso, Henry A. "A Philosophy of Fundraising." *NSFRE Journal,* Spring 1992, 55–57.

Schön, Donald. *Educating the Reflective Practitioner.* San Francisco: Jossey-Bass, 1987.

Schön, Donald. *The Reflective Practitioner: How Professionals Think in Action.* New York: Basic Books, 1983.

Sullivan, William M. *Reconstructing Public Philosophy.* Berkeley: University of California Press, 1986.

Sullivan, William M. *Work and Integrity: The Crisis and Problem of Professionalism in America.* New York: HarperBusiness, 1995.

# 2 The Management of Nonprofit Organization Resources

Dennis R. Young, PhD

*Case Western Reserve University*

If it's a quiet life you seek, managing a nonprofit organization is probably not for you these days. The institutions with large endowments and modest imperatives that can go quietly about their business without too much distress from environmental pressures are a rare, if not endangered, species. Most nonprofits have been blown significantly by the winds of change over the past two decades, requiring them to pay more and more attention to the cultivation and stewardship of their resources.

In the United States, and increasingly around the world (Salamon & Anheier, 1994), nonprofits have been buffeted most strongly by changes in the role of government. In particular, the paring of social welfare programs and the privatization of public services have called on nonprofits to provide more services, often with reduced public sector support. Moreover, changes in the forms of public financing (e.g., greater reliance on contracting, voucher, and insurance schemes), now often require nonprofits to compete vigorously for that financing, among themselves and with for-profit vendors.

The new environment with which nonprofits must now cope may be fairly described as highly competitive and market-driven, and sometimes crassly commercial. Not only do nonprofits compete for a diminishing pool of public sector funding, but they rely increasingly on earned income derived from fees for their mission-related services and from ancillary commercial ventures. Moreover, the quest for charitable dollars has become fiercely contested and frequently tinged with commercial overtones. Indeed, fund raising has become a very profitable business for some consulting firms, while corporations have discovered that their corporate contributions programs can be effective arms for marketing commercial products and services. Thus, if nonprofits have not themselves succumbed to the imperatives of this new market-driven world, they must certainly deal with the commercial pressures surrounding the organizations with which they do business.

The dynamic economic environment in which nonprofits now operate offers a host of opportunities for research aimed at understanding the plight of these organizations and helping them cope. The purpose of this chapter is to identify some of those research opportunities. While this chapter will not present a comprehensive literature review, the feasibility of conceptualizing a research agenda for the future reflects the increasingly rich and sophisticated body of research on the economic aspects of nonprofit management that has developed over the past decade. Future contributions to research on the management of nonprofit organization resources will be built, if not on the shoulders of giants (although history may single out some contributors more than others), then at least on the findings and frameworks assembled by a modest congregation of early research pioneers in this field.

In this chapter, research will be considered on three broad aspects of the management of economic resources of nonprofit organizations. The first section focuses on the *strategic* implications that nonprofit leaders face in positioning their organizations to depend on alternative sources of support: charitable, governmental, or market-based. The second section is an examination of research on the *development* of particular sources of nonprofit organization support, including charitable cash contributions, sales revenues, government funding, and in-kind contributions. The third section presents a discussion of research on the *stewardship* of economic resources and the challenges of maintaining the overall financial health of nonprofit organizations.

A full research agenda on the management of nonprofit resources would also include analysis of the implications of public policies affecting nonprofits, including tax and regulatory policy. However, this chapter is focused more narrowly on issues directly within the purview of nonprofit managers and development officers.

## Strategic Issues

Several researchers, including Bielefeld (1992), McMurtry, Netting, and Kettner (1991), and Liebschutz (1992) have studied how nonprofit organizations cope with the turbulence in their funding environments. These researchers have identified a number of broad and creative ways in which nonprofit leaders managed to navigate their organizations through the fiscal storms of the 1980s. Such strategies included generating new revenue streams, retrenching and finding new efficiencies, and discovering ways to manage organizational environments to reduce future uncertainties. Researchers have also identified reasons for organizational failure in turbulent environments, including reliance on too few strategies or sources of income (Bielefeld, 1994; Chang & Tuckman, 1994). While this class of research is still in its early stages, it makes clear the value of continuing to study how and why some nonprofits survive and others do not (Tuckman

& Chang, 1993), and what combinations of managerial strategies work best to conserve and enhance a nonprofit organization's economic base in dynamic situations.

However, economic survival of nonprofit organizations is not the only, nor arguably even the most important, consideration at the strategic level of research on nonprofit resource management. Perhaps a more critical question is how reliance on different sources or combinations of revenue affects the ability of nonprofit organizations to continue to effectively address the missions for which they were established. Concerns of this kind are now manifest both with respect to nonprofit organizations' relationships with government and their relationships with business.

The concerns over nonprofits' relationships with government have a longer history. Since the 1960s, when government expanded its social programs largely through purchase of services of nonprofit organizations, fears have been raised over whether heavy reliance on government funding has undermined nonprofits' abilities or inclinations to maintain independent postures, pursue their advocacy functions, and continue to address their historical missions. Were nonprofit organizations merely becoming delivery agents for the state (Kramer, 1994)? While levels of government funding for social services have slackened in recent years, concerns over government distortion of nonprofit operations have, if anything, become more intense (Smith & Lipsky, 1993). This may be due, in part, to the fact that the form of government funding has continued to change, moving further in the direction of contracts and insurance arrangements in which government calls the shots and forces nonprofits to compete on the same terms as for-profit suppliers.

The issue of corporate influence on the behavior of nonprofits has been even less well studied, although serious concerns have been raised about "cause-related marketing" and other such practices (Giroud, 1991). First, it is unclear what impacts nonprofits have felt as a result of the corporate world's clear turn toward "strategic giving" (Smith, 1994). Corporations are withdrawing support from activities that are merely charitable in nature and do not advance their business interests. Moreover, business now wants more to say about the conduct of nonprofit activities that they do support. Yet, corporate contributions constitute only a small fraction of private contributions to nonprofits, and this fraction has not been growing. Thus, an interesting research question is whether the recent turn in businesses' approach to philanthropy is really very important to either the financial welfare of nonprofits or their ability to maintain focus on their missions. Alternatively, corporate contributions may be concentrated in certain areas of service that are particularly vulnerable, such as the arts. If so, are nonprofits subject to the same kinds of mission distortion from corporate support that has been feared from government funding? And, if nonprofits rely on declining corporate funding, what strategies can they use to maintain their economic stability and mission focus?

The same kinds of questions can be asked of foundation support and charitable giving by major donors. The recent case of Yale having to return $20 million to a donor who claimed that the university had failed to carry out his intent, provides a titillating example. However, the diffuse and dilute nature of the agendas of these other private sources of support appears to have made mission distortion less of an issue here than in connection with support from other sectors.

Finally, the effects of nonprofits' reliance on market-based revenues in itself represents a strategic issue worthy of much further study. Do nonprofits reliant primarily on selling their wares in the marketplace become coopted by the market mentality and lose sight of the missions they were established to address? This has certainly become a salient point for the hospital industry (Gray, 1991), and is an issue of increasing concern as nonprofits become ever more dependent on sales revenues for their sustenance (Salamon, 1992a).

Because of the strategic concerns associated with both the uncertain revenues from government, the market, or philanthropy, and the distortionary pressures that may emanate from these sources, a key research concern is how important it is for nonprofits to diversify their portfolios of funders and types of funding. On this question, researchers have identified competing concerns. Gronbjerg (1991) has chronicled the complexity of managing an organization that receives funds from many different sources, particularly different governmental programs. On the other hand, some researchers argue that diversification itself provides protection from financial instabilities associated with reliance on too few sources (see discussion later in this chapter). Another key strategic question, however, is whether revenue source diversification helps nonprofits avoid mission distortion.

## Resource Development Issues

A rich research agenda surrounds the question of how nonprofit organizations can best develop particular types of revenues sources. For example, what approaches will optimize charitable fund raising or earned income programs? Use of the word "optimize" rather than "maximize" is intentional here. While in many instances, the objective may be to generate the greatest possible net revenues of any particular type, other factors often cause nonprofits to modify this goal. The following discussion considers some research questions that emerge in connection with the optimization of charitable fund raising, market-based earned income, income from government sources, and in-kind resources.

### CHARITABLE FUND RAISING

A growing body of research addresses the understanding of donor motivations and ways to segment donor markets and cultivate the interests of particular groups (Lindahl & Winship, 1992; Pink & Leatt, 1991; Prince, File, & Gillespie, 1993). While such donor-focused research continues to be fruitful, the greater need is for research on the economics of fund raising.

At least three issues in this area require further study: how much to spend on fund raising, the interaction of charitable fund raising with other forms of revenue generation, and the implications of changes in collective fund raising at the community level.

## SPENDING ON FUND RAISING

Popular wisdom about fund raising argues that the ratio of donations to fund-raising costs must be kept low so that charities may claim that the vast bulk of contributions goes directly to finance programs and services rather than administration. Steinberg (1986) has demonstrated the conceptual flaws in this argument, showing that this ratio does not accurately reflect the price of giving faced by donors. Young and Steinberg (1995) show that charities interested in raising as much money as possible should essentially approach fund raising in the same way that a business firm views its activities, as an exercise in profit maximizing. Thus, charities should invest additional dollars in fund raising so long as the net return on that investment is positive, disregarding arbitrary ratios of donations to costs. This is not to say that charities should be insensitive to donor concerns. It always makes sense to look for efficiencies that might lower the costs associated with raising any given level of funds. Moreover, donor preferences must be taken into account in estimating what level of donations will be forthcoming for a given level of fund raising expenditure.

The foregoing arguments suggest a number of different research questions. First, what do the cost and donor revenue functions for fund raising actually look like, and how do they vary among different charities and methods of raising charitable funds? Second, how can the marginal costs of fund raising be described so that donors receive accurate information about how much of their contributions actually goes to fund programs? It is also important to know what effect that information would have on donor behavior, compared with information about simple but misleading fund raising ratios.

Related to fund raising costs is the question of optimal fund raising strategy when more than one method of fund raising is available to a particular organization. For example, organizations may wish to choose between direct mail and telephone solicitation. Young and Steinberg (1995) suggest that such choices are not necessarily discrete but that optimum combinations of methods may raise the most net funds. However, implementing such combinations again requires more refined knowledge of fund raising economics, including possible "economies of scope" in pursuing more than one method at a time, as well as donor responses to each method of solicitation.

## CROWD-OUT

Charitable fund raising normally takes place within the context of an organization that has other sources of revenue as well. Thus, the possibility exists that the pursuit of one revenue source will diminish or enhance the yield on another. Researchers have called this phenomenon "crowd-out." As reviewed by Steinberg (1993), substantial research has been done on the crowd-out of charitable contributions by government funding. Generally, government funding is found to have a modest dampening effect on charitable contributions. However, relatively little research has focused on whether charitable contributions are diminished by revenues from sales. In one study of American Red Cross health and safety services, Kingma (1995) found a sizable dampening effect of sales revenues on donations. If nonprofits are to position their fund raising activities within the context of their overall financial strategies, nonprofit managers must understand these effects, and research is needed to refine the estimates of these interactions.

## COMMUNITY FUND RAISING

Historically, social service organizations have depended on United Way to finance a substantial portion of their operations. Over time, however, the level of this dependence has diminished as other sources of funding have grown. Moreover, there have been basic changes in the united fund movement itself, including the development of alternative funds competing with United Way and the emergence of "donor option" policies that allow donors to designate how they want their funds to be used (Brilliant, 1990). Future changes in the way United Ways do business are likely to be even more profound as a result of the recent turmoil within the United Way system. This unrest has stemmed in part from the scandal at United Way of America but more fundamentally from grassroots questioning of the responsiveness of United Ways to current community needs. It is possible that many United Ways will soon abandon their traditional approach of giving regular annual allocations of funds to their own "members" in favor of a system resembling that of a community foundation in which applicants will be judged on the merits of proposals.

A research program devoted to the various profound changes taking place in the united funding movement could provide important information for nonprofit organization leaders, not only in connection with their individual fund development strategies, but also with respect to how they choose to participate in United Way or in alternative community funding arrangements.

## EARNED INCOME

As nonprofits rely more on market-based sources of revenue, they need to become more knowledgeable about how to determine the price of their services, and what levels of output they should produce. The potential crowd-out of charitable contributions by sales revenues is just one example of this. If sales revenues diminish charitable contributions, then this effect must be taken into account in determining the price and quantity of services that will maximize overall revenue from the combination of these sources.

In general, very little is known about how nonprofits determine, or should determine, the prices of their services and their levels of output for sale. Standard economic texts, keyed to the operations of profit maximizing business firms, provide only limited guidance. Young and Steinberg (1995) show that the pricing and output decisions of nonprofit organizations can be complicated by a number of factors including differences in objectives, crowd-out effects, external benefits associated with the services they produce, and fairness or equity considerations. Under various circumstances, nonprofits may wish to price particular services to maximize profits (e.g., if there are no externalities and surpluses that can be put to efficient use), to maximize output (e.g., if there are external benefits not captured in the price that justify producing marginal units at a financial loss), to price discriminate among consumers able to pay different prices (e.g., if fairness is an issue or if this policy helps make service provision financially feasible), or to cross-subsidize between one service and another (e.g., if profits from a private good can be used to support a public good).

Without clear principles, nonprofit managers often fly by the seat of their pants in making their pricing and output decisions. Thus, a robust field of research exists, not only to articulate clear general theoretical principles for the pricing and production of nonprofit services but also for the empirical study of these issues within a variety of service contexts.

## GOVERNMENT FUNDING

This is an era of deepening governmental retrenchment. Thus, however significant public sector spending is now in various nonprofit service fields (Salamon, 1992a), it is likely to diminish significantly over time as a proportion of nonprofit organizations' budgets. Thus, it may not seem worthwhile, on the surface, to emphasize the development of government funding for nonprofit services as a dimension for future research. Yet, the current environment does open up some new vistas. For some time, it has been apparent that the locus of government funding is shifting from the federal to the state and local levels. Moreover, the shift from categorical to block grants promises to accelerate dramatically. How will these changes affect the ability of nonprofits to garner public resources? Liebschutz (1992) suggests that a process of "management by groping along" led nonprofit social service agencies in the 1980s to cope with federal cutbacks by incrementally shifting from federal to local sources of government support. However, as a new regime of public funding takes hold in the states, it may require more focused long-term political and organizational strategies and skills for nonprofit leaders to secure their shares of public funds. For example, if states, freed of federal categorical constraints, redefine their funding streams around client groups and social problems, such as crime or community renewal, rather than particular services, such as foster care or meals on wheels, then would-be nonprofit providers will have to adjust their approaches as well, perhaps emphasizing new creative problem-solving programs rather than provision of traditional services. The implications of the new decentralized regime of public funding is an unstudied area with potentially profound changes for the approaches nonprofit managers must use to seek government funding.

In addition to decentralization of public finance, the continued privatization of public services through contracting and insurance schemes, is also altering the potentials for nonprofit organizations to secure public funding. A continuing puzzle is whether privatization will result in more ample public sector resources available to nonprofit organizations, a constriction of that funding, or increases insufficient to support the new obligations that accompany potential funding increments. Three factors converge to make this a complex question. First, if government withdraws from delivering services itself but maintains the financing of public services, new resources will become available for private sector agencies to deliver those services. Second, however, if government simultaneously reduces the financing of such services, private agencies may have to supplement government funds with other sources to meet new service delivery obligations. Third, if contracts or insurance schemes are designed in a manner that allows for-profit firms to effectively compete for government funding, nonprofits will find themselves in contention with for-profits, not only for new business but even for the services they have traditionally delivered with government support.

In fact, all these effects appear to be taking place simultaneously. Particularly in the social services, conventional sources of government funding are shrinking, while financing through healthcare programs (Medicaid) has both increased and opened the market for for-profit providers. This complex picture of shifts in the nature and magnitude of public funding programs warrants careful study if nonprofit providers are to design sensible strategies for seeking, maintaining, or in some cases abandoning their sources of public support in the future.

## IN-KIND RESOURCES

An important but underattended area of resource development research is the cultivation of in-kind resources by nonprofit organizations. Volunteered time is the major resource in this category (Hodgkinson et al., 1992). Substantial research on the recruitment and retention of volunteers has emerged in recent years (Clary, Snyder, & Ridge, 1992; Puffer, 1991). However, research on the costs of administering volunteer programs, and the consequence of such costs on the demand for volunteers, is still in an early stage of development (Wolff, Weisbrod, & Bird, 1993). Moreover, the valuation of volunteer time versus financial or other resources, and the implications of such valuation for determining where volunteer recruitment fits into a nonprofit's overall resource development strategy, is an issue requiring substantial further study. As Young and Steinberg (1995) show, proper valuation of volunteer time is not simply a matter of attaching the market wage for similar paid work, but requires a more precise assessment of the opportunity value of that time.

Even less well understood is the solicitation and use of in-kind material goods and services by nonprofit organizations. Little study has been given to the extent or nature of in-kind donations to nonprofits, or the costs of soliciting or using them. While common experience suggests that in-kind donations can sometimes be more trouble than they are worth, in-kind donations also represent an important source of nonprofit support. Some attention has been given to the practice of bartering among nonprofits and between nonprofits and for-profit businesses. Reisman (1991) demonstrated the common use and vast potential for the direct exchange of goods and services among nonprofits and for-profits, while Ben-Ner (1993) provided an economic explanation of why bartering for goods and services seems to be more common among nonprofits than among for-profit businesses. Generally, however, this is an important research area of virtually untapped potential.

## Stewardship Issues

A series of research issues can be framed around the question of how nonprofits can best manage, maintain, and nurture the financial resources entrusted to them. Many of these issues, such as management of debt or financial surpluses, or design of investment policies, are conventional matters of financial management and control, but they take on special nuances and raise unresolved questions for nonprofit organizations.

### PROFITS

One important issue is the desirability of generating operating surpluses (profits). Profits are a straightforward matter in the business sector—basically, the more profit the better. In the nonprofit sector, the issue is much more nuanced. Small surpluses may be desirable but large surpluses raise concerns that resources are not being used as intensively as possible to address the mission of the organization. Aside from raising regulatory concerns over conformity with requirements for tax exemption, the generation of substantial operating profits per se may have an inhibiting (crowd-out) effect on charitable donations (Kingma, 1995; Young & Steinberg, 1995). Nonetheless, researchers have found that the generation of operating surpluses by nonprofit organizations is a common and helpful practice. Chang and Tuckman (1990) found that surpluses were used by nonprofits to subsidize important but loss-making services, to build up reserve funds for hedging against uncertainty or to make future investments, and even to measure organizational success. On the other hand, Young (1994) has pointed out that modest levels of deficit can also stimulate charitable support for a nonprofit organization. Overall, the issue of what policy should guide nonprofits' pursuit of operating surpluses remains unresolved.

## DEBT

Similarly, the question of nonprofit practices with respect to debt remains relatively unstudied. Here, Tuckman and Chang (1993) found that although nonprofits may have more difficulties securing loans than businesses, most nonprofits do hold debt and use it in responsible and productive ways to finance their operations. Still, research on this topic has just begun. Nonprofit leaders could use substantially better information on strategic uses of debt, appropriate levels of debt under alternative circumstances, and methods for successful borrowing.

## EQUITY BALANCES

The issue of operating surpluses is related to the development and management of significant equity balances and endowments. Chang and Tuckman (1990) demonstrated that nonprofits generate operating surpluses, in part, to create funds for future investment in new programs or facilities, and to hedge against uncertainty in future operations. However, the establishment of large equity funds raises additional unresolved but important issues. For example: How large should these funds be? How should their uses be restricted? And how should they be invested?

Few researchers have analyzed the wisdom of maintaining large endowments or equity balances or the considerations that should be taken into account in determining the degree to which such funds should be built up or spent down. Hansmann (1990) has questioned whether it is sensible to maintain large endowments when serious operational problems exist. Presumably, the phenomenon of crowd-out may also come into play if donors perceive the existence of such funds as a deterrent to further giving. Alternatively, researchers have not provided a good explanation for the "Boys Town" phenomenon under which institutions are able to continue generating large sums of donated money despite the combination of substantial accumulated funds and only modest service levels.

## INVESTMENT POLICIES

The maintenance of equity balances also raises the issue of investment policy for resources devoted to these funds. Lester Salamon (1992b, 1993) has pioneered the study of investment policies of foundations, finding that many foundations, especially the smaller ones, do not follow modern investment portfolio practices that would maintain or enhance the real (inflation-adjusted) value of their assets. By implication, Salamon's work raises other, more fundamental questions as well. For example, is it always appropriate for foundations to maintain the value of their assets? If a foundation determines that its existence should be time-limited, what should its investment policies be? And where do "program-related investments" (PRIs) fit into the picture (Renz, Massarsky, Treiber, & Lawrence, 1995)? What trade-offs should foundations be willing to make between risk and financial return on their capital, and social benefits produced by PRIs?

All these questions apply not only to foundations but also to other kinds of nonprofit organizations, such as universities, hospitals, and major cultural institutions, that maintain endowments or other large equity balances. What policies should these institutions follow in maintaining, growing, or spending-down their financial assets?

## FINANCIAL STABILITY

Researchers have examined a number of considerations that affect the ability of nonprofit organizations to maintain their operations and finances on an even keel from year to year. Indeed, one reason that nonprofit organizations maintain endowments is that they generate relatively reliable sources of current revenue. As such, endowments constitute a desirable and important element in the revenue streams of many nonprofit organizations.

As previously noted, diversification of revenue sources is another approach to financial stability. Chang and Tuckman (1994) support the view that diversification offers less risk than does reliance on any particular source of income. They found that nonprofit organizations with multiple revenue sources are more likely to be financially strong than those that depend on fewer sources. Kingma (1993) also developed a portfolio analysis for revenue diversification of nonprofits that takes into account interactions (crowd-out) among alternative revenue sources. These analyses contrast, however, with that of Gronbjerg (1993) who found that organizations relying on government funding or ongoing relationships with a few steady private funders perform better than those relying on multiple or unsteady funding sources. Gronbjerg (1991) also noted that diversification has other disadvantages including the costs of maintaining a management capacity able to administer the diverse cash flow and reporting requirements of alternative sources of funds.

Unreliable cash flow is a particular source of financial instability for nonprofit organizations, especially those relying on government funding. Grossman (1992) found that payment practices of state governments can create major operating difficulties for their nonprofit social services contractors. Cash flow problems associated with other specific sources of nonprofit income have not been well studied, though such issues as uncollected charitable pledges remain an important concern for nonprofit managers.

## FINANCIAL HEALTH AND ORGANIZATIONAL SUCCESS

Stability is just one aspect of a larger issue—how to determine whether a nonprofit organization is financially healthy. This is a relatively straight-forward question for profit-making businesses and even for government (see Young, 1994), but a much more perplexing one for nonprofit organizations. Several researchers, including Tuckman and Chang (1991) and Herzlinger (1994), have addressed this issue but key questions remain unresolved.

Tuckman and Chang (1991) base their analysis of nonprofit organization financial health on the concept of "vulnerability." These researchers ask whether a financial shock of some kind would lead an organization to reduce its output. They identify four measures of flexibility that would allow an organization to absorb a shock without reducing output: the level of its equity balances; the diversification of its revenue sources; the level of its administrative costs; and the level of its operating (profit) margins. In this framework, an organization with substantial equity balances, high administrative costs, diversified revenue sources, and high profit margins would be able to cut into these resource cushions in times of trouble without having to reduce its output. Tuckman and Chang specify quantitative indices for each of these criteria and then rate the financial health (vulnerability) of a given organization by its scores relative to other (comparable) nonprofit organizations.

Herzlinger's (1994) approach to measuring a nonprofit organization's financial health is somewhat more general. She posits four key questions and identifies financial ratios to gauge the answers. The questions are:

1. Are the organization's goals consistent with the financial resources it needs to finance them?
2. Is the organization maintaining intergenerational equity?
3. Is there an appropriate match between the sources of resources and the uses to which they are put?
4. Are present resources sustainable?

In question 1, Herzlinger is concerned with whether the organization is overextended, on the one hand, or not living up to its potential, on the other hand. She proposes measures of both short-term and long-term solvency to gauge overextension and activity or asset-turnover measures to determine whether an organization is using its assets effectively to meet its potential.

In question 2, Herzlinger is asking whether the organization is preserving its assets so that these assets maintain their value for future generations. Here she relies on measures of operating profit and returns on fund balances to determine whether the organization is preserving or enhancing its assets to compensate for inflation.

In question 3, the author asks whether the organization's sources of revenues are well matched over time with the particular expenses they are supposed to pay for. She posits that long-run expenses should be coupled with long-term sources of revenue, and short-term expenses should be matched with short-term revenues. Otherwise, the organization risks shortfalls at various points in time and difficulties in adjusting its resources to support its expenses in particular program areas. Herzlinger develops measures of the variability and controllability of different revenue sources to gauge their dependability for covering longer run expenses.

Under question 4, the author asks to what degree the organization's revenue sources are diversified, on the theory that greater diversification increases financial stability.

The Herzlinger framework has a number of points in common with other analyses. Like Chang and Tuckman (1994), she views revenue diversification as a source of stability and is also concerned with whether an organization's resources can continue to support its activities (outputs). However, Herzlinger also raises other issues that appear to require further investigation. For example, to what extent is it necessary to align the time frames of revenues and expenses? To what degree are nonprofits really unable to use their revenue bases in a holistic way to carry out their overall missions? Can they, through borrowing or actual conversions from one revenue source to another, utilize their revenues fairly flexibly, or are they severely constrained by the limitations of particular revenue sources?

Question 2 raises still other issues, reminiscent of those arising in connection with foundation investment policies. To what extent should a given nonprofit organization be driven to preserve its assets for the next generation versus spending them down to achieve a shorter term goal? Moreover, could not achievement of a short-term goal be in the best interests of future generations? For example, if an organization were to find a cure for AIDS by spending all of its assets now, would that not be intergenerationally fair?

The latter conundrum reflects the overall limitation of financial measures to gauge the health and performance of nonprofit organizations. Without specific reference to the outputs of these organizations, one cannot really tell if an organization's operations, no matter how structured financially, are in the best interests of society as a whole, or those of the organization's particular stakeholders. Similar problems arise with respect to Herzlinger's stipulation that the organization's resources be sufficient to sustain its activities, and with Tuckman's and Chang's (1991) concern that an organization be able to maintain its output in the face of financial shock. Ideally, one should first ask if it is indeed desirable to maintain such output, or whether reductions (or expansions) of output are called for. This involves much more difficult research territory, however. Conceptually, Young and Steinberg (1995) show that a nonprofit's production level should reflect the marginal value of its output to society. Moreover, achieving a level of production at which the value of output is just offset by its marginal cost may either be well within, or beyond, the organization's capacity. In any case, the appropriate approach is to estimate the benefits and costs of organizational output before determining the level at which an organization should be able to sustain its effort.

The science of identifying the real costs and the social value of the outputs of nonprofit organizations remains primitive, and it is in this area where much important research is still to be done. Since nonprofits often produce social goods and utilize donated resources whose values are not always well represented by observable market prices, standard financial measures are not sufficient to capture economic performance in the most general sense. However, more general cost-benefit calculations will require substantial research on how to measure the outputs, impacts, and resource use of nonprofit organizations, and how to value these variables in dollar terms.

## Conclusion

This chapter has presented a brief tour of research issues bearing on the management of economic resources of private, nonprofit organizations. Those areas where better information and understanding are needed by those responsible for developing the resources of these organizations and for managing them effectively have been explored.

Many other important resource-related issues exist at the policy level, including the effects on nonprofits of changes in federal, state, and local government tax and regulatory policies. Proposed modifications of the federal income tax or local property or sales taxation of nonprofit organizations will affect the environment in which managers and development officers of nonprofit organizations do their work. In this chapter, however, focus has been placed on those issues directly under the control of organizational managers and leaders. These issues have been described at three levels: (1) strategic positioning of the organization with respect to alternative sources of financial support; (2) effective development of particular sources of public and private support; and (3) management of overall organization resources to maintain financial health and stability. Along each of these dimensions, major opportunities exist for research to illuminate the issues and guide management decision making.

The future environment of nonprofit organizations almost certainly will feature less governmental support, greater reliance on earned income and other private sources, and a more demanding public. These constituents will insist that nonprofits manage their scarce resources with increasing effectiveness. In this context, research on the critical issues of resource management can make an exceedingly important contribution to the health and productivity of nonprofit organizations and their constituents in the decades ahead.

## Bibliography

Ben-Ner, Avner. "Obtaining Resources Using Barter Trade: Benefits and Drawbacks," In *Nonprofit Organizations in a Market Economy*. Eds. David C. Hammack and Dennis R. Young. San Francisco: Jossey-Bass, Inc., 1993. 278–293.

Bielefeld, Wolfgang. "Funding Uncertainty and Nonprofit Strategies in the 1980s." *Nonprofit Management and Leadership*, 1992, 2:4, 381–401.

Bielefeld, Wolfgang. "What Affects Nonprofit Survival?" *Nonprofit Management and Leadership*, 1994, 5:1, 19–36.

Brilliant, Eleanor L. *The United Way: Dilemmas of Organized Charity*. New York: Columbia University Press, 1990.

Chang, Cyril F., and Tuckman, Howard P. "Financial Vulnerability and Attrition as Measures of Nonprofit Performance," In *The Nonprofit Sector in the Mixed Economy*. Eds. Avner Ben-Ner and Benedetto Gui, Ann Arbor: University of Michigan Press, 1993. 163–180.

Chang, Cyril F., and Tuckman, Howard P. "Revenue Diversification among Non-Profits," *Voluntas*, 1994, 5:3, 273–290.

Chang, Cyril F., and Tuckman, Howard P. "Why Do Nonprofit Managers Accumulate Surpluses, and How Much Do They Accumulate?" *Nonprofit Management and Leadership*, 1990, 1:2, 117–136.

Clary, E. Gil, Snyder, Mark, and Ridge, Robert. "Volunteers' Motivations: A Functional Strategy for the Recruitment, Placement, and Retention of Volunteers." *Nonprofit Management and Leadership*, 1992, 2:4, 333–350.

Giroud, Cynthia G. "Cause-Related Marketing: Potential Dangers and Benefits." In *The Corporate Contributions Handbook*. Ed. James P. Shannon. San Francisco: Jossey-Bass, 1991. Ch. 11. 139–152.

Gray, Bradford H. *The Profit Motive and Patient Care*. Cambridge: Harvard University Press, 1991.

Gronbjerg, Kirsten A. "How Nonprofit Human Service Organizations Manage Their Funding Sources." *Nonprofit Management and Leadership*, 1991, 2:2, 159–176.

Gronbjerg, Kirsten A. *Understanding Nonprofit Funding*. San Francisco: Jossey-Bass, 1993.

Grossman, David A. "Paying Nonprofits: Streamlining the New York State System." *Nonprofit Management and Leadership*, 1992, 3:1, 81–92.

Hansmann, Henry. "Why Do Universities Have Endowments?" *Journal of Legal Studies*, 1990, XIX, 3–42.

Herzlinger, Regina E. "Effective Oversight: A Guide for Nonprofit Directors," *Harvard Business Review*, July-Aug. 1994, 52–60.

Hodgkinson, Virginia A., Weitzman, Murray S., Toppe, Christopher M., and Noga, Stephen M. *Nonprofit Almanac 1992–1993.* San Francisco: Jossey-Bass, 1992.

Kingma, Bruce R. "Do Profits 'Crowd-out' Donations? or Vice Versa," *Nonprofit Management and Leadership,* 1995, 6:1, 21–38.

Kingma, Bruce R. "Portfolio Theory and Nonprofit Financial Stability." *Nonprofit and Voluntary Sector Quarterly,* 1993, 22:2, 105–119.

Kramer, Ralph M. "Voluntary Agencies and the Contract Culture: Dream or Nightmare?" *Social Service Review,* March 1994, 33–60.

Liebschutz, Sarah. "Coping by Nonprofit Organizations in the Reagan Years," *Nonprofit Management and Leadership,* 1992, 2:4, 363–380.

Lindahl, Wesley E., and Winship, Christopher. "Predictive Models for Annual Fundraising and Major Gift Fundraising." *Nonprofit Management and Leadership,* 1992, 3:1, 43–64.

McMurtry, Steven L., Netting, Ellen F., and Kettner, Peter. "How Nonprofits Adapt to a Stringent Environment." *Nonprofit Management and Leadership,* 1991, 1:3, 235–252.

Pink, George H., and Leatt, Peggy. "Fund-Raising by Hospital Foundations." *Nonprofit Management and Leadership,* 1991, 1:4, 313–328.

Prince, Russ A., File, Karen M., and Gillespie, James E. "Philanthropic Styles," *Nonprofit Management and Leadership,* 1993, 3:3, 255–268.

Puffer, Sheila M. "Career Professionals Who Volunteer: Should Their Motives be Accepted or Managed?" *Nonprofit Management and Leadership,* 1991, 2:2, 107–124.

Reisman, Arnold. "Enhancing Nonprofit Resources through Barter," *Nonprofit Management and Leadership,* 1991, 1:3, 253–266.

Renz, Loren, Massarsky, Cynthia W., Treiber, Rikard R., and Lawrence, Steven. *Program-Related Investments.* New York: Foundation Center, 1995.

Salamon, Lester M. *America's Nonprofit Sector.* New York: Foundation Center, 1992a.

Salamon, Lester M. "Foundations as Investment Managers Part 1: The Process." *Nonprofit Management and Leadership,* 1992b, 3:2, 117–137.

Salamon, Lester M. "Foundations as Investment Managers Part 2: The Performance." *Nonprofit Management and Leadership,* 1993, 3:3, 239–253.

Salamon, Lester M., and Anheier, Helmut. *The Emerging Sector: An Overview.* Baltimore: Johns Hopkins Institute for Policy Analysis, 1994.

Smith, Craig. "The New Corporate Philanthropy." *Harvard Business Review,* May/June 1994, 105–116.

Smith, Steven R., and Lipsky, Michael. *Nonprofits for Hire.* Cambridge: Harvard University Press, 1993.

Steinberg, Richard. "Does Government Spending Crowd Out Donations? Interpreting the Evidence." In *The Nonprofit Sector in the Mixed Economy.*

Steinberg, Richard. "Should Donors Care about Fundraising?" In *The Economics of Nonprofit Institutions.* Ed. Susan Rose-Ackerman. New York: Oxford University Press, 1986. 347–364.

Eds. Avner Ben-Ner and Benedetto Gui. Ann Arbor: University of Michigan Press, 1993. 99–125.

Tuckman, Howard P., and Chang, Cyril F. "A Methodology for Measuring the Financial Vulnerability of Charitable Nonprofit Organizations." *Nonprofit and Voluntary Sector Quarterly*, 1991, (Winter), 20:4, 445–460.

Tuckman, Howard P., and Chang, Cyril F. "How Well Is Debt Managed by Nonprofits?" *Nonprofit Management and Leadership*, 1993, 3:4, 347–362.

Weisbrod, Burton A. *The Nonprofit Economy*. Cambridge: Harvard University Press, 1988.

Wolff, Nancy, Weisbrod, Burton A., and Bird, Edward J. "The Supply of Volunteer Labor: The Case of Hospitals." *Nonprofit Management and Leadership*, 1993, 4:1, 23–45.

Young, Dennis R. "Measuring the Financial Health of the Nonprofit Sector: Some Preliminary Thoughts." Draft prepared for the Nonprofit Sector Research Fund Conference on Financing the Nonprofit Sector, Wye, Maryland, 1994, November.

Young, Dennis R., and Steinberg, Richard. *Economics for Nonprofit Managers*. New York: Foundation Center, 1995.

# Fund Raisers, Ethics, and Equity

# The Fund Raising Profession

MARGARET A. DURONIO, PhD

*University of Pittsburgh*

By conservative estimates, fund raising expenditures by American nonprofit organizations may be as high as $2 billion annually. Typically, 60 percent of the total cost of raising money is for personnel, meaning that there exists in this country a work force earning in excess of $1 billion each year about which relatively little is known. This workforce provides the vital link between donors and recipients and is responsible for a sizable portion of the billions of dollars in philanthropic gifts contributed each year. Professional fund raisers, including both in-house staff and consultants, are among the most highly compensated employees in the nonprofit sector and often have significant influence in determining direction and policy for the organizations for which they work. Nevertheless, fund raising as an occupation is not well understood, nor, as some believe, fully valued.

In 1988, Virginia Hodgkinson, Vice President for Research at INDEPENDENT SECTOR, serving as a member of the Research Committee of the National Society of Fund Raising Executives (NSFRE) Foundation, suggested that if fund raisers wished to be taken seriously as professionals, they needed to know much more about themselves. The Research Committee decided to champion such a study and collaborated with the Indiana University Center on Philanthropy to organize the study and secure funding. Eugene Tempel, Vice Chancellor for External Affairs at Indiana University-Purdue University at Indianapolis, and Dwight Burlingame, Director of Academic Programs and Research at the Center on Philanthropy, convened an advisory group to help design the study and asked me to serve as principal investigator and codirector of the project with them. The Lilly Endowment Inc. and an anonymous donor provided the $220,000 budget for the study. This research:

- Presents a comprehensive, detailed picture of contemporary fund raisers at all levels of professional achievement, working for and on behalf of the entire range of nonprofit organizations.

The author wishes to acknowledge with appreciation the contributions to this chapter of Eugene R. Tempel, Indiana University—Purdue University at Indianapolis.

- Describes fund raising practitioners, their education and other work experiences, and the issues they face in their work.
- Explores what motivates fund raisers and how they find rewards and satisfaction in their work.
- Identifies the trends and environmental conditions that currently influence fund raisers in their work.
- Explains how fund raisers, fund raising managers, chief executive officers, and professional organizations can utilize knowledge and information about professional fund raisers to enhance and improve the management, practice, and contributions of fund raising.

The design of this study was heavily influenced by three kinds of previous research:

1. *Surveys completed by professional organizations serving fund raisers.* These include the Association for Healthcare Philanthropy (AHP) 1992, 1993; the Council for the Advancement and Support of Education (CASE) 1982, 1986, 1990; and the National Society of Fund Raising Executives, 1981, 1985, 1988, and 1992. For summaries of this work, see Association for Healthcare Philanthropy (1992, 1993); Turk (1986a, 1986b) and McNamee (1990a, 1990b, 1990c) describing CASE studies; and Bohlen (1981) and Mongon (1985, 1988, 1992) for NSFRE. In addition, both CASE and NSFRE conducted membership surveys in 1995, reported in Williams (1996) and Mongon (1995). These surveys, describing basic demographic characteristics of members, are invaluable contributions to the historical record of the growth and other changes in the field since the 1980s. Survey reports indicate, for example, that membership in NSFRE grew 77 percent from 2,913 members in 1981 to 12,644 members in 1992.
2. *Studies completed by Carbone (1987, 1989).* The 1987 study focused on a sample of 206 fund raisers who were CASE members. In addition to demographic characteristics, this study included information on career histories of fund raisers. The 1989 study of 754 fund raisers from membership lists of AHP, CASE, and NSFRE assessed fund raisers' opinions about their professional status.
3. *Projects on people in philanthropy completed by researchers at the Oral History Research Center at Indiana University.* These included a study of key figures in private foundations (Lichtenberg, 1993) and a study of three generations of fund-raising consultants (Harrah-Conforth & Borsos, 1991).

In this chapter, a general overview of findings, with a particular focus on information about fund raisers that has not been previously available from earlier studies, is presented. A book-length discussion of the results of this research appears in *Fund Raisers: Their Careers, Stories, Concerns, and Accomplishments.*

## Survey Findings

### METHODOLOGY AND OVERALL RESPONSE

This research involved a survey of a random sample of 2,501 members of the major professional organizations serving fund raisers (AHP, CASE and NSFRE), which elicited 1,748 responses. The consistency of the findings for topics covered in previous studies gives us confidence that our respondent sample accurately reflects fund raisers who are members of professional organizations. However, since the large population of fund raisers who are not members remains unavailable for study, the major limitation of this study is that its findings can be generalized with confidence only to fund raisers who are members of professional organizations.

Respondents to our survey included 955 women (54.6%) and 793 men (45.3%). The earliest available surveys indicated that the male/female ratio among the ranks of fund raisers shifted dramatically in the past decade, with the number of women increasing by more than 50 percent by 1992. Therefore, to the extent that organizational membership reflects the entire population, evidence indicates that women have come to outnumber men in the field.

### "AVERAGE" FUND RAISERS

According to this survey, average female and male fund raisers had the following characteristics:

|  | *Female* | *Male* |
| --- | --- | --- |
| **Ethnicity** | White | White |
| **Present Age** | 42 | 45.5 |
| **Education** | Bachelor degree in education | Graduate degree in business or education |
| **Nonprofit Area** | Education | Education |
| **Salary** | Under $39,999 | $40,000–$59,999 |
| **Title** | Director of Annual Fund | Director of Planned Giving |

These average fund raisers were similar to those identified in the most recent CASE (Williams, 1996) and NSFRE (Mongon, 1995) surveys. Of interest is that the present study and the most recent CASE and NSFRE surveys indicate that the average male and female fund raisers were older than they were a decade ago and had more years' experience in the field. These findings confirm that the field, which grew so rapidly during the 1980s, is maturing.

## OTHER GENERAL CHARACTERISTICS OF RESPONDENTS

- One of the few areas in which fund raisers are not demographically diverse is in ethnic origin: 95.4 percent of all respondents to this survey were white. Of the 68 minority respondents, 28 were African American, 10 were Asian American, 11 were Hispanic American, 12 were Native American, and 7 were "Other."
- Most respondents worked in education (49.7%) and healthcare (23.9%). An additional 11.7 percent worked in human services, and the remaining 14.7 percent worked in other kinds of nonprofit organizations including the arts, religion, public benefit, and the environment. While education and healthcare organizations have the largest fund raising departments, fund raisers from these kinds of organizations are most likely to be members of professional organizations. Therefore, we are more confident about how accurately education and health care fund raisers are portrayed in these survey results than we are about fund raisers in other areas of the nonprofit sector.
- Among these respondents, 48% had undergraduate degrees; 46% had undergraduate and graduate degrees; 6% had less than a four-year college degree. Male fund raisers in general had more formal education than female fund raisers. Seventy-three percent of male fund raisers had education beyond the undergraduate degree while only 44 percent of female fund raisers did. Of those without degrees, 83 percent were female.
- The most frequently reported fields of formal study were business and education. Most respondents (64%) had completed studies in the professions; of those remaining, 21 percent had studied in the humanities, 14 percent in the social sciences, and 1.2 percent in the natural sciences.
- "Director" was the most frequently reported title for both men and women. However, titles conveying higher organizational status, such as vice president or assistant vice president, were more likely to be reported by men, and titles conveying lower organizational status, such as assistant director or coordinator, were more likely to be reported by women.
- Women were more likely to report working in the annual fund, alumni relations, prospect research, and special events; men were more likely to report working in athletics, corporate and foundation relations, major and planned gifts, and public affairs.
- This research indicated that fund raisers make philanthropic contributions and volunteer more often than do members of the

general population. Among all Americans, an estimated 46 percent (Hodgkinson & Weitzman, 1992) of all households make philanthropic contributions and engage in volunteer activities. Among respondents to this survey, 79 percent reported making philanthropic contributions and engaging in volunteer activities.

- Although fund raising may be a "hot career" (the March 1995 edition of the *NSFRE News,* the newsletter of the National Society of Fund Raising Executives, noted that a national magazine was calling fund raising one of the "25 Hottest Careers" in the country), (Lewis, 1995) the majority of fund raisers enter the field after they have had experience in some other field. Only 15 percent of respondents reported having had no occupation other than fund raising as an adult or since college.
- Respondents most often formerly worked in education, business, advertising/promotion, and the media. Teaching of some form was the single most frequently reported former specific occupation for both men and women.
- Most fund raisers (70%) earned less than $60,000: 32 percent earned less than $40,000 and 38 percent earned between $40,000 and $59,999. Of those earning more than $60,000, 17 percent earned between $60,000 and $79,999, 7 percent earned between $80,000 and $99,999, and 4 percent earned $100,000 or more.
- The highest salaries were reported by those with the most prestigious titles, the most education, and the most seniority in fund raising. In general, fund raisers working in education and health reported higher salaries than those working in the arts, religion, or human services.
- Although female respondents to this survey outnumbered male respondents by a ratio of 1.21:1, women in the lowest salary range outnumbered men by a 3:1 ratio and men outnumbered women by 5:1 in the highest salary range. Although male respondents in general were older, had been in the field longer, and had more formal education, when men and women were matched for age, education, and experience, women still earned less. For 52 matched pairs, or 50.9 percent of the cases, men were paid more than women of the same age, education, and experience.

## FUND RAISERS' CAREER HISTORIES

It is a frequent charge that fund raising has a high turnover rate as a result of fund raisers changing jobs frequently to earn more money. Since conventional wisdom maintains that long tenure and continuity of staff are major factors in long-term fund raising success, high turnover suggests that fund raisers are more interested in personal aggrandizement than in the success of their employing organization. Some critics, both within and outside the field, believe that too many fund raisers are motivated primarily by values that are inimicable to philanthropic values and purposes. In general, most of the discussion in the fund raising literature about turnover of fund raising staff treats the phenomenon as a factor more related to the character of fund raisers than to conditions in the job market or in nonprofit organizations.

Some research indicates that turnover in fund raising is higher than for some other fields. In a 1987 study of administrative staff at educational organizations that were CASE members, the annual turnover rate for advancement staff was 17.3 percent, 50 percent higher than the 11.8 percent turnover found among staff in such areas as finance and student affairs (Thomas, 1987). Within the functional areas of advancement, turnover was higher for development (19.5%) than for public relations (18.2%) and alumni relations (13.9%). A more recent survey (Mooney, 1993) indicated that chief development officers and alumni relations professionals switched jobs more often than other higher education administrative staff. The study noted that 22 percent of chief development officers and alumni directors left their jobs each year and had an average tenure of 4.6 years, compared with the group with the lowest turnover, head librarians, who had turnover at 11 percent and average tenure at 9 years.

Based on the findings of the present survey, are fund raisers interested in career advancement? Yes. Are the majority of fund raisers transients, driven by greed for personal advancement? No. Do the majority of fund raisers have stable career histories? Well, not exactly, but I do not think that greed or other morally suspect motives are responsible for this. The tremendous growth of the field and the demand for experienced fund raisers are more likely to be responsible, as explained in this section.

Several variables related to career histories were examined: number of jobs in fund raising, years in present job, total years in fund raising, and average years per fund raising job. Questions about respondents' plans for staying with their organizations and in the field of fund raising and whether respondents had moved from one type of nonprofit organization to another were also asked. Operationally, job stability is defined for this survey as fewer job changes, high average years per fund raising job, and high average years in present job. It is important to note that it was not always possible to tell whether a respondent's job change was a promotion within the same organization or a move to another organization. In the minds of many, these are two very different kinds of changes because when fund raisers leave one organization to go to another, their knowledge of and relationships with donors cannot be retained by the organization. However, when fund raisers change jobs within an organization, the organization retains those "assets."

As indicated on Table 3.1, women had an average of 2.8 jobs, 8.3 total years' experience in fund raising, and 3.3 average years per job; men had an average of 3.1 jobs, 12.3 total years' experience, and 4.4 average years per job, indicating that, overall, men had slightly more job stability than women. Conventional wisdom suggests that persons in entry level positions change

**TABLE 3.1. Career History Statistics**

| Group | Number | Percent | Average Number of FR Jobs | Average Years in Present Job | Average Years in Fund Raising | Average Years per Job |
|---|---|---|---|---|---|---|
| *Females* | | | | | | |
| All | 900 | 100 | 2.79 | 3.25 | 8.25 | 3.31 |
| 10 or More Years' Experience | 324 | 36 | 3.82 | 4.51 | 14.12 | 4.60 |
| Fewer than 10 Years' Experience | 576 | 64 | 2.21 | 2.55 | 4.98 | 2.60 |
| *Males* | | | | | | |
| All | 764 | 100 | 3.06 | 4.35 | 12.33 | 4.42 |
| 10 or More Years' Experience | 420 | 55 | 3.85 | 5.77 | 18.35 | 5.72 |
| Fewer than 10 Years' Experience | 344 | 45 | 2.10 | 2.76 | 5.14 | 2.89 |

jobs more frequently. The fact that women as a group more often work in lower level positions in fund raising probably accounts for most of the differences in the career history data of male and female respondents.

More than half of all respondents, 55.3 percent (64% of women and 45% of men), had fewer than 10 years' experience in fund raising. It is not surprising that job stability increased for men and women as total years in the field increased. Career history patterns for people with more or fewer than 10 years' experience in the field were very different from the patterns that emerged when all respondents were grouped together without regard for length of time in the field. As indicated in Table 3.1, persons with 10 or more years' experience in the field had considerably more job stability than those with fewer than 10 years' experience. Because of the rapid growth of the field in the past decade, the differences in career history data for various lengths of time in the field are critical to evaluating and interpreting turnover in fund raising. None of the other studies on turnover specify length of time in the field, so there is really no way to determine whether turnover for those with fewer than 10 years' experience in fund raising is excessive when compared with persons who have equal tenure in other fields.

After first sorting respondents into two groups, those with 10 or more years of total experience and those with fewer than 10 years, those with stable, marginal, and transient career histories in each group were identified. Transients were those with an average of under 3 years' tenure per fund raising job. Table 3.2 contains a summary of this analysis. (Full details of this analysis will be presented in a later publication.) As indicated, only 540 or 32.5 percent were transients or respondents with career histories that show evidence of job-hopping. Of these, 387, or 71.7 percent of all transients, had less than 10 years' experience. Only 153, or 20.6 percent of the transients, had 10 or more years' experience in the field. These findings indicate that most job changes were made by people with less experience in the field, and job stability increased as people became more experienced. These findings suggest that as growth of the field levels off, and more people in the field are experienced practitioners, the rate of turnover will decrease. The percentage for those with stable career histories is conservative and probably too low. Many job changes counted here were certain to have been promotions within the same organization, which do not have the same meaning as job changes that result in employment in a different organization. In general, the findings of this study support the position that turnover in the field is more attributable to the growth of the field and current high demand for experienced practitioners than to a basic character flaw that differentiates fund raisers from other occupational groups.

Other findings regarding turnover included:

- Job stability as indicated by average years per job increased as salary increased. Men and women earning the highest salaries had

**TABLE 3.2. Stable, Marginal, and Transient Career Histories**

| Label | Years Exp. | Years per Job | Total Number | Total Percent | Female Number | Female Percent | Male Number | Male Percent |
|---|---|---|---|---|---|---|---|---|
| Stable | 10 or more | 5 or more | 281 | 16.9 | 97 | 10.8 | 184 | 24.1 |
| | 3 to 9 | 3 or more | 341 | 20.5 | 199 | 22.1 | 142 | 18.6 |
| | Total | | 622 | 37.4 | 296 | 32.9 | 326 | 42.7 |
| Marginal | 10 or more | 3–4.9 | 310 | 18.6 | 130 | 14.4 | 180 | 23.6 |
| | Fewer than 3 | [1] | 32 | 19.5 | 23 | 2.6 | 9 | 1.2 |
| | Total | | 342 | 20.6 | 153 | 17.0 | 189 | 24.7 |
| Transient | 10 or more | under 3 | 153 | 9.2 | 97 | 10.8 | 56 | 7.3 |
| | 3 to 9 | under 3 | 387 | 23.3 | 249 | 27.7 | 138 | 18.1 |
| | Total | | 540 | 32.5 | 346 | 38.4 | 194 | 25.4 |
| Unknown | Fewer than 3 | [2] | 160 | 9.6 | 105 | 11.7 | 55 | 7.2 |

[1] More than one fund raising job.
[2] Only one fund raising job.

the highest average years in their present job, indicating that the highest paid fund raisers stayed put, even though we know that fund raisers at the top of the field are actively recruited, many receiving offers that would substantially increase their already top-of-the-line salaries. This indicates that the lure of the market fails to attract after a certain point.

- The majority of respondents had not changed subsectors within the nonprofit sector. Their average number of jobs were lower and years in present job and average years per job were higher than for those who had changed subsectors, meaning that fund raisers who had not changed subsectors had more job stability than those who had changed from one subsector to another.

- Job stability decreased as the number of subsector changes increased. Both men and women with experience in four or more subsectors had longer careers in fund raising than those in any other group but they also had more jobs and lower average years per job. This seems to indicate that people who are willing to make more radical changes also make more changes, but it could also mean that people who have worked in more than one sector have more value in the market, with more opportunities for advancement.

## FUTURE WITH ORGANIZATION AND FUND RAISING

The survey asked respondents to indicate if they planned to stay with their present organizations and in the field of fund raising for the next year. About 68 percent had no intentions of leaving their present organizations and about 80 percent had no intentions of leaving fund raising in the next year. More women than men planned to leave their organizations and the field of fund raising; these differences are probably related to the fact that women are in lower level jobs where turnover is higher.

One survey respondent wrote that she thought asking such questions of fund raisers was useless because people would not tell the truth. We are not sure why this respondent thought that other survey respondents might want to disguise their intentions in a confidential survey. Why does this negative characterization of fund raisers, suggesting, in this case, that fund raisers lack candor or intend to deceive, keep cropping up? Actually, the survey respondents predicted that they hoped to make more job changes than were likely to occur, according to the other studies that have reported turnover of 17 percent (Thomas, 1987) to 22 percent annually (Mooney, 1993). Furthermore, given the fair amount of active recruiting going on in the field, there must be numbers of fund raisers who change jobs each year because they are recruited when they actually had no plans to change jobs. The number among interviewees in this study who indicated that all of their job changes were the result of being recruited when they were not seeking jobs was very high.

Future research should attempt to collect more specific information on this issue.

Other information about respondents' future plans included the following:

- Those who planned to stay at their organizations and in fund raising had more stable career histories than those planning to leave fund raising and their organizations. This finding suggests that there is a group of fund raisers who are less concerned about job stability than others, but these fund raisers are not in the majority, and again, we have to ask why this attribute is generalized to the field at large.
- The majority of respondents, 59 percent, planned to stay in fund raising and with their present organizations; 22 percent planned to stay in fund raising but leave their present organizations, which is consistent with other reported studies on turnover in development; 8.7 percent of all respondents planned to leave both their present organizations and the field of fund raising; and 3.2 percent planned to leave fund raising but stay with their present organizations.

## Interview Findings

As a follow-up to the survey, I conducted personal interviews with 82 survey respondents to collect information that would be difficult to acquire through written surveys—information about fund raisers' backgrounds and careers, their attitudes about their work, and their thoughts about the strengths and weaknesses of the field. This stage of the research was strongly influenced by the transcripts of interviews from the projects on people in philanthropy at the Oral History Research Center at Indiana University (Harrah-Conforth & Borsos, 1991; Lichtenberg, 1993). These earlier transcripts confirmed three impressions about the field of fund raising:

- In spite of the evolution of now somewhat standard techniques and processes, the work of fund raising has always been, and is today, extremely value-laden.
- Fund raising has always been, and is today, characterized by "the tension between fund raising as business and fund raising as mission" (Harrah-Conforth & Borsos, 1991, p. 27).
- As a group, the people who make their living as fund raisers are colorful, knowledgeable people of substance who love to talk about their work.

From a research perspective, interviews certainly were justified, given the subjective, nonscientific, aspects of the work that have not been fully studied. Furthermore, talking to almost 100 such interesting people seemed like too much fun to miss.

The interviews covered four general areas: Family Background, Education and Career History, Present Position, and Issues in Fund Raising. To stay within budget and time constraints, I selected nine areas across the country: Massachusetts and Connecticut; New York City, Western Pennsylvania; Washington, DC area; North and South Carolina and Georgia; Illinois; Wisconsin and Michigan; Houston area; and Southern California. Interviewees, who were selected at random from survey respondents in these geographic areas, worked in large and small cities, suburbs, and rural areas, and in organizations with national reputations and with local or regional influence.

Forty interviewees (48.8%) were women; 42 interviewees (51.2%) were men. Seventy-seven interviewees (93.9%) were white. Of the remaining interviewees, two were African American women, one was an African American man, and two were East Indian women. The only way to provide a summary of the interview data, brief enough for this chapter, is to present some general observations. To assist in that process, I subjectively rated interviewees using a scale of 5 (high), 3 (medium), or 1 (low) to assess the following characteristics:

1. *Personal Ambition.* Has this person's career been characterized by a strong interest in personal advancement?
2. *Knowledgeable.* Did this person appear to be knowledgeable about the fund raising field?
3. *Warmth.* Was this person pleasant, friendly, comfortable to be with?
4. *Authenticity.* Did this person sound credible and appear to be trustworthy?
5. *Communication Skills.* Was this person articulate, well-spoken, and expressive?
6. *Intensity for Organization.* Did this person appear to have passion for his/her organization?
7. *Intensity for Fund Raising.* Did this person appear to have passion for fund raising?

The results of my subjective evaluations are shown in Table 3.3. As the table indicates, I rated the majority of all interviewees high on all factors and ratings for high ranged from 90 percent for "Intensity for Fund Raising" to 52 percent for "Personal Ambition."

Since it is reasonable to assume that most people who would volunteer to spend two hours talking about fund raising would have a strong interest in the work, I was not surprised to find a high degree of "Intensity for Fund Raising" among 90 percent of the interviewees. I was somewhat more surprised to find a high degree of "Intensity for Organization" among 79 percent of interviewees. Of the 11 to whom I did not

**TABLE 3.3. Subjective Evaluations of Interviewees**

| Factor | High | | Medium | | Low | |
|---|---|---|---|---|---|---|
| | Number | Percent | Number | Percent | Number | Percent |
| Ambition | 43 | 52 | 32 | 39 | 7 | 8 |
| Knowledge of Field | 62 | 76 | 20 | 24 | 0 | 0 |
| Warmth | 53 | 65 | 26 | 32 | 3 | 4 |
| Authenticity | 67 | 82 | 9 | 11 | 6 | 7 |
| Communication Skills | 70 | 85 | 12 | 15 | 0 | 0 |
| Intensity for Organization[1] | 65 | 79 | 10 | 12 | 3 | 4 |
| Intensity for Fund Raising | 74 | 90 | 7 | 9 | 1 | 1 |

[1] 4 interviewees were consultants and not affiliated with a single NPO.

give high ratings in this area, 3 had recently lost their jobs and 4 were planning career changes. It was clear that the remaining 3 perceived their present positions as stepping-stones to other jobs. For the rest, the 79 percent with high ratings, caring deeply about the organization was an important part of the work. Over and over again, I heard "I couldn't do this work for an organization I didn't believe in or respect" or "I wouldn't work this hard if I didn't care about this organization." For most of these thoughtful people, a strong and personal commitment to their employing organizations was one of the most important conditions *they* required to feel satisfied and be effective in their work. Both within and outside the field, many believe strongly that fund raisers should have more organizational commitment than might be expected or required from other staff. Not discussed is the idea that fund raisers themselves may require and expect more of their organizations than other staff. Fund raisers may be more discerning and demanding employees than staff in some other areas.

The items "Warmth" and "Communication Skills" are related, both having to do with how much I enjoyed being with each person and if the interview was easy to conduct. I rated the majority of interviewees high on both items. These were, for the most part, charming, articulate people who talked easily and who made me laugh a great deal. I gave other than high ratings for "Communication Skills" to a few people because they talked too much, or they were difficult to interview because they did not listen well or otherwise did not respond to my attempts to structure the interview. I gave only three low ratings for "Warmth" to people who were quite unusual in this group.

I gave no low ratings for "Knowledge of Fund Raising." Even those with "troubled" career histories projected confidence regarding their experience in the field. Notwithstanding resumes that would document frequent job changes, it was easy to see how these people would be convincing in job interviews, particularly with persons who themselves were not knowledgeable about the field.

Regarding "Authenticity," 82 percent of these interviewees were people whose trustworthiness led me to believe they were people I might hire, like to work with, or work for. I was not completely certain about the credibility of the others, mostly because of contradictory statements or what appeared to be exaggerated claims of their achievements.

I gave fewer high ratings for "Personal Ambition" than for any other characteristic. I found that this was the characteristic on which interviewees were most diverse. As for the 43 (or 52%) interviewees whom I rated high on "Personal Ambition," these were people whose primary motivations were to be successful in their careers, to earn progressively more money, and to have progressively more responsible positions and progressively higher status. For most of these interviewees, however, the definition of "successful" also included a strong component of making a contribution to something they thought was really important. While these people may have had a stronger commitment to their success than to their organizations, they would not work for organizations they did not respect and value. Because they were experienced people with successful track records, they were in demand and could and did exercise considerable judgment and discretion in making job changes. Furthermore, many of them had very high standards for their own productivity and results.

One interviewee said, "It is important to care about one's work, but what pushes me to do my best are my three boys and the life I and my wife are building for them. I would sell life insurance or cars to provide for my family if I had to, but it is a real luxury to be able to do something meaningful." This person was 37 years old, had had two fund raising jobs in eight years, earned about $65,000 as a major gifts officer for a private university, and hoped someday to move into a position of vice president for development at an educational institution. He struck me as a principled, compassionate, competent, intelligent person who respected the university he worked for. He worked long hours at his job, was a volunteer in community activities, and was closely involved with his family. He was honest in indicating that his desire to earn more money to provide the best for his family was the most compelling motivation for him.

Overall, my interviews left the same general impressions I was left with after reading transcripts of earlier interviews with fund raisers conducted by the Indiana University Oral History Research Center. The work of fund raising is value-laden. Most people, whatever their perspective, are emotional about fund raising. Fund raising is not a science conducted according to rules and logic. The tension in fund raising between mission and business is endemic and inherent, and it will never go away. It will always be part of the excitement, the burden, and the challenge. For this reason, those people who have strong values regarding their own success and excellence in their work, as well as a strong desire to contribute to something beyond themselves, may be the best people working in the field. And I will vouch that fund raisers are colorful, interesting, substantial people who love their work.

## Implications for Fund Raisers

Based on this research, Gene Tempel and I have identified what we believe are at least among the most crucial issues currently facing the fund raising field. These issues not only generate considerable frustrations and concerns among practitioners, but they are also ones that have profound implications for the future of the field. Because fund raising is value-laden, all of these issues are controversial, evoking strong reactions from many different perspectives.

## NEGATIVE FEELINGS ASSOCIATED WITH FUND RAISING

Snake oil salesman, used car salesman, bad apple, charlatan, hired gun, pickpocket—these words turned up over and over again on surveys and in interview transcripts. Survey respondents and interviewees used these words both to describe how they were perceived and how they perceived other fund raisers. We are concerned about the extent and breadth of negative feelings associated with fund raising that prevail within and outside the field. These negative feelings have serious consequences for the field, affecting to some extent how people choose the field, the kinds of people attracted to the field, and the whole environment in which fund raisers work.

Although fund raisers are expected to exhibit strong organizational commitment, many fund raisers believe that their acceptance as serious, equal, and valued colleagues in their host organizations is not very high and that unflattering stereotypes still prevail. Although some persons with years of experience in the field noted that perceptions are improving, widespread discomfort about fund raisers continues to be the norm in many nonprofit organizations.

Additionally, some people reported that, when the subject of occupations comes up for the first time with a new acquaintance, they receive reactions ranging from aversion and loathing to incredulity ("How could you bring yourself to ask someone for money?"). Many who have received such reactions believe that a lack of understanding about what fund raisers do is at the root of these negative reactions. Another kind of negative perception of fund raisers comes from fund raisers themselves about others in the field. Over and over again, the interview transcripts reveal a certain and subtle kind of distancing that many fund raisers engaged in to differentiate themselves from other fund raisers. When talking about fund raisers in general, many interviewees used the pronoun "they" instead of "we." And almost everyone told a version of the story about how he or she happened to end up in the field, in spite of having felt earlier that fund raising was an unattractive occupation.

The last and perhaps most serious kind of negative feeling associated with fund raising was that expressed by fund raisers for the actual work of fund raising: making solicitations. A number of fund raisers who worked in situations where all direct solicitations were made by volunteers indicated they would not (or in some cases would not be able to) work as fundraisers if they were themselves required to ask for money. Among those fund raisers who were responsible for making direct solicitations, in some cases there was—despite years of successful experience—a high degree of anxiety, reluctance, and discomfort about "making the ask."

There is nothing mysterious about the negativity surrounding fund raising: Many of these reactions are the result of our culture-bound attitudes toward money and philanthropy. What is noteworthy about this negativity, in addition to how widespread it is, is that it is just not taken very seriously within the field. In fact, the most common way of dealing with it is to joke about it. The failure to take the problem seriously results, at a minimum, in missed opportunities to examine negative perceptions and reactions for whatever truths may be present, to help fund raisers cope more effectively with the feelings such reactions generate, and perhaps most important, to assist fund raisers in developing critical skills they need to more effectively accomplish their goals.

## COMPENSATION

Nowhere is it more apparent that fund raising is value-laden work than it is when addressing the issue of compensation for fund raisers. Compensation in the entire nonprofit sector has become a controversial front-page issue since William Aramony was forced to resign as head of the United Way of America because of charges of financial mismanagement and use of United Way funds to enhance his personal lifestyle. His $463,000 annual salary outraged the press and general public as well as many (but not all) persons working in the nonprofit sector. Although no one defended Aramony's alleged misuse of United Way funds, some fund raisers were not disturbed by his large salary, believing that it was consistent with the scope of his accomplishments and responsibilities. One interviewee said, "We don't have good coherent arguments to make about why a six-figure salary for a United Way director isn't excessive. Managing a billion-dollar enterprise requires skills and abilities that are very competitive in the marketplace. The field has to be better at dealing with these issues."

While many believe that nonprofit salaries should be equal to salaries for comparable positions in the for-profit sector and that comparable salaries are needed to attract the best people, for some fund raisers, high salaries are a source of discomfort (although I have only heard of one fund raiser who has negotiated for a lower salary). One interviewee said, "For the first time in my life I am being paid handsomely. I worked for so long in the nonprofit world where I was told that I gave up higher pay for a noble cause, and I was happy to do that. Sometimes my salary is stressful for me now. I wonder whether I really deserve my paycheck and if I'm overpaid for what I do." Some observers believe that, as fund raising salaries continue to climb, the field is more at risk, more likely to attract persons with inappropriate values or motives. One interviewee noted, "Money taints virtue, money taints motivation, and as we pay people more, we're going to have people in the sector who are there for perhaps different motivations, but that doesn't mean we shouldn't pay people appropriately."

The fund raising field faces a major conundrum. Market mechanisms of supply and demand operate to drive up salaries as more nonprofit organizations experience more urgent needs for successful fund raising programs and compete for the limited number of qualified, experienced fund raisers. At the same time, as overall fund raising costs increase, prospects, donors, and other constituencies including the general public, become more skeptical and more critical. Will increased costs, including higher salaries for fund raisers, serve to decrease giving or substantially diminish the net value of gifts for meeting actual philanthropic needs?

## ETHICS

One interviewee who said that the most divisive issue among fund raisers was the ethics of gift accounting, added, "Fund raisers are like some farmers. They're independent as hell and they always lie to you." Do fund raisers always, or usually, or often, lie, or otherwise seek to deceive, regarding how much they raise?

There is an interesting parallel to be drawn between fund raising and collegiate athletics. Sometimes looking at a problem in a different context can be illuminating. Because higher education organizations are under extreme pressure to generate more revenues from all sources and because fund raising and athletics both present significant opportunities for increasing revenues, staff in these areas experience constantly expanding pressure to "win"—to meet the constantly more demanding bottom line, at a time when resources to support the work are more and more limited. In addition, both fields, by their nature, seem to require and attract people who are aggressive, competitive, and ambitious. These conditions ensure that people who work in these areas will encounter abundant ethical risks and dilemmas.

A study on scandal and reform in collegiate athletics (Cullen, Latessa, & Byrne, 1990) provides some insight about ethical problems in fund raising. This study found that head coaches thought that although "cheating is generally tolerated and fairly widespread" in collegiate athletics, they nevertheless believed that "nearly all" or "most" of their coaching colleagues "are very honest and have very high ethical standards" (p. 53). (It would be interesting to see the results of this kind of research among fund raisers. In light of widespread negative perceptions of fund raisers within the field, I wonder if fund raisers would respond with as much confidence in the honesty of their colleagues.)

Cullen and colleagues (1990) suggested that this apparent contradiction could be understood by the additional finding that the coaches believed the primary reason for cheating was not related to "flaws in the character of coaches," but "the intense pressure to win that is inherent in the role of a head coach" (p. 53). The authors concluded, "Reducing misconduct will depend on implementing reforms that diminish the persistent, intense pressures on coaches to win and accrue profits for their universities" (p. 63).

Generalizing from research on coaches to fund raising, the conclusions suggest that the focus on increasing ethical behavior in fund raising should shift from the behavior and character of fund raisers to an examination of how their roles are structured and the organizational environments in which they work. The research on coaches strongly suggests that fund raisers cannot resolve ethical dilemmas effectively or deal with the conflicts of interest endemic to the work without the full support and commitment to ethical behavior of their organizations.

## PREPARATION FOR WORKING IN FUND RAISING

Fund raisers are divided about whether there should be standardized formal preparation and credentials for working in the field. Opinions on this issue are broad and diverse, ranging from a not infrequently reported belief that fund raisers are born, not made, and that fund raising cannot be taught, to the belief that fund raisers should be licensed and that completing formal educational requirements should be only one part of this process.

The content of the work of fund raising is not perceived to be intellectually rigorous. After all, many kinds of volunteers do this work all over the world. This reality of the nature of the work contributes a great deal to the lack of clarity and consensus among fund raisers about preparation and entry issues. Also, many practitioners reasonably conclude that since they have been successful personally and on behalf of their organizations without such formal requirements, these kinds of standards and requirements are unnecessary for others.

Nevertheless, the relative simplicity of the "mechanics" of fund raising belies the overall complexity of the work, especially at senior levels. Additionally, it is important to take note that the lack of formal avenues for preparation and entry to the field results in the lack of systematic methods for providing enculturation and socialization experiences for those who work in the field. This field will not truly come of age until we take as much responsibility for the socialization of fund raisers as we now do for providing opportunities for the development and enhancement of skills and techniques relevant to effective practice.

## GENDER AND MINORITY ISSUES

All the research to date clearly indicates that significant sexism and even more significant racism operate in the fund raising field. Diversity issues have attracted the attention of for-profit organizations because it has been demonstrated that failure to diversify the workforce will have an increasingly serious and negative impact on the bottom line. Research has indicated that by the year 2000, there will be more and more women and minorities in the workforce and far fewer white males. How will a diversified workforce affect the work of fund raising? Perhaps not enough thought has been given to the possible impact on the bottom line if we fail to diversify our workforce and to eliminate gender-based salary disparities.

## Conclusion

Although many different kinds of research from various disciplines will be useful and are needed in the field of fund raising, progress in our efforts to define effective performance in fund raising will inform the discussion and help people to act responsibly and strategically. Studies of effectiveness and accountability in fund raising should be designed to address the process and content for evaluating, rewarding, and recognizing fund raisers. Research to describe current practices as well as to define "ideal" or preferred practices would be useful. Also helpful would be empirical data regarding what fund raisers actually do in carrying out their functions and roles. This kind of information not only would help others to understand fund raising, but also would be useful in the development of standard competencies defining acceptable practice and performance at basic, intermediate, and advanced levels of practice.

## Bibliography

Association for Healthcare Philanthropy. *Salary and Benefits Report—U.S.A.* Falls Church, VA: Association for Healthcare Philanthropy, 1992, 1993.

Bohlen, J. R. *National Society of Fund Raising Executives 1981 Survey Results.* Alexandria, VA: National Society of Fund Raising Executives, 1981.

Carbone, R. F. *Fund Raisers of Academe.* College Park, MD: Clearinghouse for Research on Fund Raising, 1987.

Carbone, R. F. *Fund Raising as a Profession.* College Park, MD: Clearinghouse for Research on Fund Raising, 1989.

Cullen, F. T., Latessa, E. J., and Byrne, J. P. "Scandal and Reform in Collegiate Athletics: Implications from a National Survey of Head Football Coaches." *Journal of Higher Education,* Jan./Feb. 1990, 50–64.

Duronio, M. A., and Tempel, E. R. *Fund Raisers: Their Careers, Stories, Concerns, and Accomplishments.* San Francisco: Jossey-Bass, 1997.

Harrah-Conforth, J., and Borsos, J. "The Evolution of Professional Fund Raising: 1890–1990." In *Taking Fund Raising Seriously: Advancing the Profession and Practice of Raising Money.* Eds. D. F. Burlingame and L. J. Hulse. San Francisco: Jossey Bass, 1991.

Hodgkinson, V. A., and Weitzman, M. A. *Giving and Volunteering in the United States: Findings from a National Survey.* Washington, DC: INDEPENDENT SECTOR, 1992.

Lewis, P. "President's Message." *NSFRE News,* March 1995, 1.

Lichtenberg, N. *American Foundations Oral History Project Final Report.* Unpublished paper. Bloomington, IN: Indiana University Oral History Research Center, 1993.

McNamee, M. "The Feminization of CASE." *Currents,* September 1990, 8–12.

McNamee, M. "The Outlook for Women." *Currents,* September 1990, 13–14.

McNamee, M. "The Salary Surge." *Currents,* September 1990, 15–21.

Mongon, G. J., Jr. *NSFRE Profile 1985 Membership Career Survey.* Alexandria, VA: National Society of Fund Raising Executives, 1985.

Mongon, G. J., Jr. *NSFRE Profile 1992 Membership Survey.* Alexandria, VA: National Society of Fund Raising Executives, 1992.

Mongon, G. J., Jr. *NSFRE Profile 1995 Membership Survey. Preliminary Report.* Alexandria, VA: National Society of Fund Raising Executives, 1995.

Mongon, G. J., Jr. "Profile 1988 NSFRE Membership Career Survey." *NSFRE Journal,* Winter 1988.

Mooney, C. J. "Study Examines Turnover Rates in 12 Campus Jobs." *Chronicle of Higher Education,* Feb. 10, 1993, A16.

Thomas, E. G. "Flight Records." *Currents,* October 1987, 6–11.

Turk, J. V. "The Changing Face of CASE." *Currents,* June 1986, 8–13.

Turk, J. V. "The Shifting Salary Scene." *Currents,* June 1986, 15–20.

Williams, R. L. "Survey on Advancement." *Currents,* Feb. 1996, 8–22.

# 4 ▼ The Ethical Dimensions of Fund Raising

MICHAEL O'NEILL, EdD
*University of San Francisco*

Peter Drucker once remarked that even though management theory and research are only a century old, management itself is at least as old as the pyramids. Similarly, while philanthropic theory and research are only about 20 years old, philanthropy itself goes back to the beginnings of recorded history. The ethics of philanthropy is no exception to this time gap. There is almost no research on the ethics of philanthropy, even though people have practiced or violated philanthropic ethics, and have discussed the issue, for many centuries. Moses Maimonides's comments on *tzedekah;* many passages from the Bible (Jeavons, 1991), the Koran, and Eastern wisdom; Aristotle's discussion of the virtue of generosity in the *Nichomachean Ethics;* and the reflections of other thinkers, East and West, have presented rich insights into the ethical dimensions of giving and soliciting gifts.

While the recency of the fund raising profession largely explains the absence of research on its ethics, the rapid growth of fund raising activity in United States and a few other countries suggests the need for research on the ethical dimensions of this activity. This need is a subset of the larger need for more theory and research on effective fund raising. Carbone's comment (1986, p. 21) is still largely true a decade later: "The field of fund raising has an enormous body of lore and experience, and even a modest amount of research findings. Its fund of theoretical knowledge, however, is limited."

Given the almost complete absence of research on fund raising ethics, this chapter summarizes the few studies that exist and suggests possibilities for further research. An important definitional issue is the distinguishing between three overlapping but different aspects of fund raising: ethical, legal, and professional. Failing to thank a donor for a gift is neither unethical nor illegal, but it is certainly poor practice. Siphoning off part of a grant for personal use is unprofessional and unethical but, more to the point, it's illegal. Some codes of ethics fail to distinguish clearly between these three areas. We dilute the significance of ethics if we focus instead on what is illegal or simply poor professional practice (*Honorable Matters,* 1991).

Several leaders in the fund raising field have initiated the search for a theory of fund raising, including its ethical aspects. The collection of papers in *Taking Fund Raising Seriously* (Burlingame & Hulse, 1991) is particularly helpful in this regard. Former Harvard president Derek Bok has made some interesting comments on the ethics of fund raising (Bok, 1982, Chapter 11, "Accepting Gifts"). Thompson (1992) has emphasized the relationship of fund raising ethics to the specific institutional setting, an important theoretical point. O'Neill (1993) has argued that Western philosophy provides several excellent starting points for developing a theory of the ethics of fund raising.

These beginnings of a theory of fund raising ethics need to be matched by research on the same topic. One promising area of study is discovering what "ethics" means to fund raisers, what ethical standards they see as relevant to their work, and what ethical decisions they face. There have been several studies of the actual ethical standards, the "moral rules-in-use," of business and government managers, beginning with the classic 1961 *Harvard Business Review* article, "How Ethical are Businessmen?" by Raymond Baumhart, a Jesuit priest reporting on his Harvard Business School doctoral dissertation (Baumhart, 1961, 1968; see also Bird & Waters, 1987; Gortner, 1991; Jackall, 1988; Toffler, 1986; Waters & Bird, 1987). These studies find variations in ethical perceptions and practices, but they all document the existence and importance of ethical standards even in work situations where no explicit mention is made of ethics. People working in the business, government, and presumably nonprofit worlds face ethical decisions and dilemmas whether or not their coworkers or supervisors ever talk about ethics and whether or not the organizations have explicit ethics codes. A key finding of these studies is that workers who must make ethical decisions often experience ambiguity, confusion, and anxiety: What should I do? How do my peers act in such situations? What does my boss think I should do? Another conclusion is that the same "moral rules-in-use"—principles such as honesty in communications, fair treatment, giving special consideration to particular individuals and groups, fair competition, and respect for law—are found in many different organizational settings. These studies, done in the business and government sectors, have relevance for the nonprofit sector and offer, among other things, the possibility of cross-sector and cross-occupational ethical research: What are the similarities and differences between ethical decisions that fund raisers and other managerial and professional workers face?

Two studies include some data on the ethical perceptions and experiences of fund raisers. Carbone (1989) surveyed 754 members of the Association for Healthcare Philanthropy (AHP), the Council for the Advancement and Support of Philanthropy (CASE), and the National Society of Fund Raising Executives (NSFRE), the three largest professional associations of fund raisers. Two questions in the survey dealt with ethical perceptions. The first statement was "Fund raisers are intimately aware of the code(s) of ethics in their field of work and almost without exception these standards guide the work that they do." Only 34 percent of the respondents agreed with this statement; 25 percent disagreed; and 41 percent said they were unsure. These responses are particularly striking in that fully 87 percent of the respondents rated the code of ethics issue as important. The second statement was "Fund raisers who violate ethical standards established by national organizations are penalized by other fund raisers for these violations." Only 5 percent agreed with this factual assertion; 58 percent disagreed; and 37 percent said they were unsure. There was less consensus on whether this was an important issue: 57 percent said yes, 10 percent no, and 33 percent were unsure. The anecdotal responses indicated that many people felt sanctions and penalties were impractical, impossible, or unwise.

Duronio (1995) surveyed a sample of 2,501 members of AHP, CASE, and NSFRE. Of those surveyed, 1,476 (59 percent) responded, along with 272 who received copies of the survey from colleagues, for a total of 1,748 responses. When asked what the "best" fund raisers are like, the two descriptors receiving the largest number of responses were "has integrity" (326) and "honest" (274). The descriptions with the next highest ranking were, in descending order, "intelligent," "outgoing," "committed to cause," "friendly," "self-confident," "enthusiastic," "personable," "ethical" (114), "committed to organization," "is a 'people' person," and "creative." When asked to suggest how the practice of fund raising could be improved, the strategy chosen most often was "promote/'stand for' ethics, honesty, and integrity" (194). Other top responses concerned educating the public about the importance of fund raising, education programs for fund raisers, certification programs for fund raisers, and the like. As a follow-up to the mail questionnaire, Duronio conducted 82 personal interviews with survey respondents and five interviews with "experts" selected because of their positions or experience in the field. Like the survey, the interviews covered a wide range of aspects of fund raising work, including salaries, advancement, preparation, and needed skills. Duronio (1995, p. 14) reported: "Almost every interviewee made at least some mention of ethical issues in fund raising." Ethical issues mentioned included standards for reporting gifts, the scandal involving William Aramony of United Way of America, disclosing fund raising costs, and commission-based compensation.

The Carbone and Duronio studies provide a much-needed beginning of research on the ethical beliefs and perceptions of fund raisers. There has been great attention in recent years to codes of ethics for fund raisers, but almost nothing is known about what fund raisers think of such codes or to what extent these codes actually guide behavior. The fact that only a third of the respondents in Carbone's study were comfortable on these issues clearly suggests that this is an area that needs more attention. Such research could pursue in depth not only the questions previously mentioned, but also such questions as the following: What ethical dilemmas do fund raisers face? How do they deal with them? What do they feel are the most important ethical principles involved in fund raising? How much agreement or disagreement is there among fund raising professionals as to ethical standards and practices?

A related issue of considerable theoretical and practical interest is whether certain demographic variables affect ethical perception and decision making among fund raisers. Carol Gilligan (1977, 1982, 1988; Gilligan, Lyons, & Hanmer, 1990) and others have argued that women and men approach ethical problems differently, that women tend to give more relative weight to the interpersonal dimensions of an ethical situation as distinguished from universal moral principles applicable to the situation. There is evidence both for and against this theory, and it is debated among psychologists, ethicists, and feminists; but it raises a question of possible relevance to an occupation that is already more than 50 percent female and moving increasingly in that direction (Mixer, 1994). Other demographic questions could be raised—for example, do age, professional experience, educational level, social class, minority status, religious background, and other such variables shape the ethical perceptions and behavior of fund raisers?—but none of these areas is as well developed conceptually and empirically as the gender issue.

There is need for research on donor perceptions of fund raising ethics. A January 1990 Opinion Research Corporation survey found that only 37 percent of Americans, when asked to rate eight professions for trustworthiness on a scale of one to five (five being the most trustworthy), ranked fund raisers at the four or five level ("Less Than Half . . . ," 1990). While fund raisers did better in the poll than lawyers, stockbrokers, insurance salesmen, politicians, and car salesmen; and while such isolated research findings need to be interpreted with caution, the results would seem relevant to an occupation whose success depends heavily on trust. Research on donor perceptions could clarify what the people and institutions who donate $125 billion a year to charity think about the ethical characteristics of fund raisers and fund raising. Client perceptions of practitioner ethics are important in all professions and most areas of business. Such perceptions seem especially significant for fund raising given its trust-related dimensions.

Research on the perceptions of major donors is particularly needed. How do wealthy people view the ethics of fund raising? Questions of this type could be an interesting and practical adjunct to studies of the philanthropic attitudes and behavior of the wealthy.

The relationship of giving and culture is another fruitful area of research on fund raising ethics. Anthropologists have found that in some cultures gift-giving is a form of exhibiting status and increasing dominance over the recipient, a finding that may have implications, including ethical implications, for fund raising. For example, donor control motives can raise ethical issues in contributions to universities (Bok, 1982). Naming an endowed chair after a donor might present no problem, but if the donor wanted to control what was taught and even who taught, accepting such a gift would violate the principle of academic freedom. Another example relates to the process of fund raising. In some cultures, asking for a donation is a shameful thing, an abdication of personal and family responsibility. Using normal fund raising procedures with such a group might violate normative standards in that group.

Analysis of fund raising codes is another research possibility. The major fund raising professional organizations and many nonprofit organizations have codes of ethics relating to fund raising behavior. What are the common themes in such codes? What are the significant differences? What insight do such codes give us into fund raising? Ylvisaker suggested that ethical codes reveal something about the professions that develop these codes, including the observation that "the closer the profession is to the market and reality, the longer and the more complicated the code" (Ylvisaker, 1991, p. 158). It may be that fund raisers are particularly focused on ethical questions and ethics codes partly because of their "closeness to the market and reality."

Case studies of fund raising ethics would be useful. The media has focused attention on ethical disasters such as the scandals at United Way of America, the National Association for the Advancement of Colored People, Covenant House, and the like. It would be more illuminating and representative to study the fund raising process in action in a sample of nonprofit organizations, with a special view to the ethically relevant aspects of fund raising behavior.

Such case studies might clarify whether there are significant differences in ethical values and perceptions among the major participants in the fund raising process. A certain amount of anecdotal evidence suggests that fund raisers, CEOs, boards, and key volunteers sometimes feel ethically compromised by actions of one of the other parties. There is no *a priori* reason to assume that major participants in the fund raising process view ethical issues in the same way. Answers to this research question could have major theoretical and practical value.

The "tainted money" issue is another potential area of research. What values and moral standards do people use in deciding whether to solicit and accept gifts from particular donors? A few years ago, a student in a nonprofit management Master's program stated emphatically that he would never accept a gift from a certain oil company. Asked if he would accept a grant from the Rockefeller Foundation, he replied, "Of course!" Aside from its historical weakness, the student's answer raises an important ethical research question: By what principles should fund raising be guided with respect to the appropriateness of donations from certain persons or industries? Does the type of recipient organization or the purpose of the gift make a difference? Does time make a difference? Is it ethical to accept a grant from the Rockefeller Foundation and unethical to accept a gift from one of the oil companies that originally generated that fortune? Is it ethical to accept a grant from the Duke Endowment and unethical to accept a gift from a tobacco company? Should women's groups, or any groups, accept grants from the Playboy Foundation? How do major participants in the fund raising process think about these things? What principles do they use to decide that one gift is acceptable and another is not?

It would be helpful to have empirical studies of the ethical dimensions of prospect research and what people, including donors, think of such research. Foley (1995) surveyed 127 prospect researchers in 1991, including the question "Do you feel your job requires the making of ethical decisions regarding prospect information?" to which 113 answered "Yes" and 9 answered "No." Foley also interviewed six major donors to determine their reaction to prospect researchers gathering information from public records such as probate records, divorce files, and property assessments. The response of the six donors was mixed: Most understood and accepted that such research meant the fund raisers were "merely doing their homework," whereas other respondents expressed discomfort and dismay that fund raisers were gathering information the donors considered highly personal, even if contained in public records.

Another topic worth studying is the history of attention to fund raising ethics. Interest in the ethics of fund raising seems to have increased greatly in the last decade or two. This may be simply a function of the increased amount of activity in this field, but there may be other factors as well. A study documenting and analyzing this phenomenon might be a useful part of the history of this "emerging profession" (Carbone, 1989, p. 46).

The preceding comments represent a brief exploration of the possible areas of research into the ethics of fund raising. There is great need for both theory and research on this important topic. Ethical analysis could clarify the moral dimensions of the fund raising role, and empirical research could test some of the common assumptions about fund raising ethics. This is a subset of the larger need for more theory and research on fund raising in general, a case that has been well made by Mixer (1993), Carbone (1986, 1989), and others. That effort, in turn, is essential for the further professionalization of the fund raising role.

## Bibliography

Baumhart, R. C. "How Ethical Are Businessmen?" *Harvard Business Review,* 1961, 39, 6–19, 156–176.

Baumhart, R. *An Honest Profit: What Businessmen Say about Ethics in Business.* New York: Holt, Rinehart, and Winston, 1968.

Bird, F., and Waters, J. A. "The Nature of Managerial Moral Standards." *Journal of Business Ethics,* 1987, 6, 1–13.

Bok, D. *Beyond the Ivory Tower: Social Responsibilities of the Modern University.* Cambridge, MA: Harvard University Press, 1982.

Burlingame, D. F., and Hulse, L. J., eds. *Taking Fund Raising Seriously: Advancing the Profession and Practice of Raising Money.* San Francisco: Jossey-Bass, 1991.

Carbone, R. F. *An Agenda for Research on Fund Raising.* College Park, Md.: Clearinghouse for Research on Fund Raising, University of Maryland College Park, 1986.

Carbone, R. F. *Fund Raising as a Profession.* College Park, Md.: Clearinghouse for Research on Fund Raising, University of Maryland College Park, 1989.

Duronio, M. A. Personal communication. 1995.

Foley, K. Personal communication. 1995.

Gilligan, C. "In a Different Voice: Women's Conceptions of Self and of Morality." *Harvard Educational Review*, 1977, 47, 481–517.

Gilligan, C. *In a Different Voice: Psychological Theory and Women's Development*. Cambridge, MA: Harvard University Press, 1982.

Gilligan, C., ed. *Mapping the Moral Domain: A Contribution of Women's Thinking to Psychological Theory and Education*. Cambridge, MA: Harvard University Press, 1988.

Gilligan, C., Lyons, N. P., and Hanmer, T. J., eds. *Making Connections: The Relational Worlds of Adolescent Girls at Emma Willard School*. Cambridge, MA: Harvard University Press, 1990.

Gortner, H. F. "How Public Managers View Their Environment: Balancing Organizational Demands, Political Realities, and Personal Values." In *Ethical Frontiers in Public Management: Seeking New Strategies for Resolving Ethical Dilemmas*. Ed. J. S. Bowman. San Francisco: Jossey-Bass, 1991, pp. 34–63.

*Honorable Matters: A Guide to Ethics and Law in Fund Raising* Chicago: National Society of Fund Raising Executives, Chicago Chapter, 1991.

Jackall, R. *Moral Mazes: The World of Corporate Managers*. Oxford University Press, New York, 1988.

Jeavons, T. H. "A Historical and Moral Analysis of Religious Fund Raising." In *Taking Fund Raising Seriously: Advancing the Profession and Practice of Raising Money*. Eds. D. F. Burlingame and L. J. Hulse. San Francisco: Jossey-Bass, 1991, pp. 53–72.

"Less Than Half of Americans Rate Fundraisers Trustworthy." *Non-Profit Times*, March 1990, p. 17.

Mixer, J. R. *Principles of Professional Fundraising: Useful Foundations for Successful Practice*. San Francisco: Jossey-Bass, 1993.

Mixer, J. R. "Women as Professional Fundraisers." In *Women and Power in the Nonprofit Sector*. Eds. T. Odendahl and M. O'Neill. San Francisco: Jossey-Bass, 1994, pp. 223–253.

O'Neill, M. "Fundraising as an Ethical Act." *Advancing Philanthropy*, 1993, 1, 30–35.

Thompson, D. F. "Ethical Fundraising: An Educational Process." *Educational Record*, 1992, 38–43.

Toffler, B. L. *Tough Choices: Managers Talk Ethics*. Wiley, New York, 1986.

Waters, J. A., and Bird, F. "The Moral Dimension of Organizational Culture," *Journal of Business Ethics*, 1987, 6, 15–22.

Ylvisaker, P. "Summary of Statement." In *Ethics and the Nation's Voluntary and Philanthropic Community: Obedience to the Unenforceable*. Washington, DC: INDEPENDENT SECTOR, 1991.

# 5 Respecting the Individual, Valuing Diversity

## Equity in Philanthropy and Fund Raising

Marilyn Fischer, PhD

*University of Dayton*

Three 70-year-old African American cousins came to my predominantly white philosophy of music class to talk about gospel music. They recalled their earliest memories of music in the black church and traced how it changed through time. They recounted their experiences with gospel music in rural black churches and urban churches, in "class" churches and "mass" churches. They laughed, remembering how gospel music had been celebrated from the beginning in some churches, yet viewed with suspicion in others. Finally, at the end, one cousin said, "You know, gospel music really isn't my thing."

My students learned a lot about diversity that day. They learned that to understand an individual they had to understand the social and historical contexts through which he or she shapes a life. Gospel "isn't my thing" in a very different way for the cousin than for many of the white students because it is not a part of their history. Yet, among those who share a social and historical context, individual differences will be found.

There are paradoxes in thinking about equity and diversity together. We think of equity in terms of fairness, which we often translate as treating people "the same." We also call for sensitivity to diversity, acknowledging that various cultural groups are different in important ways, and to treat everyone "the same" ignores or erases these differences. Then, when we finally get our sensitivities right about group differences, we realize we can't see the individual for the group. In this chapter, I will begin to work through some of the many layers of complexity that this issue poses.

The fund-raising profession has made clear its commitment to diversity. Pat Lewis, President and CEO of NSFRE, in her editorial for *Advancing Philanthropy's* Winter 1994 issue devoted to diversity, writes, "If we are truly committed to advancing philanthropy . . . we must be equally committed

**65**

to cultural and social inclusiveness." She concludes the column, "Let us do all we can to strengthen the diverse tapestry of philanthropy" (p. 9).

A number of contributors to that issue remind us how a commitment to diversity is a matter of ethical import. Charles Stephens (1994) stresses that in this country all actions have significance in terms of race, ethnicity, and gender. To the degree that philanthropic decisions are made without regard for these differences, philanthropy is undemocratic. R. Roosevelt Thomas, Jr. (1994), finds it imperative that organizations manage diversity so that all participants can contribute to their full potential.

Understanding and valuing diversity involves both equity and ethics. I will focus on two subtle, yet pervasive forms of inequity that are perpetuated when diversity is not acknowledged and will discuss why it is hard to recognize that everyone is diverse.

## Equity and Respect

There are many ways to think about the basic equality of all people. Aristotle articulated the fundamental Western understanding of equity: Justice or fairness is a matter of treating equals equally and unequals in proportion to their inequality. Kant identified the basis of human equality: Whatever else we are, however we may differ as individuals, humans qua humans are infinitely precious and worthy of respect. Respect is owed to people simply on the basis of their shared humanity. Treating people equitably is a matter of treating all people in a manner that respects their intrinsic worth and dignity. Here, treating people equitably means treating them the same, where "same" is based on our shared, universal humanity. Because we are fundamentally the same in terms of basic human worth, we all deserve to be treated accordingly.

The tradition of classical liberalism, from John Locke, to the Declaration of Independence, and throughout the history of the U.S. Constitution, reinforces this tradition of equity as treating people equally. The familiar idea here is to treat everyone equally, *regardless* of their sex, race, religion, ethnic origin or condition of disability. This notion is usually applied in terms of political and civil rights, such as rights to vote, to a fair trial, to freedom of speech and religion, and to equal legal recognition of basic needs to education, healthcare, and so on. Honoring these rights is a way of demonstrating equal respect. This provides background conditions on which individuals can then act autonomously, pursue their vision of the good life, and seek to realize their potential.

All of this sounds fine. The puzzle comes when we pair this understanding of equity with current calls for increased sensitivity to diversity issues. Affirmative action gives a paradigmatic example of this puzzle. We say that in hiring and promotion, it is equitable that everyone be judged on merit alone, and not on their skin color, ethnic origin, gender, sexual orientation, or religious beliefs. Yet the factors on this list are precisely those important for sensitivity to diversity. The puzzle is, how can we be sensitive to and value diversity, while also treating people equitably?

When puzzles appear, it is time to question assumptions. While respect for "humans qua humans" is fundamental to equity, it is incomplete. For persons come into the world, and live and grow with a history, functioning within multiple cultural groups. One individual may be Hispanic, Catholic, a woman, a lesbian, and able-bodied. None of these factors determines what a person is, but they do give a heritage and history of circumstances to which that person responds in the process of forming his or her own personal identity. Here we arrive at the response to defining equity as treating people the same. To treat persons *regardless* of gender, sexual orientation, degree of disability, and ethnic background is *not* to treat them as an individuals, but to ignore factors crucial in understanding who they are. Hence the insult my friend feels when a white person says to her, "I don't even see you as black; to me you are just Pat."

## Perceptual Inequities

Inequities stemming from prejudice are easy to evaluate from an ethical point of view—they are morally wrong. The ethics of prejudice are simple; identifying prejudice and rooting it out are much more difficult. However, when diversity is not recognized and valued, more subtle and deeply rooted forms of inequity are apt to be perpetuated, often by reasonable, decent, well-meaning people. Two of these forms can be called "perceptual inequities" and "institutional inequities."

Perceptual inequities may occur when people misunderstand, and consequently misjudge what another person thinks or does. This is particularly problematic when the person who misjudges is in a position of power, or has the ability to make choices that will dramatically affect the life-chances of the other.

A number of perceptual inequities have been identified in recent work on philanthropy and fund raising. One has to do with understanding ethnic traditions in giving. When survey questions are framed in terms of money and time donated to philanthropic organizations, many ethnic groups in the United States appear less philanthropic than the white population. But the assessment changes when informal giving customs are included. For example, Smith, Shue, Vest and Villarreal in *Ethnic Philanthropy* (1994), write of the Mexican tradition of "compadrazgo," or fictive kinship. Extended families are created, and with them, strong responsibilities to care emotionally, spiritually, and materially for members outside the nuclear family. An anthropologist, commenting on "compadrazgo," writes, "It exists in the gap between the absolute, formal rigidity of the family and the absolute flexibility of friendship. . . . In other societies this gap is filled by such institutions as voluntary associations" (Foster, 1967, p. 79).

To overlook traditions of giving in ethnic communities while collecting data on philanthropy, is to impose cultural patterns of the dominant society on communities where these do not fit. When giving through voluntary organizations is assumed to be normal and definitional, rather than as *one* way of being philanthropic, other patterns are judged deficient or not even seen.

Emmett Carson (1991) gives another example of perceptual inequities. He observes:

> By allowing the unchallenged perpetuation of the myth that blacks are not engaged in efforts to help themselves, public attention has focused on whether the poorest members of the black community are deserving of assistance, rather than on the more salient issue of what resources are required to address the needs of poor blacks. Whether intentionally or not, the lack of scholarly interest in black philanthropy has helped to perpetuate these beliefs by signaling either that blacks have no philanthropic traditions worthy of study or that their participation in the nonprofit sector is negligible. (p. 222)

What scholars choose to study is an equity issue in that scholarly attention certifies an issue as "worthy," and uncovers historical and empirical data upon which public and private initiatives are based. The misperception that African Americans have no tradition of philanthropy can thus perpetuate a number of continuing inequities.

Perceptual inequities can also be seen in hiring and compensation patterns in nonprofit workplaces. Julie C. Conry's (1991) study, "The Feminization of Fund Raising," explores how the field is changing as the percentage of women in the profession increases. In other fields such as public relations, bank telling, teaching, and library science, as relatively more women entered a profession, salary levels and prestige declined. Many of these changes reflect "perceptual inequities." Conry cites several studies that compare men's and women's salaries, with all other factors being equal such as same job title, type and size of institution, and educational and experiential background. A 1990 CASE study found that being male added $5,136 to annual salary, up from $3,686 in 1986. Here the same tasks are perceived as less valuable if performed by a woman rather than a man.

A second type of perceptual inequity has to do with how various job-related skills are assessed and valued. Skills that are traditionally associated with being female, such as listening well and nurturing, are viewed as "natural" rather than acquired skills, and their value is downgraded accordingly. Conry concludes, "The characteristics attributed to women as making them more effective fund raisers—being more verbal, more sensitive, less afraid of emotion, more detail-oriented, more nurturing and more creative—are also cited as the very reason many barriers exist to being taken seriously by management, trustees, and donors" (p. 164).

These perceptual inequities are further reflected in the extent to which occupations are segregated by gender; for the most part men and women do not do the same work. This is true in nonprofit organizations, as well as in business and government. Women make up 65 to 70 percent of the nonprofit workforce, yet they hold only 15 percent of executive and managerial positions (Conry & McDonald, 1994). Even within the same profession, men and women do different work. Conry cites evidence of "female ghettos" developing within the fund-raising profession, with high concentrations of women in prospect research and annual fund, two areas of relatively low compensation and status (1994).

In the preceding examples, perceptual misjudgments lead to genuine inequities. People are not assessed fairly and they suffer social, economic and psychological costs as a result.

## Institutional Inequity

A second form of inequity I will call "institutional inequity," patterned after Gertrude Ezorsky's notion of "institutional racism." In *Racism and Justice: The Case for Affirmative Action*, Ezorsky (1991) defines institutional racism this way. "Institutional racism occurs when a firm uses a practice that is race-neutral (intrinsically free of racial bias) but that nevertheless has an adverse impact on blacks as a group" (p. 9). Examples of practices which can perpetuate institutional racism include recruitment by personal connections and using personality traits as qualification requirements.

Ezorsky stresses that these policies are not inherently inequitable, and would probably be used in a society free of discrimination. A personal connection regarding a prospective employee can give valuable information that is difficult to obtain in other ways. Yet when wealth and power are distributed inequitably, using personal connections in this way excludes people who lack such connections. Also, on the face of it, it is eminently sensible to want to hire someone who will be able to function comfortably with the current team of employees. But if the team functions effectively because of shared socialization as whites, or as middle-class women, or as jocks, then the impact of this hiring qualification is to perpetuate inequities. While these institutional practices may themselves be free from overt prejudice, they may have the effect of reinforcing prejudice. People may think, if there are so few black, female, or disabled CEOs, perhaps people in those groups genuinely lack qualification.

Ezorsky focuses on racism, but we can think by analogy to other inequities. One source of institutional inequity in nonprofits that is particularly troubling is the way "friendship" functions. Now friendship is a vital human good, as Epicurus reminds us, "Of the things which wisdom provides for the blessedness of one's whole life, by far the greatest is the possession of friendship" (1994, p. 34). Yet the argument could be made that friendship functions in nonprofits to perpetuate institutional inequities. The best solicitor is the person who has, or can easily develop, a personal relationship with a prospect. Thus begins a potentially long-term relationship between the prospect and the organization, leading to larger gifts and deeper involvement, influence, and power. The inequity here is that friendship patterns in this country reek of historical discrimination. Housing, education and employment patterns, and participation in churches and social organizations all are heavily influenced by gender, ethnicity, race, and class. We know and feel comfortable with people like us—our friends. People in positions of power and influence have friends who also are in positions of power and influence. Even when overt prejudice is absent, social inequities are perpetuated when friendship is an influential basis for organizational function.

## We Are All Diverse

Read and listen carefully to expressions of concern about diversity. In most cases, one hears about women, African Americans, Hispanics, and other ethnic groups, gays and lesbians, and perhaps the disabled. These are valid and needed calls for increased sensitivity to those among us with diverse backgrounds, experiences, and cultures. But the unstated assumption is that some of us are not diverse, that some of us are "normal." Deep in the background, rarely brought to consciousness, we have the contemporary version of the question W.E.B. DuBois (1990) in 1903 felt always fluttering around him though never stated explicitly, "How does it feel to be a problem?" (p. 7) Today the unstated, but underlying question is, "How does it feel to be diverse?" Notice the presupposition, that there are some who are not diverse, who are not the problem.

As long as this is the case, no matter how "sensitive" we become to diverse cultures, inequity will persist. Until those who consider themselves "normal" replace that mentality with the clear understanding that their perspective is but one among many, the schema for stigma remains.

Inequities are perpetuated by the notion that one or one's group is nondiverse (normal). I ask my white students what it means to be black, and they have quite a lot to say (but not nearly enough). I then ask them what it means to be white, and they have absolutely nothing to say. In this case, their ignorance is a reflection of their privileged social status. Persons of color need to know what it means to be white as a matter of survival (Collins, 1990). For white people, being able to get on all right in life without knowing what it means to be white is a sign that the social world is so constructed in their own image, that they need not see their reflection.

Peggy MacIntosh (1993) comments, "I have come to see white privilege as an invisible package of unearned assets that I can count on cashing in each day, but about which I was "meant" to remain oblivious" (p. 31). She gives many concrete examples of what this package contains, including: "I can do well in a challenging situation without being called a credit to my race"; "I can be reasonably sure that if I ask to talk to 'the person in charge,' I will be facing a person of my race"; "I can be late to a meeting without having the lateness reflect on my race"; and, "If I have low credibility as a leader, I can be sure that my race is not the problem" (pp. 33–34). Knowing what it means to be white includes being concretely aware of how having white skin eases one's way through the day.

There are reasons the "normal" perspective needs to be made explicit. I do not think those with the "normal" perspective will be able to understand diversity until they can see how those from "diverse" perspectives view them. This is not easy, and often requires a wrenching reconstruction of oneself. Diversity isn't simply that some people celebrate Christmas, while others have Hanukkah or Kwanzaa. In the United States, it didn't happen that diverse cultures one day dropped in and settled in proximity. The history of diversity is a history of oppression and domination, a history in which benefits and burdens of social life have been distributed most inequitably.

What are the implications of these concerns for fund raising research? Many efforts are being undertaken to research historic and contemporary giving patterns among ethnic communities (see, e.g., Hamilton & Ilchman, 1995). These efforts are critical, both as a matter of equity, and to increase effective philanthropic endeavors among these populations. However, the point of this chapter is that "valuing diversity" cannot be simply a matter of adding ethnic or gender concerns to ongoing institutions. Dominant cultural philanthropic institutions need to scrutinize their own histories, institutional structures and culture to identify perceptual and institutional inequities. They need to examine, for example, how biased perceptions have shaped hiring and job assessment patterns, or how friendship and institutional power have been linked. Thomas's (1991) analysis of how changing root culture is fundamental to managing diversity gives one pattern for how extensive change needs to be.

Yes, to deal with inequity, we must understand and value diversity. But understanding diversity is more than appreciating diverse customs and points of view. It is also understanding our mutual history of diversity, and the inequitable power structures at the base of that history. Rooting out perceptual and institutional inequities rests on our ability to confront explicitly this history and its contemporary legacies.

## Bibliography

Carson, E. D. "Contemporary Trends in Black Philanthropy: Challenging the Myths." In *Taking Fund Raising Seriously.* Eds. D. F. Burlingame and L. J. Hulse. San Francisco: Jossey-Bass, 1991.

Collins, P. H. *Black Feminist Thought*. New York: Routledge, 1990.

Conry, J. C. "The Feminization of Fund Raising." In *Taking Fund Raising Seriously*. Eds. D. F. Burlingame and L. J. Hulse. San Francisco: Jossey-Bass, 1991.

Conry, J. C., and McDonald, J. E. "Moving Toward a Matrix: Gender and the Nonprofit Culture of the Nineties." In R. C. Hedgepath (Ed.), *New Directions for Philanthropic Fundraising: Nonprofit Organizational Culture*, No. 5, San Francisco: Jossey-Bass, 1994.

DuBois, W. E. B. *The Souls of Black Folk*. New York: Vintage Books, 1990.

Epicurus. *The Epicurus Reader*, trans. by B. Inwood and L. P. Gerson. Indianapolis: Hackett, 1994.

Ezorsky, G. *Racism and Justice: The Case for Affirmative Action*. Ithaca, NY: Cornell University Press, 1991.

Foster, George M. *Tzintzuntzan: Mexican Peasants in a Changing World*. Boston: Little, Brown, 1967, pp. 75–77.

Hamilton, C. H., and Ilchman, W. F. *Cultures of Giving II: How Heritage, Gender, Wealth, and Values Influence Philanthropy. New Directions for Philanthropic Fundraising*. No. 8, San Francisco: Jossey-Bass, Summer 1995.

Lewis, P. "Diversity: Challenge and Opportunity." *Advancing Philanthropy*, Winter 1994, 2, 9.

MacIntosh, P. "White Privilege and Male Privilege." In A. Minas (Ed.), *Gender Basics: Feminist Perspectives on Women and Men*. Belmont, CA: Wadsworth, 1993.

Smith, B., Shue, S., Vest, J. L., and Villarreal, J. *Ethnic Philanthropy*. San Francisco: University of San Francisco, Institute for Nonprofit Organization Management, 1994.

Stephens, C. R. "Is Philanthropy Democratic?" *Advancing Philanthropy*, Winter 1994, 2, 21–24.

Thomas, Jr., R. R. *Beyond Race and Gender*. New York: American Management Association, 1991.

Thomas, Jr., R. R. "Managing Diversity and the Philanthropic Community." *Advancing Philanthropy*, Winter 1994, 2, 31–33.

# PART III Giving

# ▼ 6 The Demographics of Giving Patterns

## JULIAN WOLPERT, PhD

*Woodrow Wilson School—Princeton University*

Giving patterns are of interest to many groups. Development officers and fund raisers are concerned with what these patterns reveal about short- and long-run donor trends and donor response to changes in the economy and tax laws, news about charity improprieties, and shifts in political and social attitudes and values that affect giving. Nonprofit officials worry about the same factors but are also concerned about whether donors will augment or retarget their gifts to make up for cutbacks in government grants and contracts.

Researchers who have been observing long-term giving patterns have the challenge of assessing the degree of stability in donations and interpreting the incremental shifts taking place among donors. How are demographic and social shifts, changes in income distribution, population redistribution, and political change reflected in donation levels and the targeting of donations? Are the American people developing donor and volunteer fatigue? Have we Americans become so fragmented into special interest groups and so self-serving in the targeting of our contributions that we give only to organizations whose services we benefit from directly? The answers to these questions and concerns can be found only in part from surveys and analysis of giving patterns. The survey findings tell us some basic facts about continuity and change, but they raise additional questions.

## Donor Profiles

Students of donor behavior and practicing fund raisers share a common dream, which is to discover robust and consistent clues to behavioral determinants of charitable giving. The task of eliciting gifts would be much simpler and more efficient if we knew the factors that determine donor intentions and the factors that affect the level and targeting of contributions. The dream of fund raisers is to identify stable profile groups of donors who can be expected to respond homogeneously to a precisely worded solicitation. That would make it far easier to alter the messages systematically to elicit a higher rate of giving or a change in the targeting of gifts. This enhanced skill should enable fund raisers to raise U.S. giving levels from the current modest 2 percent level to the "Give Five" goal or even higher. Some practitioners may protest that increasing the level of precision and predictability about donors would spoil the fun and challenge of fund raising. They needn't worry on that account. We are far from achieving this pinnacle of accuracy and are not likely to develop a magic solicitation formula within the next few years.

Information on national patterns of giving by profile groups has improved our understanding of why people are generous or not. Donor surveys, such as the INDEPENDENT SECTOR's series on *Giving and Volunteering* (Hodgkinson & Weitzman, 1994), permit us to begin to relate specific socioeconomic, life-cycle, ethnic, and religious attributes with giving levels and targeting of donations. The breakdowns reported in the 1994 volume show us the percentage of respondents who contribute, their average contribution, and the percentage of household income represented by their contributions (see Table 1.9 in *Giving and Volunteering*, Vol. I, 1994). For example, males contribute a higher share of their income than females, whites more than minority members, the elderly more than the young, the poor and the rich more than the middle class, Protestants and others more than Catholics, married people more than singles. Appendix D of Volume II provides the demographic profiles for donors who contribute to: the arts; education; environment; health; human services; and religion. Readers are referred to these tables and to the accompanying discussion for further information and survey findings.

But these tabulations by single or dual household attributes (e.g. the giving patterns of the elderly affluent) still contain a great deal of variance. The elderly affluent vary a great deal in their giving patterns. More sophisticated analysis and much larger donor surveys will allow us to develop profile groups based on multiple socioeconomic and other characteristics that can be assumed to have somewhat more predictable patterns of giving. Multivariate analyses of giving patterns would allow classifying donors into profile groups that are more homogeneous. However, the profile analyses at best would provide marginal improvements in predictability. An adequate donor profile analysis for the nation in all its diversity would require much larger samples and more expensive surveys than the 1,500 households in the Gallup sample for *Giving and Volunteering*.

The inherent limitations of this approach, however, are the shortcomings of relying solely on demographic and social variables as determinants of giving. Donor behavior is also affected by emotional, cognitive and context factors that do not necessarily vary consistently with socioeconomic attributes. Some of these context variables are covered in the *Giving and Volunteering* survey, such as the effect of being solicited for a contribution. The more subtle but vitally important behavioral characteristics and context factors are more difficult to discern and assess. For further insight on these factors, we need to rely on our social psychology colleagues and their expertise in designing experiments and questionnaires. These factors are more difficult to elicit in surveys or even in personal interviews.

This is not to deny the valuable information obtained from the *Giving and Volunteering* survey whose value is enhanced by the opportunity to examine changes over two-year intervals. The data provide helpful clues about national giving tendencies and their shifts that merit further investigation. For example, evidence of recent donor and volunteer fatigue among subgroups of the population is an important warning sign to the need for further validation and targeting of strategies for remedial action. People do not donate at specific levels because they are male, affluent, and Catholic. But if giving and volunteering declines substantially over a two-year period among this group, we can attempt to verify the observed pattern among recipient agencies. If true, we can retarget our fund raising efforts to ease the impacts, if at all possible.

Analysis of donor behavior by demographic characteristics or donor profiles is presumably guided by assumptions about household resources that affect the ability to give and habitual giving patterns. After all, it is generally more efficient to solicit the rich than the poor and those who give regularly than the impulse donor who may only get the impulse on rare occasions. Thus, demographic characteristics are most helpful in reaching those easiest to solicit for continued giving. However, donations are also affected by solicitation and social contexts. The solicitation context is the interaction between fund raiser and potential donor whether through mail, phone, or personal interview. There are many specialists who study the solicitation context and I readily defer to their greater expertise.

While waiting for additional research, however, much can be learned from currently available data about the demographic characteristics of donors and how we can do an ever better job of augmenting contribution levels. A lot can be learned as well about the new fund raising challenge attributable to demographic changes occurring in the metropolitan areas that contain most of our nonprofits.

## Donor Patterns in America's Metropolitan Areas and States

I have been examining demographic and community patterns of American generosity over the past several years. My rationale is that national data about giving patterns is of concern primarily to that small minority of charities that raise funds nationally. Since more than 90 percent of contributions are raised and spent locally, giving patterns examined in their local social and economic contexts can provide additional insight. This nation is so diverse and so locally oriented that national patterns of giving tell us only part of what we need to know. The community studies have included both charitable and public sector expressions of generosity. The analyses have been aimed at helping fund raisers understand first how and why Americans and their communities differ so profoundly in their levels of generosity and second how and why these differences matter and what to do about it.

A brief synopsis of findings from the community studies (Wolpert, 1993) shows that:

- Americans are not uniformly generous but vary greatly from place to place in their level and targeting of donations.
- Generosity differences between communities have their greatest impact on services targeted to the lowest income population.
- Disparities in generosity levels have been declining but principally due to the harsher economic environment in the more generous places rather than greater generosity in the more parsimonious places.
- Generosity is greater where per capita income is increasing, the political and cultural ideology is liberal rather than conservative, and in the smaller metropolitan areas where distress levels are lower.
- Greater generosity is associated with greater targeting for educational, cultural, and health services rather than social assistance to the needy.
- The increased sorting of Americans into socially homogeneous communities has reproduced public and nonprofit service infrastructures in the suburbs often at the expense of support for center city and rural institutions (the real growth of service provision is quite small).
- Gaps in basic services and quality of life are widening between the growing and declining states and metropolitan areas.
- Our severely fragmented and atomized nonprofit sector contributes effectively to the variety and quality of life in American communities but lacks the resources and is not structured to address major service and regional disparities.

The findings show that some American communities are a lot more generous than others (e.g., an 18-fold difference in United Way contributions, even greater disparities in others), just as some socioeconomic, age, cultural, and religious groups are more generous than others (Wolpert, 1993). Some differences in generosity both in charitable giving and willingness to support public sector services are to be expected in this large and diverse nation. Minor differences do not need much attention. We analyze the extremes or the outliers in donor differentials by place or by socioeconomic attributes not to label or stigmatize some as generous or stingy but to assist in probing the *why* and the *so what* issues and to improve fund raising efforts and outcomes.

Regional and community analysis allows us to examine how donor behavior is related to community size and composition, historical and social development, the level of economic well-being or distress or other factors presumably linked to generosity. We have been able to verify that American generosity is greater in smaller communities, in places where resources are greater and distress less severe, greater in center cities than suburban communities, greater in blue than white collar communities, and greater in politically liberal than conservative places. Because of the changing economic environment and political shifts, giving level differences have been declining.

We also find from these analyses that profound differences in generosity between places persist even after allowing for these economic and social factors (e.g., Midwest communities are more generous than those in the Sunbelt). Apparently, *regional cultures of generosity* exist that are analogous to civic and political cultures. However, we still understand little about how generosity and civic culture emerge and develop and how to intervene to foster more of it. In-depth demographic and community studies are needed to improve our knowledge base of institutional, behavioral, and context factors.

## Discussion

The social context for donors relates to community and provides the rationale for studying how giving patterns differ from place to place. We cannot assume that demographic or profile groups will behave similarly in all environments. Donations presumably are affected by the value that people place on the services and benefits provided by local nonprofits and their resource needs to carry on programs and activities. If donors of a given demographic profile behaved uniformly in all communities, then the fund raising task would be infinitely simpler. But they do not. Thus, we are forced to supplement the analysis of donor profiles by observing the locational patterns of giving. Community study thus provides an opportunity to capture an additional set of variables for observation.

The added justification for community studies is that other dimensions of giving behavior can be revealed by examining donations on a place-by-place basis. This strategy allows us to observe patterns of giving for places that differ not only in the demographic and social composition of their populations but in their complements of nonprofit institutions and giving traditions. Additional hypotheses can be validated as well, such as the notions that smaller or more socially homogeneous places are more generous than larger and more diverse places; or that generosity is greater in longer established communities; or where income is more evenly distributed; or where nonprofits play a more prominent role in service provision; or that places have distinctive and enduring cultures of generosity; or that donor tendencies are crowded out by public sector generosity.

# Bibliography

Hodgkinson, Virginia, and Weitzman, Murray. *Giving and Volunteering in the United States.* Washington, DC: INDEPENDENT SECTOR, 1994.

Wolpert, Julian. *Patterns of Generosity in America: Who's Holding the Safety Net?* New York: Twentieth Century Fund, 1993.

# 7 Philanthropic Giving and Fund Raising in Europe

## Patterns and Current Developments

HELMUT ANHEIER
*Rutgers University & Johns Hopkins University*

STEFAN TOEPLER
*Johns Hopkins University*

This chapter offers a basic overview of fund raising patterns and practices in Western Europe by illustrating a broad spectrum of sources of private support that includes individual giving, corporate contributions, and foundation support, and also less commonly used sources, such as lotteries and fine collections. This is followed by a look at current trends in fund raising. There is a growing diversification of funding sources in many European countries, combined with increased professionalization of fund-raising approaches and techniques. To a large extent, this first trend is a reflection of the greater need among nonprofit organizations to generate higher levels of private support in a fiscal environment characterized by cutbacks in public budgets, and subsequent reductions in government support. The second trend, professionalization, while feeding on the greater demand and the wider opportunities for fund raising services in recent years, is, in no small measure, also related to calls for improved accountability of grant-making practices among donors, the nonprofit community, and the public at large.

Throughout this chapter we point out similarities and differences in European fund-raising compared with the situation in the United States. While all European countries can look back to long traditions of charity, individual giving, and philanthropic institutions, the term "fund raising" has typically been absent in their cultural repertoire. This is not to say, however, that no fund-raising practices and techniques exist in Europe; to the contrary, we observe a rich set of such practices throughout the region. The point is that fund raising in Europe takes place in a different cultural and institutional environment: For example, the role of religion

**81**

in individual giving behavior is markedly different from that in the United States, as are popular expectations attributed to the role of the state. European countries generally have populations that are far less religious and more secular in cultural orientation than the United States; similarly, European countries have allocated a greater role to the state for the social, cultural and economic well-being of their citizens, leading to a more comprehensive system of public and private institutions in fields such as social protection or arts and culture. Since both factors, religion and state, are significantly related to the size and scope of a country's nonprofit sector (Anheier & Seibel, 1990; Salamon & Anheier, 1996), we expect fund raising patterns and practices to vary accordingly.

As in the United States, albeit with a considerable time lag, fund raising has become more important over the past 15 years and is likely to emerge as one of the central themes among European nonprofit managers in the future. We have already hinted at some of the reasons for this (e.g., cutbacks of government funds and increased professionalization). While these may appear familiar to students of American fund raising, it would be wrong to assume that fund raising will take on the same importance and centrality for nonprofit organizations in Europe as in the United States. Of course, American fund-raising techniques have been, and will continue to be, imported by Europe. However, they are then usually adapted to fit a cultural and social context that may be very different from that of the United States.

## Why Fund Raising Is an Issue in Europe

More than 2,000 years ago, Gaius Maecenas, a nobleman and friend of the Roman emperor Augustus, sponsored the works of the poets Ovid, Horace, and Virgil. Many centuries later, Maecenas was adopted as the cultural role model for Europe's patrons supporting cultural, educational, and charitable initiatives. Indeed, largely stripped of the patrician, conservative image it carried for much of the nineteenth and twentieth centuries, the term "maecenatism," or *Mäzenatentum* in German and *mécénat* in French, as private patronage has come to be called, has undergone a remarkable revival in recent years. Judging from current debates, it appears as if European citizens as well as business corporations are taking renewed interest in supporting common causes through private contributions rather than via public channels, (i.e., taxation).

One underlying reason for this trend is the growing disenchantment with the welfare state among the political and economic elites of European countries. Irrespective of the wide variation in current public sector policies across Europe, it is commonly assumed that the state's technocratic bureaucracy has become too ineffective and too inflexible to respond adequately to changing social needs, and that it has proven incapable of initiating the innovations necessary to meet the current and future challenges facing European countries, such as high unemployment, aging populations, or inertia in the educational system.

Therefore, a reappraisal of private initiative and voluntary action is taking place, combined with significant increases in the size of the nonprofit sector in virtually all European countries (Salamon & Anheier, 1996). Throughout the 1980s, nonprofit organizations expanded their presence in traditional fields, such as child care and social services, and moved into new ones like the environment or, increasingly, the self-help movement. Similarly, the birthrate of foundations has accelerated significantly in recent years, as has the growth of corporate contributions, providing a new, albeit still quite limited, potential for professional fund raising activities.

Furthermore, far-reaching shifts in the policy environments across Europe have been affecting the traditional mix of revenue sources. With the advent of conservative governments in most of Europe in the 1980s, significant changes in the relationship between the public and nonprofit sectors emerged. In some countries such as Denmark, the Netherlands, or Belgium, the nonprofit sector was hit by outright cutbacks of social welfare spending. In the United Kingdom, decentralization policies vested greater responsibility in the voluntary sector, and the change from block grant funding to contract-based schemes introduced higher degrees of competition among nonprofit providers. Likewise, the process of reunification in Germany fostered a climate of fiscal austerity that leaves the nonprofit sector with new challenges, but without significant increases of public support. Furthermore, with the introduction of the Common Market, nonprofit organizations stand to lose their national privileges, and are likely to face increased international competition. The case for fund raising rests, therefore, on general reductions of government support, and growing competition among nonprofits as well as from commercial providers.

In this context, it is important to note that private donative sources represent only a small part of nonprofit revenue in Europe. In fact, individual and corporate giving and foundation support combined account only for 7 percent of total nonprofit sector revenue in France, 4 percent in Germany and Italy, and 12 percent in the United Kingdom (Exhibit 7.1). The comparable figure for the United States is close to 20 percent. By contrast, income from sales, fees, and charges ranges between 28 percent in Germany and 53 percent in the United Kingdom, whereas government support averages around 52 percent for these four countries (Salamon & Anheier, 1996). Two implications flow from these data: first, the composition of nonprofit revenue differs significantly across European countries; and second, donative income is the least important source of income for the nonprofit sector throughout the region. This means that irrespective of considerable further increases in fund raising activities that seem likely to take place in Europe over the next few years, the importance of private donative income will remain lower than in the United States.

## EXHIBIT 7.1 Nonprofit Revenue Sources

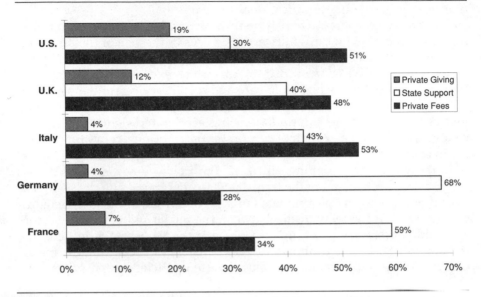

Source: Salamon & Anheier, 1996.

## *Sources of Private Giving*

### INDIVIDUAL GIVING

National surveys of giving behavior were undertaken in France and Germany as part of the Johns Hopkins Comparative Nonprofit Sector Project (Anheier, Salamon, & Archambault, 1994; Salamon & Anheier, 1996). These surveys can now be compared with similar studies conducted by INDEPENDENT SECTOR in the United States (INDEPENDENT SECTOR, 1992) to get a better sense of cross-national similarities and differences.

In comparing the results of these surveys, however, certain crucial differences in the handling of key social problems and in the treatment of important aspects of charitable giving must be kept in mind. As mentioned earlier, European countries have developed far more complete public systems of social welfare protection than the United States. Problems that are typically left for private charitable support in the United States are therefore more commonly handled, and handled more completely, through state support in Europe. This does not mean, however, that the European countries have no nonprofit sector as it is known in the United States. To the contrary, Germany has one of the most highly developed nonprofit sectors in the world (Salamon & Anheier, 1996). However, as mentioned, European nonprofit sectors rely more heavily on governmental support than on private charitable giving.

Also, tax regulations for giving vary across countries. Compared with Europe, the United States has a generous tax regime, with tax deductibility of donations to public charities up to a ceiling of 50 percent of taxable income. French tax law is less generous: up to 5 percent of taxable income to *"associations reconnus d'utilite publique,"* or public benefit associations, which number only a few hundred, largely well-established and traditional charities; donations to the well over 600,000 other nonprofit organizations are deductible to a limit of 1.25 percent of taxable income. It seems obvious that the low ceilings impair the ability to attract large lead gifts which are the cornerstone of the classic fund raising formula in the United States. The ceilings for tax-deductible donations in Germany are somewhat higher than in France: as a general rule up to 5 percent can be deducted for contributions to tax-exempt organizations; and for some specific charitable purposes, the ceiling is raised to 10 percent (Anheier & Seibel, in press).

Another crucial difference between the United States and Germany concerns the handling of religious giving. In the United States, giving to religious institutions (churches, temples, synagogues, mosques) represents over 60 percent of all the giving reported. In Germany, however, the bulk of religious contributions flows through a completely different channel: they are collected through the state in the form of a church tax that is levied against the income of those who indicate they are church members and distributed to the religious group designated by the individual.[1] These contributions to churches in Germany typically do not show up in giving surveys. Comparing the results of giving surveys in Germany with those in the United States without adjusting for this fundamental difference in the handling of religious contributions can thus produce highly misleading conclusions. It is therefore necessary to incorporate estimates of religious contributions into the German data wherever possible.

*Variations in Giving*

Table 7.1 offers an overview of the major dimensions of giving in three countries. About 7 out of 10 Americans donated money in the previous 12 months, compared with about 4 out of 10 in the two European countries. The average sum of money donated during the past year amounted to about $850 in the United States, $120 in Germany, and $96 in France. Thus, not only is the overall proportion of givers in the population significantly higher in the United States, but also the amounts given differ even more, with the average U.S. contribution outweighing the French and German one 7 to 8 times. And, whereas half of all donations in the United States are $300 or higher, the median German and French sums are about $40, or 13 to 15 percent of the U.S. figure. The significantly higher amounts of giving in the United States are also borne out when we take income into account.

---

[1] The church tax is a privilege granted to the major churches as part of the political settlement toward the separation of church and state in the 19th and early 20th centuries.

## TABLE 7.1. International Dimensions of Giving, 1991/92

| | United States | Germany (with Church Tax) | Germany (without Church Tax) | France |
|---|---|---|---|---|
| % of Respondents Making Contributions Previous 12 Months | 73% | over 90% | 44% | 43% |
| Average Sum of Donation | $851 | n/a | $120 | $96 |
| Median Sum of Donation | $300 | n/a | $44 | $40 |
| Donations as % of Annual Income; All Respondents | 1.20% | 1.12% | 0.31% | 0.15% |
| Donations as % of Annual Income; Givers Only | 1.91% | n/a | 0.85% | 0.39% |

Source: INDEPENDENT SECTOR, 1992; Salamon, Anheier, & Sokolowski, 1996.

Americans donated about 1.2 percent of their annual income, and for contributors, the figure increases to almost 2 percent. By contrast, Germany respondents donated 0.3 percent of their income, amounting to about one-fourth of the U.S. figure. In France, the level is 0.15 percent (i.e., half the German proportion and one-eighth of the U.S. share). As noted earlier, however, the figures reported above are somewhat misleading because they fail to include religious contributions in Germany, which are collected on behalf on the churches by tax authorities as a 7 to 9 percent surcharge on the income taxes of those who indicate they belong to a church. Although one might question whether the church tax is a truly voluntary contribution, it is nonetheless important to take the church tax into account to avoid misleading conclusions about the level of giving across different countries. In 1990, the Catholic Church received DM 6.6 billion ($4.1 billion) in church taxes, and the Lutheran Church DM 6.5 billion, or $4.1 billion.[2]

If we use our survey data to estimate the total sum of donations for the West German population, we arrive at about DM 4.3 billion, or $2.6 billion. This sum amounts to 33 percent of the church tax total, roughly similar to the share that religion represents of total giving as reported

---

[2] As with religious giving in the United States, church tax revenue is used in part to support charitable activities. Most notably, the German churches provide partial funding for their affiliated welfare organizations, but the extent is unknown.

on the INDEPENDENT SECTOR surveys in the United States. Factored into the figures presented in Table 7.1, the German giving data would in some instances certainly surpass those for the United States. The proportion of givers would jump to at least 90 percent, assuming that 86 percent of the population are members of either the Catholic or the Protestant Church; the average donations would increase substantially and, likewise, the proportion of income donated would inflate by a factor of 3.6 to 1.12 percent, a figure close to the U.S. situation of 1.2 percent for all respondents.

## Scope of Giving

Table 7.2 offers a breakdown for the incidence of giving by fields or areas, following in large measure the International Classification of Nonprofit Organizations (Salamon & Anheier, 1993). Looking at giving first, we find that in terms of the share of respondents active in them, three fields dominate in the United States: religion, health, and social services, followed by education and research. One out of every two respondents in the United States reported contributions to both religion and social service activities; and every third person supported the health sector. In Germany, by contrast, a different, more evenly spread pattern of private contributions by field prevails, whereby religion, international activities, health and social services are the most frequent targets of contributions. In France, with the exception of health, no other field stands out to the extent that religion and social services do in the United States. The pattern in these two European countries reveals more secular private giving behavior, especially in France.

### TABLE 7.2. The Incidence of Giving, 1991/92

| Field | United States (%) | Germany (%) | France (%) |
|---|---|---|---|
| Culture & Recreation | 16 | 9 | 2 |
| Education & Research | 21 | 2 | 8 |
| Health | 33 | 13 | 23 |
| Social Services | 50 | 13 | 10 |
| Environment | 16 | 9 | 2 |
| Advocacy | 12 | 3 | 2 |
| Philanthropy | 16 | 1 | 1 |
| International | 4 | 15 | 7 |
| Professional | 16 | 2 | 2 |
| Religion without Church Tax | 51 | 24 | 9 |
| Religion with Church Tax | n/a | over 90 | n/a |
| Other | 3 | 3 | 1 |

Source: INDEPENDENT SECTOR, 1992; Salamon, Anheier, & Sokolowski, 1996.

## Religious and Nonreligious Giving

Religion emerges as one of the significant differences between the United States and the two European countries. Table 7.3 explores this further. Leaving the issue of the German church tax aside, 6 out of 10 dollars in U.S. contributions are made for religious purposes, as opposed to 3 out of 10 in Germany and 2 out of 10 in France. A look at religious giving as a share of annual income shows the same pattern. Whereas U.S. givers donate 1.91 percent of their income, about 60 percent of this represents religious contributions (0.95%). For Germany, the share of religious giving as a percentage of annual income is 0.33 percent, or somewhat more than a third of the 0.85 percent donated totally, excluding the church tax. Finally, in France, the religious component of giving represents only one fifth of total contributions, which amount to 0.39 percent of annual income. The average and the median sum of religious contributions are fairly close to those for total giving. While the United States shows much higher levels of giving overall, the three countries are somewhat closer when nonreligious giving is considered.

## Who Donates?

Table 7.4 reveals several striking similarities and differences across countries in terms of who donates. In all three countries, women are more likely

### TABLE 7.3. Religious Giving, 1991/92

|  | United States | Germany (with Church Tax) | Germany (without Church Tax) | France |
|---|---|---|---|---|
| Sum of Religious Giving as % of Total Sum of Giving | 60% | 80% | 33% | 22% |
| Religious Giving as % of Annual Income of Givers | 0.95% | 0.8%–0.92% | 0.33% | 0.08% |
| Average Total Sum of Religious Donations for Givers, Previous 12 Months | $800 | n/a | $119 | $107 |
| Median Total Sum of Religious Donations for Givers, Previous 12 Months | $300 | n/a | $40 | $40 |

Source: INDEPENDENT SECTOR, 1992; Salamon, Anheier, & Sokolowski, 1996.

## TABLE 7.4. Selected Characteristics of Givers, 1991/92

| | % of Respondents Who Reported Giving during the Previous 12 Months | | |
|---|---|---|---|
| | United States (%) | Germany (%) | France (%) |
| *Sex* | | | |
| Male | 70 | 40 | 39 |
| Female | 74 | 50 | 46 |
| *Religion* | | | |
| Protestant | 74 | 44 | 56 |
| Catholic | 76 | 49 | 48 |
| Other & None | 64 | 39 | 34 |
| *Religious Activity* | | | |
| Frequent | 84 | 58 | 62 |
| Less Frequent | 63 | 43 | 47 |
| Rarely or Never | 57 | 29 | 40 |
| *Occupation* | | | |
| Farmer | 80 | 40 | 49 |
| Professional | 86 | 66 | 49 |
| Self-Employed | 85 | 47 | 48 |
| White Collar Employee | 77 | 42 | 47 |
| Blue Collar Worker | 66 | 39 | 21 |
| Not Economically Active | 68 | 50 | 50 |
| *Education* | | | |
| Primary | 48 | 47 | 39 |
| Secondary | 73 | 46 | 44 |
| Tertiary | 84 | 41 | 53 |

Source: INDEPENDENT SECTOR, 1992; Salamon, Anheier, & Sokolowski, 1996.

to make contributions than men. At the same time, however, such differences within each country are never larger than 10 percent, which seems to indicate that, overall, giving levels do not differ too greatly along gender lines.

Religious affiliation, too, seems to have little effect on giving. Specifically, Catholics and Protestants show very similar patterns; and also the catch-all category *Other and None,* while somewhat lower overall, does not strikingly deviate from the general picture. What seems to matter, however, is the degree of religiosity, measured by the frequency of church, temple, mosque or synagogue attendance. Here, accordingly, a significant drop in levels of giving occurs as levels of religious activity decline. One reason for this is that much religious giving actually occurs in churches. Those who do not go, therefore, have less of an opportunity to give.

Occupational characteristics reveal that giving tends to be below average for blue-collar workers and above average for the self-employed, white-collar workers, and professionals. Moreover, the economically inactive portions of the population, most notably homemakers and retirees, reveal higher shares of givers than blue-collar workers. Across the three countries, giving appears as a dual phenomenon: On the one hand, it seems linked to professionals and white-collar employees, and on the other, housewives and the elderly, too, play prominent roles. Giving is less a phenomenon associated with the blue-collar work status.

Looking at the relationship between levels of education and giving, respondents in the United States are nearly twice as likely to give if they have completed a college degree (tertiary level) than those with primary education only (less than high school). The data suggest that the share of givers in Germany declines as people become more educated. It seems most plausible to assume that this deviation is the result of the lower share of givers among tenured civil servants[3] and a higher frequency of givers among homemakers and the elderly. Since the former tend to be better educated than the latter, this would help account for the reverse relationship.

Concerning the relationship between giving and income, research in the United States suggests that lower-income groups tend to donate the highest share of their income, followed by higher-income groups, and then middle income groups, which tend to give the lowest proportion on average (see Auten & Rudney, 1990).[4] This results in a curvilinear relationship between income and contributions. To some extent, this relationship is borne out by the U.S. data in Table 7.5: As incomes initially increase, the share of donations declines and begins to increase slightly, albeit fluctuating, for higher incomes. This, however, is typically not the case for the two European countries. Here the share of contributions is relatively stable for the three lowest income groups (ranging between 1.16% and 1.52% for Germany and 0.43% and 0.63% for France), drops off for middle incomes, and remains at low levels for higher income groups. Thus, the well-to-do in Europe tend to give relatively less than lower-income groups.[5]

---

[3] In Germany, the state grants a lifetime employment guarantee to civil servants after a few years in public service, conditional upon passing an examination.

[4] For the United States, the point has been made that the very affluent not only give out of income, but also out of wealth (see Schervish, Chapter 8, this volume). While this may hold true for Europe as well, no data exist to examine this relationship.

[5] When considering the relationship between giving and income we should introduce one important caveat. Were we to include the church tax for the German data, we would observe an automatic increase in total giving as income increases, due to the progressive nature of income taxation. At the same time, this would also imply that lower income groups in Germany pay relatively less in church tax when compared with higher income groups, but donate relatively more as a share of disposable income.

**TABLE 7.5. Donations as Proportion of Annual Income for Givers, 1991/92**

| Income Groups | United States (incl. rel. giving) % | United States (excl. rel. giving) % | Germany (without church tax) % | France % |
|---|---|---|---|---|
| Lowest | 4.17 | 2.09 | 1.52 | 0.43 |
| - | 2.80 | 0.70 | 1.16 | 0.63 |
| - | 1.97 | 0.60 | 1.24 | 0.61 |
| - | 1.60 | 0.49 | 0.52 | 0.44 |
| - | 1.85 | 0.62 | 0.67 | 0.29 |
| - | 2.11 | 0.94 | 0.44 | 0.24 |
| - | 1.72 | 0.71 | 0.37 | 0.25 |
| - | 1.68 | 0.56 | | |
| Highest | 2.22 | 1.10 | | |

Source: INDEPENDENT SECTOR, 1992; Salamon, Anheier, & Sokolowski, 1996.

## CORPORATE GIVING

Corporations have only recently become more significant players in the field of nonprofit revenue in Europe. In France, the notion prevailed until the 1980s, that philanthropy would be an outright misuse of corporate resources (Essig & de la Taille Rivero, 1993). In Germany, as in many other countries, corporate activities traditionally focused on the provision of social, educational, or entertainment services for employees, with occasional spillover effects to benefit the larger local community. Although larger corporations began to establish foundations to support education and research as early as the 1920s, this was typically in response to the specific needs of firms in a particular industry. Overall, however, corporate involvement in philanthropy remained largely low-key and local in character, and tied to the charitable inclinations and cultural interests of individual entrepreneurs and CEOs.

Since the 1970s, however, major changes have been taking place. Business leaders saw themselves confronted with stagnant markets, and began to look for strategies to cope with emerging consumer attitudes that were considerably different from those of the prior decades. Ronald Inglehart's (1977) well-received study *The Silent Revolution* highlighted the widespread value change in Western societies toward a greater awareness of social responsibility in what was diagnosed as the "post-materialistic" society. Accordingly, corporations became more receptive to new visions in marketing, and began to reassess their role in society. Leslie Dawson's (1969) influential "Human Concept of Marketing" suggested that corporations had to be able to respond to challenges outside the market place to secure long-term survival. Furthermore, with the internationalization of the marketplace, U.S. corporations began to set the pace by making first attempts at introducing American-style corporate giving programs to their European subdivisions.

However, without a long-standing tradition of systematic and relatively large-scale corporate philanthropy in place, these early attempts were hampered by a lack of experience and understanding on both sides. For example, the decision of a well-known German theater to reject, on ethical grounds, the corporate sponsorship offered by a major defense contractor received national media attention. In turn, corporations interested in sponsorships and philanthropic programs became more cautious in their approach. For recipient nonprofit organizations, particularly in the fields of arts, and culture, and humanitarian assistance, public support was held in higher regard and generally accepted as preferable to private, corporate contributions, which were easily judged as "tainted," "self-interested," or sometimes as outright "political."

In the late 1980s, however, public attitudes began to shift, and corporate giving became increasingly professionalized. Although it is almost impossible to give a comprehensive picture of corporate philanthropy in Europe due to a lack of systematic data, the following brief overview of business sponsoring in France, the United Kingdom, and Germany will nonetheless offer some initial support for the two major characteristics of current corporate philanthropy in Europe: (1) There is good reason to conclude that corporate giving initiatives have indeed increased in recent years, both in scale and scope; and (2) the approaches chosen by corporations differ significantly both across the countries of the region as well as between Europe and the United States.

In France during the 1980s, the main thrust of business giving had centered on arts and culture, and was largely oriented toward the improvement of the corporate image as part of a larger public relations effort. A diversification of French corporate giving did not take place until the early 1990s. According to rough estimates provided by Essig and de la Taille Rivero (1993), about half of corporate donations are channeled toward arts-related activities with the other half going to humanitarian, educational, and environmental causes. The scale of total company support is estimated to exceed FFr one billion, or $200 million (Rigaud, 1991). Interestingly, business funding of the arts initially evolved without any tax incentives,[6] which were introduced only later with the Maecenatism Promotion Act of 1987 (loi sur le développement du mécénat). The Act also requires corporations to distinguish clearly between primarily business-related and primarily philanthropic activities; that is to keep giving separate from marketing activities.

Besides the trend to broaden the scope of giving to allow recipients in areas other than the arts to benefit from corporate generosity, two recent developments are likely to have a significant impact on fund raising.

---

[6] Similarly, in Italy patronage of the arts is considered a good business practice despite the lack of any corresponding tax advantages (Vanhaeverbeke, 1993).

Corporations are trying to change donor-donee relations into partnerships. This involves, on the one hand, a willingness on the corporate side to engage in multiyear commitments with nonprofit organizations, as opposed to ad-hoc, one-time cash contributions in response to incoming, often unsolicited, proposals. On the other hand, such long-term commitments typically impose a wider range of conditions and other requirements on recipient organizations. These commitments come with "strings attached." The corporate partners seek active involvement and at least some degree of influence on program planning and implementation, which may lead participating nonprofit organizations to change their style of operation (Essig & de la Taille Rivero, 1993). Combined with a growing professionalization of grant making, most corporations are beginning to develop their own strategies, and to select partners and projects accordingly—thus reducing the prospects of direct funding from corporate sources for nonprofit organizations in response to unsolicited requests.

Over the past two decades, corporate giving expanded significantly in Great Britain, in part due to active encouragement by government, industry and business associations (Kendall & Knapp, 1995). Under the traditional covenant system, corporate donors were required to commit funds to charities—other than sponsorships and noncash donations—for a period of at least four years to qualify for tax incentives; in 1986, an exception to the covenant was granted to non-closely-held corporations, which now can deduct charitable donations as long as the amounts given do not exceed 3 percent of dividends (Weisbrod & Mauser, 1991). In addition to these tax incentives, a variety of programs encourage corporate support, most of which have been established in cooperation with government and businesses. The Association for Business Sponsorship of the Arts (ABSA) administers a government-supported program, called Business Sponsorship Incentive Scheme, which offers matching funds for new sponsorships to encourage first-time corporate sponsors, and makes fund raising methods and techniques available to arts institutions (Tweedy, 1992). Another scheme is the rapidly growing "Per Cent Club"—organized by Business in the Community—in which corporate members initially give 0.5 percent of pretax profits (Lane, 1994).

The state of corporate support in the United Kingdom is fairly well documented. In a recent survey among the top 500 corporate donors, cash donations emerged as the single most important form of support, accounting for 40 percent of total support. Sponsorships, the next most frequent support method, comprise nearly 20 percent. The remainder went to other forms of noncash assistance such as secondments, training, and in-kind assistance (Passey, 1995).[7] While cash donations represent truly philanthropic giving, sponsorships provide financial or material assistance for activities or events as part of an arrangement that also holds commercial

---

[7] It must be noted that the participating companies had not been able to assign roughly 18 percent of total support.

**EXHIBIT 7.2. U.K. Corporate Donations, by Recipient Group, 1993/94**

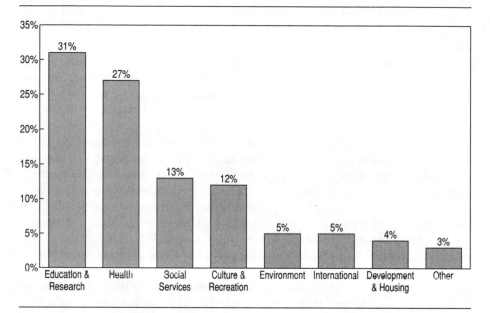

Source: Passey, 1995, Tab. 7.2.

benefits for the sponsoring company. Preferred areas for sponsorships are sports and the arts, although government cutbacks opened up sponsorship opportunities in the community services field. The growing popular interest in environmental issues attracted some corporate interest into this area as well. The breakdown of the survey data on cash donations in Exhibit 7.2 shows that, in terms of value of support, British corporations allocate most nonsponsorship giving to the fields of education and research, and health (approximately 31% and 27%, respectively). Both fields were strongholds of the British welfare state in the 1950s and 1960s (Passey, 1995).

Finally, in Germany, corporate tax law generally allows charitable deductions of either 5 or 10 percent of net profits, depending on the cause to be supported. Although the tax incentives for corporate giving are in many respects more generous than in other European countries,[8] philanthropic donations are a relatively insignificant part of business support for the charitable activities. The boost of corporate assistance since the early 1980s was carried by steep increases in sponsorships. German tax law treats sponsorship as legitimate business expenses that reduce pretax profits.

---

[8] For an overview of the tax treatment of corporate contributions—with an emphasis on giving to the arts—in 16 European countries, see CEREC & Arthur Andersen, 1991.

For recipient organizations, in contrast, sponsorship revenue counts as taxable business income, and not as donations. In 1991, it is estimated that donations account for 500 million DM ($330 million), or slightly less than 17 percent of total corporate support, whereas sponsorships amount to 2.5 billion DM, or $1.6 billion (Burens, 1995).

Table 7.6 presents estimates on the development of the German sponsorship market. The total sum of corporate sponsoring expenditures increased sixfold over the past 10 years. At the same time, a shift in emphasis or field occurred, similar to that which has been observed for France and the United Kingdom. Although two-thirds of all funds are still used to sponsor sports events and activities, the overall dominance of sports sponsorship has diminished, whereas the arts and, more recently, social/community services and environment concerns have become more attractive to corporate sponsors. According to opinion polls among large and medium-size corporations, arts and environmental sponsoring show a higher potential for growth than other instruments in corporate marketing and public relations efforts (Hermanns & Püttmann, 1990).

However, cooperation between businesses and nonprofit organizations is in a state of flux, and both sides are constantly seeking to develop new avenues of assistance. Noteworthy in this context was the 1994 fund raising campaign for humanitarian relief and assistance for Rwanda. As part of this campaign, the German Red Cross teamed up with Deutsche Bank, the largest commercial bank in Germany. The bank placed advertisements in all major German newspapers announcing that it would match individual donations to the Red Cross on a one-to-one basis. Within a few weeks, the Red Cross received nine million DM ($6 million) in private contributions, which was then matched by Deutsche Bank (Burens, 1995). The campaign received widespread publicity, not only because of its fund raising success, but also because it was the first time that a major German corporation used the matching fund scheme on a large scale. Although there will be greater flexibility in the way business support is provided in the future, sponsorships are likely to continue to be the preferred mechanism for corporate contributions to the nonprofit sector.

Corporate support of the nonprofit sector in Europe has grown substantially since the early 1980s. However, outright philanthropy remains a rather

## TABLE 7.6. Corporate Sponsoring in Germany

|  | Sports (%) | Arts (%) | Social Services & Environment (%) | Estimated Expenditures |
|---|---|---|---|---|
| 1985 | 80 | 13 | 7 | DM 0.4 billion |
| 1989 | 72 | 18 | 10 | DM 1.2 billion |
| 1995 | 66 | 20 | 14 | DM 2.5 billion |

Source: MC Sponsoring, cit. in Mussler, 1991.

rare phenomenon. The business sector generally seeks a quid pro quo, usually in the form of sponsorships that link the prestige and respectability of nonprofit organizations to the corporate image as part of public relations efforts or, more directly, to brand recognition and promotion.

With the growing professionalization and specialization of sponsoring programs, raising funds from the corporate sector confronts nonprofit organizations with new challenges: First, to succeed, any fund-seeking organization has not only to present the need or cause to be addressed, but has also to describe the potential rewards for the sponsoring company, making the up-front development of specific strategies to attract sponsorships a binding necessity. Second, the tendency of business sponsors to demand some degree of active involvement leaves many nonprofit leaders uneasy. Third, sponsorships generally provide support for specific or new activities, which often include little funds for general operating expenditures. And fourth, sponsoring favors certain areas of nonprofit activity. Although there is a growing interest in social and environmental affairs among corporate grant-makers, smaller and less prestigious organizations constantly lose out in the competition for corporate support.

## FOUNDATIONS

One of the most compelling arguments for establishing a foundation—besides the prospect of tax advantages—is the opportunity to create an organization, that—at least in theory—will last in perpetuity. Although economic and political turmoil can considerably endanger the survival of foundations, a considerable number can look back to a long history. The oldest existing German foundation was established around the year 898, and about 170 foundations, still in existence, were created before the year 1500 (Toepler, 1996). These early founders, either rich merchants, patricians, or aristocrats, were not driven by tax considerations. Religious motivations, the looming possibility of social unrest, and, most frequently, concerns for the future well-being of the larger family, provided incentives to establish foundations.

Although foundations have a long-standing tradition in Europe, the size of the various foundation sectors varies considerably across countries. The relatively small country of Switzerland counts 6,500 to 7,000 philanthropic foundations (Kowner, 1993), almost as many as Germany. In France, there are only about 500 independent foundations plus 360 endowments administered by the Fondation de France (Tsyboula, 1993). Great Britain with at least 2,500 grant-making trusts (Leat, 1992) lies in between. Besides these estimates, little is known about the assets and the grant making of European foundations.[9] One of the exceptions is Germany, where a database on

---

[9] For a broad overview of the role of foundations in the European Union, see Toepler and Strachwitz, 1996.

foundations was established in 1989–1990 (Bundesverband Deutscher Stiftungen, 1991).

Almost all of the early foundations operated hospitals, which in the medieval sense meant houses for the sick, but for the poor, the disabled, the aged, and travelers as well. Although hospital foundations remained prominent, grant-making foundations began to develop in the 14th century either as eleemosynary or as scholarship trusts (Toepler, 1996). Welfare and education as the two main areas of activity remained characteristic of German foundations until the twentieth century. Today, about one quarter of all existing German foundations were established before 1900.

The German foundation sector, although relatively large compared to France or Great Britain, is still considerably smaller than its U.S. counterpart. Whereas the Foundation Center counts some 33,000 American foundations as of 1991, the German Foundation Directory listed about 6,500 at the same time. Since no public disclosure of financial data is required of German foundations, only a minority volunteered to do so for the compilation of the Directory. Based on these data, Anheier and Romo (1993) estimate that foundations in Germany hold aggregate assets in the vicinity of $21 billion, and made grants totaling at least $1.9 billion (Anheier & Romo, 1993), whereas U.S. foundations controlled almost $163 billion in assets and distributed roughly $9.2 billion in grants in 1991 (Renz & Lawrence, 1993).

In absolute terms, the U.S. foundation sector is 6 times larger in size, almost 8 times larger in assets than its German counterpart, and paid out 5 times more in grants (Anheier & Romo, 1993). However, since both the population and the economy in Germany are smaller than in the United States, absolute differences need to be put in perspective. With differences in GDP, total employment, and population size taken into account, Anheier and Romo (1993) report that the U.S. foundation sector is 1.4 to 1.8 times larger, and total grant payments represent 0.18 percent of GDP in the United States, and 0.13 percent of GDP in Germany.

German foundations show a propensity to support social services, education and research, and arts and culture, as Exhibit 7.3 shows. The main fields receiving foundation support are not unlike those in the United States; perhaps with the exception of the health area, to which American foundations direct decidedly more attention.[10] However, recent trends indicate a change of emphasis among newly established foundations. As in the United States, the 1980s saw a strong increase in foundation births. Although at a somewhat lower level in absolute numbers, the growth rate of the German foundation sector equaled that of the U.S. foundation community (Anheier & Romo, 1993; Toepler, 1996). While the arts have profited most from this growth so far, the environmental area is likely to receive an

---

[10] For a more fully developed discussion of differences in scope, see Anheier & Romo, 1993; Toepler, 1996.

## EXHIBIT 7.3. Fields of Interest of German Foundations

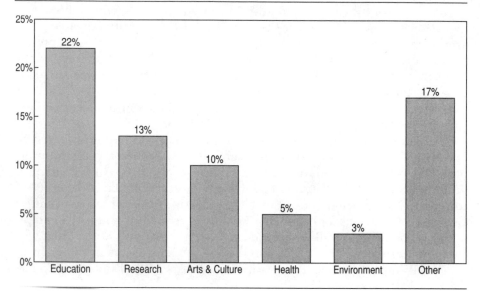

Source: Documentation Centre on German Foundations.

increasing share of foundation resources in the future. One of the reasons for this trend lies in the emergence of a new generation of donors lacking the traumatic experiences of authoritarianism, war, and social misery that formed the previous generation; they are more inclined to support activities outside the traditional fields of welfare and culture (Neuhoff, 1991).

From a fund raising perspective, one particular characteristic of German foundations reduces their overall importance as a central source of funds. German foundations, especially most of the larger ones, tend to operate their own projects and programs rather than concentrate on grant making. As funding intermediaries for the nonprofit sector, their role is thus more limited. In general, operating foundations account for roughly one-third of all foundations in Germany, while the share of these types of foundations is less than 10 percent in the United States. The comparatively high percentage of operating foundations in Germany is not only due to the historic legacy of hospital foundations alone. Most operating foundations were established in the twentieth century and their growth rate, though now below that of grant makers, almost doubled between the 1950s and the 1980s. Moreover, 5 of the 10 largest foundations are at least partially operating, among them the Bosch, Körber, and Krupp Foundations (Toepler, 1996).

The distinction between grant-making and operating foundations in Germany, however, is more functional than legal in nature. Neither general laws concerning foundations nor tax regulations establish a distinction between the two types—in contrast to U.S. tax law, which stipulates a slightly preferential treatment for operating foundations (Toepler, 1994). Legal considerations, therefore, are unlikely to influence the founder's choice.

A still relatively infrequent phenomenon is the use of foundations as fund-raising vehicles. The purpose of these organizations is typically to raise funds for either endowments or more specific projects. Usually, foundations of this kind are sponsored or chaired by dignitaries from all walks of public life. A prominent example in Germany is the Mildred Scheel Foundation for Cancer Research, which was initiated by a former First Lady—a physician who later died of cancer herself. Given her popularity, the foundation was able to raise a substantial endowment from the public at large, but still continues to rely on income from fund raising appeals. In Belgium, a foundation was established on the occasion of King Baudouin's silver jubilee in 1976. The start-up capital in this case was raised in a slightly different way: A quarter of the initial endowment was contributed by the Belgian government, another quarter came from individual and corporate donations, while the remaining half was raised through the sale of commemorative coins (Debulpaep, 1992).

Although there is some interest in using nonendowed foundations as a means of fund raising, it will take a long time to change the charitable attitudes of Europeans to incorporate such ventures into their giving patterns. In the United Kingdom, which is the only European country so far to import the concept of community foundations from the United States, of the community foundation movement had a very shaky start. Of the first six community foundations—established with seed money from the government in the mid-1980s—only four survived (Neuhoff, 1993). Ten years later, public awareness remains low, although existing community trusts are growing, and new ones are forming (Pike, 1994).

## OTHER SOURCES

Besides individual, corporate, and foundation giving, there are other sources of support for nonprofit organizations. After registering as potential recipient organizations with provincial high courts, German nonprofit organizations can receive penalty payments and other punitive fines levied against parties found guilty of misdemeanors and felonies by the courts.

Of greater importance than fines, however, are lotteries, which have a long tradition in Europe as a means of raising money for public projects. In the first half of the eighteenth century, for example, the construction of Dresden's Church of Our Lady—for which rebuilding funds are currently being raised—was in part financed through a lottery.

Basically, there are two types of lotteries: television lotteries and state lotteries. The latter primarily provide revenue for the government, and to a lesser extent, for charitable causes. TV lotteries are rarely a source of general revenue for the nonprofit sector at large. Proceeds from the lottery tied to the German version of the TV show "Jeopardy," for example, exclusively benefit the *Aktion Sorgenkind,* a national charity that provides care for disabled children.

In the case of state lotteries, revenues set apart for charitable or philanthropic purposes are most often distributed to funding intermediaries rather than to nonprofit organizations directly. Allowances from the national lotteries support the European Cultural Foundation in the Netherlands, and the King Baudouin Foundation in Belgium. In Germany, the states use lottery and gambling revenue to bolster the annual budgets of state-sponsored arts foundations (Toepler & Strachwitz, 1996; Toman, 1990).

Whereas state lotteries are long-established institutions and provide only little revenue for the nonprofit sector in most of Europe, the situation is quite different in Great Britain. A national lottery was launched there in 1994. Moreover, the purpose of the lottery is not to primarily or even exclusively benefit the government treasury; rather it is to provide revenue for five groups of beneficiaries: sports, the arts, charity,[11] national heritage, and the Millennium Fund, after a 12 percent tax has been collected. Subtracting prize money, tax, commissions, costs, and profits leaves 28 percent of total revenue for the beneficiaries, to be equally divided among the five groups via the arts and sports councils, the National Lotteries Charity Board, the National Heritage Memorial Fund, and the Millennium Fund.

Although the government made clear that lottery revenue could not be used to justify further cuts in public sector funding, the response within the nonprofit sector to the prospect of the lottery was not unequivocally positive. Charities fear that the lottery will undermine their own fund raising efforts. Whereas the purchase of tickets is promoted as a way of doing good with slogans such as "Every time you play the National Lottery, someone else gets a better chance," only 5.6 percent of the ticket prize actually goes to charity (one-fifth of 28 percent). It is therefore possible that the public might reduce charitable support in favor of buying lottery tickets (Pike, 1994). Accordingly, estimates place annual revenue losses due to reduced interest in more traditional fund raising activities in the range of £190 million to £270 million. By way of comparison, the lottery disbursed £159 million to charities during the first six months of operation (Creigh-Tyte, 1966) with the prospect of annual revenue rising to £300 million over the next years (Pike, 1994). In other words, the introduction of the national lottery might lead to a situation in which British charities will initially have less revenue at their discretion than before the lottery's inception, and will see only modest gains in the future.

---

[11] The British meaning of charity differs from the way the term is used in the United States. In the United Kingdom, charitable purposes have been classified in four groups: relief of poverty; advancement of education; advancement of religion; and other purposes beneficial to the community that fall within the spirit of the preamble to the Charitable Uses Act of 1601. Sports, the arts, and heritage are not necessarily considered to be "charitable" purposes.

In some fields like education, U.S. nonprofit organizations rely to significant degrees on income from organized constituencies, such as alumni associations or museum membership. This method of revenue generation is generally less developed in Europe. German or French students rarely identify with their alma mater deeply enough to be willing to contribute to alumni funds. On the other hand, state universities do not actively attempt to solicit donations from former graduates. As a rule, alumni associations are organized separately from the universities themselves, and—with the amount of total donations seldom exceeding the six-digit range—are not very effective as a source of support (Burens, 1995, p. 46).

With the prevailing separation of institution and alumni/member organization comes another problem: The supported organizations have little leverage to influence the membership, and patron's associations tend to follow their own agendas (Raue, 1993). Furthermore, for patron's associations, revenue maximization is not necessarily a top priority. Occasionally, contribution levels are set high enough to effectively exclude large segments of potential members in order to secure exclusiveness (Toepler, 1995). In the case of the Friends of the National Gallery Association in Berlin, for example, the preference of the founders was to seek 100 members contributing DM 1,000 a year rather than 1,000 members paying a DM 100 membership fee (Raue, 1993). It must be noted at this point that the segmentation of the membership market by providing different membership categories with increasing benefits attached still is an uncharted potential among European nonprofit organizations.

## Trends in Fund Raising: Professionalization and Accountability

With the expansion of the European welfare states after World War II, nonprofit organizations could rely on growing support from the public sector, supplemented by their own financial revenue such as fees and charges. The degree of professionalization and sophistication of fund raising remained low, and little pressure existed to put stronger emphasis on private giving. Accordingly, modern fund-raising techniques did not develop until the late 1970s, and the "tin can approach" to collecting funds from the public remained the most commonly used form of collection. Outside the churches, the collection of donations lacked a systematic approach, and fund raising consisted mainly of brief campaigns that periodically recurred but failed to foster and maintain a continuing donor base (Haibach, 1993; Vaccaro, 1993).

### SHIFT IN FUND RAISING METHODS

The traditional and still dominant methods to raise funds are street collections, door-to-door collections, and the selling of raffle tickets. Even in the United Kingdom, which has the highest degree of private giving as percentage of total nonprofit revenue in Western Europe by far most donors are reached by these three methods. According to survey results, 37 percent of respondents gave in door-to-door collections, 32 percent in street collections, and 31 percent bought raffle tickets (Martin et al., 1995). While these methods are used by most fund raising organizations regardless of their size, other forms such as appeals broadcast on public television or revenue from marketing of records or the issue of special postal stamps (where parts of profits or surcharges are allocated to specific charitable causes) only benefit large, established national organizations.

In the changing funding environment of the 1980s, however, nonprofit organizations began to approach fund raising in a more systematic manner, and adapted techniques, many of which were imported from the United States. Most notably, direct mail—and with it, the necessity of developing and monitoring a donor database—became the method of choice. Initially direct mail was primarily used to solicit donations from known previous donors to the organization. The current trend points to more use of direct mail in an effort to reach a broader audience. Furthermore, revenue generation through commercial activities, (e.g., charity shops and catalogues), while uncommon in continental Europe, is becoming popular in Great Britain, where proceeds from commercial activities have the highest share of total donations of all fund raising methods (Martin, Halfpenny, & Lowe, 1995).

While a considerable time lag in the adoption of U.S. techniques remains, and while cultural differences, and different legal and tax treatment inhibit the fuller transfer of techniques, American fund raising methods are increasingly common. Several German banks manage investment funds to support charities that offer donors the option of buying shares instead of giving directly to the charity. The proceeds (as well as capital in the case of the donor's death) are allocated to designated nonprofit organizations. Depending on the composition of the various funds, donors receive tax deductions in return. One of the oldest of these "social investment funds" was established in 1976, and manages capital of approximately $100 million (Freyberg, 1995).

However, cultural and legal differences still prohibit a full adaptation of some of the basic features of American fund raising. For example, traditionally, nonprofit boards in Europe are not supposed to give. An awareness of the potential benefits of having board members contributing themselves is only evolving now (Schöffmann, 1993), while the feasibility of implementing such requirements remains questionable. Another example concerns telemarketing. In contrast to direct mailings, European nonprofit organizations have not yet adapted telephone marketing to any significant degree, although there are indications of growing interest in this method of soliciting funds. In the United Kingdom, less than 0.5 percent of survey participants reported giving in response to telephone appeals (Martin et al., 1995). As in many other countries, cold calling by phone for commercial purposes—which includes solicitations for donations—is generally unlawful in Germany. Active telemarketing is therefore only acceptable if the person to be called had previously indicated agreement—either explicitly or implicitly by volunteering the telephone number—to receive phone solicitations. Accordingly, the debate on how to use telemarketing mainly focuses on passive telemarketing options such as the provision of "1-(800)" or "1-(900)" service numbers to induce potential donors to establish contact on their own.

## ENSURING ACCOUNTABILITY

Some countries such as Germany and Switzerland have regulations in place that require charities to obtain prior authorization for street and door-to-door collections (Fäh, Ebersold, & Zaugg, 1991). However, these laws intended to offer some degree of protection for givers, are proving inadequate. With the growing number of nonprofit organizations competing for donations, the average household receives approximately 100 fund raising appeals per year. Moreover, the public is becoming increasingly suspicious due to occasional fraudulent appeals or mismanagement and waste in large charities—topics readily covered in the press. Accordingly, there have been recent movements to implement some kind of voluntary self-regulation to rebuild trust and preempt government action in the long run.

Switzerland pioneered voluntary self-regulation and established, as early as 1934, the *Zentralstelle für Wohlfahrtsunternehmen* (ZEWO), or Clearinghouse for Welfare Enterprises. Organized as a membership organization of national charities, private corporations, and state authorities, and chartered to "protect charitable activities" and "to promote order and clarity" in the collection of donations, the ZEWO implemented a variety of programs to set a framework for fund raising (Fäh et al., 1991). In 1940, a seal of imprimatur for fund raising was developed to identify reputable charities. Interested organizations have to apply for the seal, which is only rewarded to those who fulfill certain criteria, and are willing to give ZEWO access to annual reports and financial statements for review purposes. Since 1946, an annual ZEWO-edited collections timetable details the time slots for fund raising campaigns by the various charities. A set of regulations, developed in the mid-1980s, calls for mutual understanding and cooperation among fund raising organizations, and limits to one the number of annual national fund raising campaigns per institution in an effort not to undermine the public's trust through a confusing array of uncoordinated fund raising activities (Fäh et al., 1991).

The next European country to follow the Swiss example and implement a seal of approval for fund raising was Sweden in 1989. France and Germany followed in the early 1990s. The German case proves to be interesting in that the introduction of the seal was accompanied by heavy criticism, and eventually, by competing initiatives. The seal was launched in 1992 by the *Deutsches Zentralinstitut für Soziale Fragen* (DZI), or Central German Institute on Social Issues. As in Switzerland, organizations have to apply for the seal, and allow a review of internal procedures and financial statements. The DZI's initiative was greeted with considerable interest in the media and the larger public as well. In 1992, individual inquiries at the DZI concerning fund raising issues numbered over 17,000.

For organizations with the DZI seal, it proved to be a valuable fund raising tool. However, only charitable and humanitarian relief organizations could apply for the seal; moreover, the seal applied to national or international fund raising activities only. Accordingly, local and regional charities as well as cultural, environmental, political, or religious organizations could not benefit from it. With the larger public being aware of the seal, but not of its limitations in scope, this constellation implied a serious handicap for noncharitable nonprofit organizations. This led to a veritable controversy within the fund-raising community (BSM, 1/94).

After initial attempts to reach an agreement with the DZI failed to broaden the scope and inclusiveness of its seal, larger environmental organizations explored options to launch an alternative seal in the environmental area. After some time, they decided to initiate a cooperative effort to cover the whole range of nonprofit activities. As a result, a membership association was established in 1993 to foster the ethics of fund raising, ensure accountability, and further the mutual interests of member organizations. The association sponsors a German Council on Donations, comprising a panel of 10 fund raising experts to supervise and evaluate the fund raising practices of associate members and nonmembers alike (BSM, 3/93). Although it is still too early to determine how the turf war between the DZI and the Council of Donations will end, it shows the trend within the fund raising community to take the development of professional standards seriously, which is enforced by the public's growing interest in transparency and accountability in the market for donations.

## Conclusion

This chapter could offer little more than an initial overview of fund raising patterns and practices in Europe. Perhaps more than anything else, the previous pages demonstrate how little we know about fund raising in this part of the world, and how much research remains to be done before we will gain a more complete and comprehensive understanding of fund raising practices in Europe. First, we need to know more about how different tax policies relate to donative behavior, and how different philanthropic traditions can be combined with modern fund raising methods. Moreover, we need to broaden our knowledge of how fund raising is linked to, and indeed part of, the much larger question of resource allocation in the modern, postindustrial societies of Europe: How can we combine public (i.e., taxation) and private (i.e., fund-raising) methods to achieve a better, more equitable and more efficient use of increasingly scarce resources?

The level of sophistication and professionalism of fund raising in Europe will increase over the next years. In our view, these developments are closely related to the need to find new income sources in the face of declining public sector support, at least in relative terms. They are also fueled by a growing number of professional consultants who provide their assistance to nonprofit organizations, large and small, that are unable to devise their own in-house fund raising strategies. What are the long-term implications of these trends for nonprofit organizations and the nonprofit sector at large? Since we cannot automatically assume that these changes will be positive, we suggest that research efforts put the impact on the overall well-being of both the sector and society of such private fund raising efforts under the same level of scrutiny in terms of efficiency and equity as we have come to subject any other existing or proposed taxation policy. Only then will we be able to evaluate the usefulness of substituting and supplementing existing mechanisms to cater for the public good. In other words, we need to move beyond calls for greater transparency and requests for ethical standards, and explore the overall benefits of the redistributional effects of fund raising. Private fund raising does not exist in a vacuum and must be examined against the possibility of alternative ways of revenue generation, including, but not limited to, fees for services and related commercial income, social insurance schemes, and statutory funding options. This topic does indeed represent a wide open field for future research.

Finally, an unprecedented intergenerational transfer of wealth is likely to take place in Europe over the next decade. For the first time in nearly a century, personal wealth has not been destroyed by either inflation, war, or both. In the German case alone, estimates of personal wealth in the early 1990s ranged around $3 trillion; each year 10 percent of this sum, or $300 billion will be transferred from one generation to the next (Strachwitz, 1994, p. 96). While this transfer certainly provides a fertile ground for philanthropic entrepreneurship in the future, it remains uncertain whether Europe's nonprofit organizations will indeed be able to tap the accumulated wealth to a significant degree. Since a similar transfer of wealth—also with uncertain outcomes for philanthropy—is taking place in the United States (Greene, Greene, & Moore, 1993; Murphy & Schervish, 1995), comparative research into the dynamics of these transfers might better reveal how different the framework for fund raising in the United States and Europe truly is.

## Bibliography

Anheier, H. K., and Romo, F. "Foundations in Germany and the United States: A Comparative Analysis of Size, Scope, and Variations." Chapter presented at the symposion *Trusts and Foundations: International Perspectives,* Voluntas & Laboratoire D'Economie Sociale, Sorbonne, Paris, October 21–23, 1993.

Anheier, H. K., Salamon, L. M., and Archambault, E. "Participating Citizens: U.S.-Europe Comparisons in Volunteer Action." *The Public Perspective,* 1994, 3, 16–18; 34.

Anheier, H. K., and Seibel, W., Eds. *The Third Sector: Comparative Studies of Nonprofit.* Berlin: DeGruyter, 1990.

Anheier, H. K., and Seibel, W. *The Nonprofit Sector in Germany.* Manchester: Manchester University Press, in press.

Auten, G., and Rudney, G. "The Variability of Individual Charitable Giving in the US." *Voluntas,* 1990, 2, 80–97.

Baum, H. "Der Spendenmarkt der 90er Jahre. Herausforderungen für die Kommunikationsarbeit." In *Social Sponsoring und Social Marketing: Praxisberichte über das "neue Produkt Mitgefühl."* Eds. T. Leif and U. Galle. Köln: Bund, 1993.

Bruhn, M. *Sozio- und Umweltsponsoring: Engagements von Unternehmen für soziale und ökologische Aufgaben.* München: Vahlen, 1990.

BSM (Bundesarbeitsgemeinschaft Sozialmarketing) *BSM—Newsletter.* Various issues.

Bundesverband Deutscher Stiftungen e.V. (Ed.) *Verzeichnis der Deutschen Stiftungen 1991.* Darmstadt: Hoppenstedt, 1991.

Burens, P.-C. *Die Kunst des Bettelns—Tips für erfolgreiches Fundraising.* München: C.H. Beck, 1995.

CEREC, and Arthur Andersen. *Business support for the arts in Europe: A guide through the fiscal maze.* London: Arthur Andersen, 1991.

Creigh-Tyte, S. "Building a National Lottery: A Review of British Experience." Paper presented at 9th International Conference on Cultural Economics. Boston, May 8–9, 1996.

Dabson, B., Ed. *Company Giving in Europe.* London: Directory of Social Change, 1991.

Dawson, L. M. "The Human Concept: New Philosophy for Business." *Business Horizons,* 1969, December, 29–38.

Debulpaep, J. "An Operating Foundation." In *Patronage of the Arts by Foundations and Non Government Organizations in Europe.* Ed. Kulturstiftung Haus Europa. Berlin: Maas, 1992, 69–79.

Essig, C., and de la Taille Rivero, M. "Frankreich und die Kulturförderung heute." In *Kulturförderung—Mehryals Sponsoring.* Eds. Count R. Strachwitz and S. Toepler. Wiesbaden: Gabler, 1993, 97–106.

Fäh, B., Ebersold, W., and Zaugg, R. *Geldsammeln im Dienste des Mitmenschen: Philosophie und Praxis des Fundraising.* Bern & Stuttgart: Haupt, 1991.

Freyberg, P. "Spenden statt Sparen." *Die Zeit,* April 28, 1995, 12.

Greene, E., Greene, S., and Moore, J. "A Generation Prepares to Transfer Its Trillions." *The Chronicle of Philanthropy,* November 16, 1993.

Haibach, M. "Professionelles Spendensammeln. Fundraising in USA und Deutschland." In *Social Sponsoring und Social Marketing: Praxisberichte über das "neue Produkt Mitgefühl."* Eds. T. Leif and U. Galle. Köln: Bund, 1993, 177–189.

Hermanns, A., and Püttmann, M. "Sponsoring-Barometer." *Absatzwirtschaft*, 1990, 9, 80–86.

INDEPENDENT SECTOR. *Giving and Volunteering in the United States 1992.* Washington: INDEPENDENT SECTOR, 1992.

Inglehart, R. *The Silent Revolution: Changing Values and Political Styles among Western Publics.* Princeton: Princeton University Press, 1977.

Kendall, J., and Knapp, M. "The Kent/Hopkins Project: Summary of the UK Statistical Mapping." In *Dimensions of the Voluntary Sector: How Is the Voluntary Sector Changing?* Ed. CAF. London: Charities Aid Foundation, 1995, 27–34.

Kistenfeger, H., and Plewnia, U. "Auf der Suche nach Millionen." *Focus*, 1995, 17, 118–122.

Kowner, A. "Kulturförderung in der Schweiz." In *Kulturförderung—Mehr als Sponsoring.* Eds. Count R. Strachwitz and S. Toepler. Wiesbaden: Gabler, 1993, 111–119.

Lane, J. "Corporate Support to the Voluntary Sector 1992/1993." In *Researching the Voluntary Sector.* Eds. S. Saxon-Harrold and J. Kendall. London: Charities Aid Foundation, 1994, 203–212.

Leat, D. "A Survey of Grant Making Trusts 1992/93." In *Dimensions of the Voluntary Sector: How Is the Voluntary Sector Changing?* Ed. CAF. London: Charities Aid Foundation, 1995, 63–67.

Leat, D. *Trusts in Transition: The Policy and Practice of Grant-Giving Trusts.* York: Joseph Rowntree Foundation, 1992.

LOGO-S. "Trends im Spendenmarkt." *Verein & Management,* 1994, 5, 6–8.

Martin, J., Halfpenny, P., and Lowe, D. "Individual Giving and Volunteering in Britain 1993." In *Dimensions of the Voluntary Sector: How is the Voluntary Sector Changing?* Ed. CAF. London: Charities Aid Foundation, 1995, 51–55.

Murphy, T., and Schervish, P. "The Dynamics of Wealth Transfer: Behavioral Implications of Tax Policy for the $10 Trillion Transfer." In *Nonprofit Organizations as Public Actors: Rising to New Public Policy Challenges.* Working Chapters of the 1995 Spring Research Forum. Washington, DC: INDEPENDENT SECTOR, 1995.

Mussler, D. "Sponsoring in den 90er Jahren." In *Jahrbuch Sponsoring 1991.* Ed. P. Strahlendorf. Düsseldorf: ECON, 1991, 7–19.

Neuhoff, K. "Community Foundations in den USA: Ein Vorbild?" In *Kulturförderung—Mehr als Sponsoring.* Eds. Count R. Strachwitz and S. Toepler. Wiesbaden: Gabler, 1993, 185–198.

Neuhoff, K. "Sozial- und Wohlfahrtsstiftungen in Deutschland." *Theorie und Praxis der sozialen Arbeit,* 1991, 6, 227–234.

Passey, A. "Corporate Support of the UK Voluntary Sector 1993/94." In *Dimensions of the Voluntary Sector: How Is the Voluntary Sector Changing?* Ed. CAF. London: Charities Aid Foundation, 1995, 57–61.

Pike, A. "Financial Times Survey: Charities Investment and Finance." *Financial Times,* Dec. 15, 1994, 13–16.

Raffée, H., and Wiedmann, K. P. *Dialoge: Das gesellschaftliche Bewubtsein in der Bundesrepublik und seine Bedeutung für das Marketing.* Hamburg: Gruner & Jahr, 1983.

Raue, P. "Die Rolle von Fördervereinen in der Kulturförderung." In *Kulturförderung—Mehr als Sponsoring.* Ed. Count R. Strachwitz and S. Toepler. Wiesbaden: Gabler, 1993, 229–234.

Renz, L., and Lawrence, S. *Foundation Giving—Yearbook of Facts and Figures on Private, Corporate and Community Foundations.* New York: Foundation Center, 1993.

Rigaud, J. "Company Giving in France: An Overview" In *Company Giving in Europe.* Ed. B. Dabson. London: Directory of Social Change, 1991, 57–59.

Salamon, L. M., and Anheier, H. K. "In Search of the Non-profit Sector II: The Problem of Classification." *Voluntas,* 1993, 3, 267–309.

Salamon, L. M., and Anheier, H. K. *The Emerging Nonprofit Sector: An Overview.* Manchester: Manchester University Press, 1996.

Salamon, L. M., Anheier, H. K., and Sokolowski, S. W. *The Emerging Sector: A Statistical Supplement.* Baltimore: The Johns Hopkins Institute for Policy Studies, 1996.

Schöffmann, D. "Ohne Moss nix los! Kapitalbildung für eine gute Sache." In *Social Sponsoring und Social Marketing: Praxisberichte über das "neue Produkt Mitgefühl."* Eds. T. Leif and U. Galle. Köln: Bund, 1993, 190–197.

Strachwitz, Count R. *Stiftungen—nutzen, führen und errichten: ein Handbuch.* Frankfurt: Campus, 1994.

Strachwitz, Count R. "Unternehmen als Sponsoren, Förderer, Spender und Stifter." In *Kulturförderung—Mehr als Sponsoring.* Ed. Count R. Strachwitz and S. Toepler. Wiesbaden: Gabler, 1993, 251–263.

Toepler, S. "Marketing-Management für Museen: Die amerikanische Perspektive." In *Das Museum als Nonprofit-Organisation.* Ed. A. Zimmer. Frankfurt: Campus, 1995, 155–175.

Toepler, S. *Operation in a Grantmaking World: Reassessing the Role of Operating Foundations.* Research Report. Johns Hopkins Institute for Policy Studies, 1994.

Toepler, S. *Stiftungen in der modernen demokratischen Gesellschaft—Ansätze zu einer ökonomischen Betrachtungsweise.* Munich: Maecenata Verlag, 1996.

Toepler, S., and Strachwitz, Count R. "Traditional Methods of Funding: Foundations and Endowments." In *Europe's Solidarity: Resourcing Foundations, Associations, Voluntary Organizations, and NGO's in the Member States of the European Union.* Ed. L. Doyle. Brussels: AICE, 1996, 100–108.

Toman, M. "Landeskulturstiftungen in der Bundesrepublik—Ein Überblick." In *Europäischer Kulturförderalismus—Positionen und Aufgaben der Kulturstiftungen.* Ed. Hessische Kulturstiftung. Wiesbaden: Hessische Kulturstiftung, 1990, 10–17.

Tsyboula, S. "Foundations in Europe: The View from France." Presentation at the symposion *Trusts and Foundations: International Perspectives*, Voluntas & Laboratoire D'Economie Sociale, Sorbonne, Paris, Oct. 21–23, 1993.

Tweedy, C. "Great Britain." In *Patronage of the Arts by Foundations and Non Government Organizations in Europe*. Ed. Kulturstiftung Haus Europa. Berlin: Maas, 1992, 87–96.

Vaccaro, A. "Die Spende—Ein Produkt?" In *Kulturförderung—Mehr als Sponsoring*. Ed. Count R. Strachwitz and S. Toepler. Wiesbaden: Gabler, 1993, 209–222.

Vanhaeverbeke, A. "Private Kulturförderung in europäischen Dimensionen." In *Kulturförderung—Mehr als Sponsoring*. Eds. Count R. Strachwitz and S. Toepler. Wiesbaden: Gabler, 1993, 127–135.

Weisbrod, B. A., and Mauser, E. "Tax Policy toward Non-profit Organisations: An Eleven-Country Survey." *Voluntas*, 1991, 1, 3–25.

# Inclination, Obligation, and Association

## What We Know and What We Need to Learn about Donor Motivation

PAUL G. SCHERVISH, PhD
*Boston College*

This chapter reviews the *status quaestionis* surrounding the issue of motivation for charitable gifts of money and assets—what I will call *financial philanthropy*. By *motivation*, I refer not to the moralistic distinction between so-called noble and base intentions, or between altruistic and self-serving aspirations. Rather, by motivation I refer to the array of associations, experiences, goals, and orientations that generate people's charitable giving—what I like to refer to as *mobilizing factors*. Because the same factors (such as volunteering or organizational membership) may lead to giving *and* increased giving, it is always necessary to bear in mind what place in the "pipeline" of giving we are speaking about at each point in the discussion. Therefore, in exploring the mobilizing factors that induce financial philanthropy, it is important to distinguish between those influences that lead people to become givers in the first place and those that lead some donors to make larger than average gifts or to increase their giving.

In all instances, the guiding principle of my approach to charitable giving is represented by an *identification* model rather than an *altruism* model of motivation. The altruism model is best known through the various studies on extraordinary heroism and on blood and organ donations. I have elaborated my view of the identification model in various places (Ostrander & Schervish, 1990; Schervish, 1993, 1995) and find it well articulated in a parallel fashion by Martin (1994) and Langdon (forthcoming). My fullest case for the theoretical and empirical superiority of the identification model over the altruism model is in the first chapter of my book *The Modern Medicis* (Schervish, forthcoming). Both my intensive

I am grateful to the T. B. Murphy Foundation Charitable Trust for supporting the research reported here, and to Platon Coutsoukis who graciously and competently assisted in the preparation of this paper.

interviews with wealthy donors and survey analyses of giving and volunteering persuade me that it makes little theoretical or practical sense to chase down forces of *selflessness* precisely in the areas of life in which dedication and commitment of *self-identification* are so crucial. Thus instead of investigating the quantitative *absence* of the self, I prefer to investigate the qualitative presence of the self.

I address the issue of motivation and charitable giving in four sections. First, I summarize the literature on motivations for giving. I do not intend this review to be exhaustive. Rather in reviewing a range of conceptual and empirical writings, my goal is to present a useful topical survey of the kinds of variables designated by researchers as important. Second, I will present the empirical findings my colleague John Havens and I have thus far discovered from our ongoing multivariate research on the factors that induce charitable giving. In the third section, I elaborate a research agenda aimed at substantiating what we and others have already found and at uncovering what we still need to learn. I conclude by suggesting the implications for encouraging a less judgmental and more fruitful fund raising attitude, especially in regard to wealthy donors.

## Mobilizing Factors for Charitable Giving

The current literature on the motivating factors for charitable giving is extensive; however, it is uneven in its level of theoretical sophistication and empirical complexity. For a number of reasons, including that volunteering is tied to charitable giving, the literature on motivations for volunteering is always indirectly, if not directly, relevant to the discussion of charitable giving. Also, the fund raising and prospect research literature is invariably related to the mobilizing factors for giving insofar as this literature addresses the organizational techniques and personal strategies fund raisers employ to induce donors to contribute. Also, this literature is both repetitive and partial. Although much of the literature offers useful information, the key findings seem to be periodically "rediscovered." As a result, we have a litany of well-documented factors that appear to motivate charitable giving. In the absence of more complex research, we know little about the *relative importance* of these factors; that is, how the factors are linked together in a causal chain, and which factors turn out to be more important and which turn out to be less important in the light of multivariate statistical analyses. This is true for qualitative as well as quantitative research efforts. To date, neither approach for studying charitable giving has endeavored to produce anything even approaching normal science. We have not yet reached the point at which the theories, conceptual frameworks, measurement techniques, statistical analyses, and findings of one research effort build explicitly on previous research and become the basis for subsequent research designed to confirm, disprove, or amend previous findings.

So what can we learn from the current literature? Platon Coutsoukis, a research associate at the Social Welfare Research Institute, and I have undertaken a systematic review of the literature on the factors inducing charitable giving. As yet, our efforts have not progressed sufficiently to provide an appropriately complete and coherent account of this literature. However, I am able to outline the major categories of factors found to be influential in inducing charitable giving and to indicate the most important specific variables studied within each of the categories. We have generally limited our review to the literature that deals with charitable giving. In some instances, however, we report findings from studies on the factors that lead to "charitable acts" in general, without distinguishing between volunteering and giving.[1]

As I stated, I have not found a comprehensive literature review summarizing the empirical findings concerning charitable giving parallel to what David Horton Smith (1994) and Fischer and Schaffer (1993) have provided regarding the theory and research on volunteering. The two broadest conceptual outlines of factors contributing to giving are presented in Mixer (1993) and Schervish and Havens (1997). Although developed independently, the latter two frameworks are similar. Because I am understandably more familiar with the schema I developed, and because we have now carried out a substantial amount of empirical research based on it, I have chosen to summarize current research findings according to the rubrics of my framework. My debt to Mixer's good review, however, is great. Finally, I want to mention that Virginia A. Hodgkinson is currently completing a prodigious tome in which she provides a comprehensive review not just of the research findings on motivation for charitable giving but on the full range of religious, philosophical, sociological, psychological, legal, and institutional factors that lead to care and community participation. At this point, I have not drawn upon her work.

The major categories of variables comprising my conceptual framework grew out of my analysis of intensive interviews with millionaires in the Study on Wealth and Philanthropy (Schervish & Herman, 1988) and further elaborated in the course of subsequent research. Although the specific motivations of wealthy donors differ in significant ways from those of nonwealthy donors, the broad categories of variables I found to be relevant for millionaires seem to provide an effective conceptual framework for understanding giving in general. My research indicated the following eight variables:

1. *Communities of participation.* Groups and organizations in which one participates.
2. *Frameworks of consciousness.* Beliefs, goals, and orientations that shape the values and priorities that determine people's activities.

---

[1] I recognize that I am skimming the surface of the vast literature on charitable giving and so apologize to those whose work we have thus far neglected, and request that they let us know about their work and how it relates to our conceptual framework.

3. *Direct requests.* Invitations by persons or organizations to directly participate in philanthropy.
4. *Discretionary resources.* The quantitative and psychological wherewithal of time and money that can be mobilized for philanthropic purposes.
5. *Models and experiences from one's youth.* The people or experiences from one's youth that serve as positive exemplars for one's adult engagements.
6. *Urgency and effectiveness.* A sense of how necessary and/or useful charitable assistance will be in the face of the onset of an unanticipated or previously unrecognized family, community, national, or international crisis.
7. *Demographic characteristics.* The geographic, organizational, and individual circumstance of one's self, family, and community that affect one's philanthropic commitment.
8. *Intrinsic and extrinsic rewards.* The array of positive experiences and outcomes of one's current engagement that draws one deeper into a philanthropic identity.

The first seven variables work both to induce charitable involvement in the first place and, once in place, to increase one's level of commitment. The eighth variable—reinforcing rewards—is by definition relevant in regard to increasing the level of participation of those who have already become involved and, as such, may be in the form of one or more of the first seven variables. For a particular individual, any one of the first seven factors may be sufficient to induce at least a minimal level of philanthropic care, but in most cases the path to philanthropic care is via the influence of several if not all the factors.

## ELABORATION OF VARIABLES[2]

*Communities of participation* are the networks of formal and informal relationships with which people are associated. Communities of participation may be formal organizations such as schools, soup kitchens, or weekend soccer leagues. Communities of participation may also be quite informal, such as an extended family visiting and caring for an elderly grandparent or neighbors rallying to help a family burned out of its home. Some communities of participation (such as a political party) require little voluntary activity while others (such as a cooperative nursery school) require participation as a condition of membership. Some communities of participation are entered only out of choice, such as a volunteer fire department or volunteer counseling at a shelter for battered women. Others are entered

---

[2] My discussion of the first five and the eighth variables in the following paragraphs is taken with only slight revision from my article "Gentle as Doves and Wise as Serpents: The Philosophy of Care and the Sociology of Transmission" (Schervish, 1995b).

as a result of circumstances; for example, parents with school-age children are automatically put into contact with numerous school, extracurricular, and sports programs that offer opportunities to volunteer time and to contribute money. As I indicated, many communities of participation directly request and sometimes require time and money from their participants. But the important point is that being connected to an array of such life-settings is the basis for people becoming aware of needs and choosing to respond.

*Frameworks of consciousness* are ways of thinking and feeling that are rooted deeply enough in one's awareness to induce a commitment to a cause based on political ideology, religious beliefs, social concerns, or other values. An awareness of the redemptive value of Alcoholics Anonymous' twelve-step program in one's own or a family member's life is one example. Equally common are the deeply felt convictions about political prisoners that lead concerned citizens to join Amnesty International, about homeless people or battered women that lead volunteers to work at shelters, about community violence that lead parents to patrol the streets as part of a neighborhood watch, about the value of religious faith that lead church members to work in a food bank or a program for racial justice. The list of motivating concerns is as long as the list of deeply cherished beliefs. Just as there are different types of organizations in which one may participate, there are different types of beliefs. Some mobilizing beliefs are in fact better described as general values, other beliefs are really fundamental orientations, while still other beliefs concern causes to which one is dedicated. Again, there are no impermeable boundaries separating these kinds of beliefs any more than there is a sharp demarcation between what one does because of heartfelt feelings, on the one hand, and communities of participation, on the other. Communities of participation and frameworks of consciousness almost always occur together.

The third mobilizing factor comprises *direct requests* made to individuals for contributions of time and money. Many of these invitations arise directly as a result of one's participation in an organization. Certainly, some people volunteer their time and money without being asked. For the majority of givers, being asked is cited as a major reason for their charitable efforts. We are finding evidence that while telephone and mail solicitations do get results (otherwise they would not be so incessant), those who contribute higher percentages of their income state they are not influenced by such impersonal methods. Still, there is every reason to believe that people in all income groups follow what I found among wealthy contributors, namely that being asked directly by someone the contributor knows personally or by a representative of an organization the contributor participates in is a major mobilizing factor. Once again, the linkages among the mobilizing factors are apparent. Being asked to contribute largely occurs from within existing communities of participation and appeals to existing frameworks of consciousness.

The presence of *discretionary resources* is a fourth factor leading to charitable commitment. The level of one's discretionary resources of time and money is a mixture of objective and subjective considerations. The amount of time retired people, with children out of the house, consider discretionary is likely to be greater than the amount felt to be available by members of the labor force who are still raising children. Similarly, a family of four with a household income of $75,000 presumably enjoys more discretionary spending than a family of four with an income of $25,000. Nevertheless, there are a good number of complicating factors including the amount of time needed to care for a sick spouse and the amount of money devoted to necessary expenditures such as college tuition and taxes. One family's necessity is another family's luxury, which highlights that the amount of discretionary resources is also a matter of subjective disposition. What may appear to some as a desperately urgent need for which they should sacrifice time and money may appear less compelling to others with the same objective resources. The organizations in which we participate, the cultural frameworks we embrace, the pleas to which we are attuned, and the resources we deem able to give are inextricably linked.

The same is true for the fifth determinant, namely the positive *models and experiences from one's youth* that animate adult philanthropy. By speaking of models from one's youth, I do not mean to neglect those exemplars from adulthood. But for the sake of clarity, I include such adult models (be they friends, business associates, or colleagues on a board of directors) as part of one's community of participation. To be emphasized here are those activities and lives that people are more or less drawn into in the course of growing up. To some extent, such contacts are voluntary choices. But the majority of them are more likely to have been unavoidable, put in the person's path by parents, grandparents, churches, youth groups, and schools. As such, they are occasions for initiation into the child's earliest communities of participation and frameworks of consciousness. They are part of a moral education that molds children's lives at a period when they are less guarded about priorities and more apt to accrue a feel for the charitable impulse.

The sixth mobilizing factor is the *urgency* with which needs are presented to potential donors and the effectiveness these donors perceive their charitable response to have. Such urgency usually revolves around the actual onset or introduction into an individual's purview of an unanticipated highly salient family, community, national, or international need. Such emergency needs are thrust on individuals by such events as illness, deaths, fires, and other tragedies that befall relatives and friends. But equally important are the local, national, and international natural disasters, famines, and epidemics that strike people as particularly compelling because of the dire nature of a situation and the lack of normal channels of provision. Here, perhaps more than in any other circumstance, people sense and respond to the realization, "There but for fortune go I." A response to urgency is connected to the perceived effectiveness of a response. An urgent need about which potential donors feel they can make no difference is unlikely to mobilize their time and money. In many ways, the now familiar "compassion fatigue" is a result of an emotional stalemate resulting from the intersection of repeated urgent appeals coupled with the perception that intervention is ineffective in curtailing suffering.

*Demographic* variables comprise the seventh category of influences. Such demographic variables include individuals' personal characteristics of age, education, gender, and race as well as various background or contextual characteristics associated with one's employment, community, home ownership, tenure living in a locale, and so forth. Most demographic characteristics are introduced into analyses as control variables and so are not accorded much explanatory substance. Many so-called demographic controls, however, represent important underlying causal dynamics. For example, education and age are not simply control variables. Rather they are indicators of a person's array of relationships, experiences, networks, organizational involvements, and time commitments that set in motion a range of consequences for charitable participation.

An eighth variable comes into play when we are seeking to explain the intensity of people's philanthropic commitment. This is the set of *intrinsic and extrinsic rewards* that accrue to individuals who are already active in philanthropy. The source and intensity of such satisfactions are connected to the additional communities of participation and frameworks of consciousness that philanthropists encounter in carrying out their commitments. Such reinforcing factors include getting to know other givers, formal and informal expressions of gratitude, public recognition of various sorts, and direct material benefits such as preferred seating at the symphony and decision-making clout at a welfare agency. But most important among such reinforcing rewards is the personal satisfaction from helping others and from seeing one's money and time used as an effective investment to accomplish cherished goals. In this regard, less involved philanthropists might do well to take a page from Jane Addams and from those who work directly with the beneficiaries of their philanthropy. One of the richest sources of reinforcing satisfaction is to ascertain firsthand the positive effect of one's care on the lives of others and to be able to more fully identify with one's beneficiaries as radical ends.

Exhibit 8.1 is a compendium of the various categories of mobilizing factors and specific variables examined in empirical research on the determinants of charitable giving.

## Multivariate Analysis of Charitable Giving

To my knowledge, our research at the Social Welfare Research Institute is the only effort to carry out a multivariate analysis of variables representing nearly all the general factors catalogued in the preceding section. The

## EXHIBIT 8.1. Determinants of Charitable Giving

### I. Communities of Participation
1. Church
   a. Denominational Affiliation
   b. Church Attendance
   c. General Church Involvement
   d. Volunteering for Church Organizations
2. School (school's religious orientation and emphasis of community service, student's organizational memberships and academic performance)
3. Work (size of business and organizational culture)
4. Civic Institutions (membership and general involvement)
5. Government and Political Organizations (sense of power and influence)

### II. Framework of Consciousness
1. General Values
2. Religious Beliefs and Values
3. Political Beliefs and Values
4. Attitudes about Social Responsibility
5. Attitudes about Volunteering
6. Attitudes toward the Recipient Organization

### III. Direct Requests
1. Medium of Request (face-to-face meeting, telephone call, mail)
2. Strategies of Approach (determine needs and wants of donor, describe need, use mix of rational arguments and emotional appeals, convey organizational vision, provide opportunities for donor involvement, show the example of leading supporters)
3. Mode of Petition (ask or encourage to give, document organizational efficiency and effectiveness of gift,* offer additional information and convenient financial arrangements)
4. Closure: Foundations of an ongoing Relationship (feedback on accomplishments and appropriate recognition and personal rewards—see VIII.2. Extrinsic Rewards)

### IV. Discretionary Resources
1. Income
2. Wealth and Composition of Wealth (real estate, equities, and other properties)
3. Time (hours per week, weeks per year, employment—part time, stage of entrepreneurship, retirement, age of children)
4. Expectations about Future Financial Capacity

### V. Models and Experiences from One's Youth
1. Parental Example
2. Example of Other Role Models
3. Membership in a Youth Group
4. Was a Volunteer

*(continued)*

## EXHIBIT 8.1. (continued)

    5. Door-to-Door Fund raising
    6. Helped by Others
    7. Active in Student Government

### VI. Urgency and Effectiveness
    1. Demonstration of Pressing Need
    2. Belief in the Effectiveness of Gift
    3. Perceived Organizational Efficiency

### VII. Demographic
    1. Location (geographic location, urban/rural type, size and economic status of community)
    2. Age
    3. Gender
    4. Education
    5. Race
    6. Marital Status
    7. Children (presence and number of)
    8. Employment (part or full-time)
    9. Occupational Prestige
  10. Length of Residence
  11. Home Ownership
  12. Health

### VIII. Intrinsic and Extrinsic Rewards
    1. Intrinsic Rewards
       a. Personal Elements (self-esteem, achievement, cognitive interest, growth, meaning, or purpose in life)
       b. Configurations of Personal Elements
       c. Social Elements (status, affiliation, group endeavor, interdependence, power)
       d. Negative Elements (guilt reduction or guilt avoidance, frustration, insecurity)
    2. Extrinsic Rewards
       a. Recognition Rewards (introductions in meetings, invitations to elite gatherings, publicity)
       b. Personal Rewards (immediate thank-you letters, telephone calls from leaders and officials, awards, membership in elite groups, and peer acknowledgments)
       c. Social Rewards (development of new personal relationships, an increased sense of community and status, and new awareness of group cohesion)
       d. Tax Incentives (e.g., income, estate, and capital gains taxes)

* Determinant(s) cited in more than one category.

major exception is that we have not yet modeled how intrinsic and extrinsic rewards advance additional giving. In regard to demographic variables, we have not yet attempted to incorporate the contextual variables of community and geography that Wolpert (1994, 1995a, 1995b) has skillfully analyzed.

We explored the causal relationship between the foregoing variable sets and charitable giving through a multivariate analysis of a subset of the "National Survey of Giving and Volunteering in the U.S." collected in 1992 by the Gallup Organization for the INDEPENDENT SECTOR (Schervish & Havens, 1994). The survey is of a representative cross-sectional sample of 2,671 American households whose respondent was 18 years of age or older. The survey obtains information on giving and volunteering, numerous indicators of relevant motivations and attitudes, household social characteristics, economic factors, and selected demographic descriptors. To increase the likelihood of accurate responses, we restricted our analysis to the subsample of 2,065 households in which the respondent, often jointly with their spouse, was both "most involved in deciding which charities your household will give to" and "primarily responsible for giving donations to charity."[3]

## OPERATIONALIZATION OF VARIABLE CLUSTERS

We briefly considered defining our dependent variable, charitable giving, (1) as two variables (participation and total amount contributed); (2) as the amount given to religious organizations and amount given to nonreligious organizations; or (3) as total amount contributed. In the end, we decided on the percentage of income contributed by the household as the dependent variable in our investigation.[4] Among the major considerations for this choice was that it is a continuous variable which is not, itself, overwhelmingly influenced by household income—as is the case with the total amount contributed. In addition, it has the historical advantage that we and others have worked extensively with this measure in previous research efforts.[5]

---

[3] Due to missing data in the 25 independent variables used in the final regression analysis, the sample size for this regression was reduced further to 1,375 households.

[4] Based on the subsample of households in which the respondent either solely or jointly with others (usually their spouse) in the household make decisions regarding philanthropic contributions, we estimate that 77 percent of the population of households contribute to one or more philanthropic organizations. The average of total annual contributions is $733 per household—$440 to religious organizations and $293 to nonreligious organizations. The annual total of all contributions amounts to 2.0 percent of household gross income—1.3 percent being given to religious organizations and .7 percent being given to nonreligious organizations.

[5] The contribution variables for the survey contained missing data for approximately 10 percent of the households that made a contribution. Among these households, one component of giving was usually missing, but there were often nonmissing values for several

We reviewed the questions asked in the survey several times to map particular questions into one of the conceptual clusters. At the conclusion of this process we had mapped 107 variables into the seven clusters. For a number of methodological reasons, 107 variables is too large a number even for multivariate analysis.[6] We used a highly empirical procedure to reduce the number of variables to a more manageable size. We ran a series of multiple regressions to estimate (1) the relationship between charitable giving (i.e., percentage of household income given to charity) and the variables associated with each theoretical cluster, estimated independently of variables in any other cluster; (2) the relationship between charitable giving and all 107 variables, entered in hierarchical order by cluster; (3) the relationship between giving and all 107 variables entered simultaneously; and (4) the relationship between giving and all 107 variables with the least significant variables successively eliminated until the remaining variables were all significant at the .10 level. At the end of this procedure, we included all variables that were theoretically significant at .10 level and several nonstatistically significant variables that we judged to be the most theoretically important. The resulting number of variables was reduced from 107 to 48; these are listed by theoretical cluster in Exhibit 8.2.

## FINDINGS ABOUT INDIVIDUAL CLUSTERS

Details of our multivariate analysis are presented in Schervish and Havens (1994). Our central finding is that there is broad quantitative support for major tenets of the identification theory of philanthropy. We came to this conclusion as a result of investigating two questions: (1) whether each of the clusters of variables was separately related to charitable giving and (2) which specific variables determine charitable giving when variables from all the clusters are examined simultaneously. The first step was to

---

other components. Consequently, the missing values were imputed for the missing components and then added together with the nonmissing components to arrive at an estimate of total contribution. These imputations were based on multiple regressions of age of respondent, sex of respondent, education of respondent, residential location, and household income. This method assumes that missing values within each category follow the trend relationship for that category.

[6] First, such a large number of variables is difficult for the researcher and the reader to keep straight, even within cluster groupings. Second, the 107 variables are interrelated among themselves which has the effect that the impact of any one variable is in part obfuscated by each of the others—the more variables beyond 15 to 20 in this particular analysis, the greater the degree of obfuscation. Third, each of the 107 variables were not answered by a small percentage of the sample; when any of the answers were missing, the case was eliminated from the analysis; less than 900 cases had substantive answers to all 107 variables; consequently the sample was reduced to less than 48 percent of the original subsample size. Fourth, because of the high degree of intercorrelation, the statistical methods could not, in most instances, identify which of the variables were statistically significant (although this does not necessarily cause major problems in early stages of research).

## EXHIBIT 8.2. Independent Variables within Theoretical Clusters

**Communities of Participation**

| | |
|---|---|
| Q27 | Length of time living in community |
| Q33e | Directly helped a needy person other than relative, friend, neighbor, homeless, or street person |
| Q37 | Average number of hours per week respondent spent helping friends or relatives who don't live with respondent |
| Q87 | Frequency of attending church or synagogue |
| Q901 | Number of people living in household |
| Nvol | The number of different types of organization in which the respondent volunteers time |
| Hvol | The number of hours per month that the respondent volunteers |
| Ngiv | The number of different types of organization to which the respondent's household makes a contribution in money and/or in kind |
| Rfix | Gives a fixed proportion of income to church, synagogue, or mosque |
| Ofix | Gives a fixed proportion of income to nonreligious organization(s) |

**Frameworks of Consciousness**

| | |
|---|---|
| Q67b | Giving back to society some of benefits it gave you is a personal motivation that may involve both charitable giving of money and volunteering time in general, not just last year |
| Q67f | Fulfilling a business or community obligation is a personal motivation that may involve . . . |
| Q67i | Meeting religious beliefs or commitments is a personal motivation that may involve . . . |
| Q68b | Teaching people to be more self-sufficient is a major, a minor, or not a goal of charitable giving of money and volunteering time |
| Q68e | Enhancing the moral basis of society is a major, a minor, . . . |
| Q68f | Changing the way society works is a major, a minor, . . . |

**Direct Requests**

| | |
|---|---|
| Q26 | Has been asked to give money or other property to charitable organizations, including religious organizations, in the past year |
| Q66b | Receiving a phone call asking you to give is (very important, somewhat important, not too important, or not at all important) to you for contributing to a charitable organization |
| Q66c | Someone coming to the door asking you to give is (very important, . . .) |
| Q66j | Being asked by clergy to give is (very important, . . .) |
| Q67a | Being asked to contribute or volunteer by a personal friend or business associate was a (major motivation, minor motivation, or not a motivation) for your charitable giving and volunteering |
| Q67j | Being encouraged by an employer was a (major motivation, . . .) |

*(continued)*

## EXHIBIT 8.2. (continued)

### Discretionary Resources

Q3    Degree respondent worries about not having enough money—a lot, moderate amount, or only a little

Q4    Respondent has (more, less, or the same amount of) money left over after paying bills this year compared with last year

Q77    Will be claiming a deduction for charitable contribution on federal income tax return for 1991

Q83    Is financially (better off, about the same, worse off) now compared with a year ago

Q84    Expect at this time next year to be financially (better off, the same, worse off) then than now

Inc    Household gross income

Nemp    The number of people currently employed in the household

### Models and Experiences from One's Youth

Q82A    One or both parents did volunteer work in community when young

Q82j    Helped by others in the past when young

Q82k    Saw somebody in family help others when young

### Urgency and Effectiveness

Q47a    The need for charitable organizations is greater now than five years ago—strongly agree, agree, disagree, strongly disagree

Q47b    Charitable organizations are more effective now in providing services than five years ago—strongly agree, . . .

Q47c    I place a low degree of trust in charitable organizations—strongly agree, . . .

Q47g    Generally, the U.S. is in more trouble now than 5 years ago—strongly agree, . . .

Q47h    Generally, charitable organizations play a major role in making our communities better places to live—strongly agree, . . .

Q47i    On the whole, charitable organizations do not do a very good job in helping those who need help—strongly agree, . . .

Q69h    Most people with serious problems brought their problems on themselves—strongly agree, . . .

Q69i    It is in my power to do things that improve the welfare of others—strongly agree, . . .

### Demographic Characteristics

Age    Respondent's age

Heduc    Education of Chief Wage Earner

Hret    Retirement Status of Chief Wage Earner

Race    Race Dichotomy (nonwhite or white)

Prot    Religious Affiliation Dichotomy (non-Protestant or Protestant)

Cath    Religious Affiliation Dichotomy (non-Catholic or Catholic)

Jwsh    Religious Affiliation Dichotomy (non-Jewish or Jewish)

Orel    Religious Affiliation Dichotomy (not other religion or other religion)

run multiple regressions[7] of the specific subset of variables associated with each theoretical cluster to determine whether a subset explained giving behavior as represented by the percentage of household income contributed. Each separate regression analysis estimates the combined direct and indirect impacts of the cluster of variables on percentage of income contributed. It also estimates the relative combined direct and indirect impact of each of the variables associated with the cluster.

## Communities of Participation

Our analysis also demonstrates that participation in associational communities induces charitable contribution. The set of 10 variables corresponding to participation in a variety of communities is significant at the .0001 level of statistical significance. The strength of the relationship, measured by $R$-Squared, is a rather substantial .288. Given the empirical methods used to reduce the number of variables in the analysis, it is interesting that most variables measuring general levels of social participation (e.g., membership in a variety of clubs and organizations) were not sufficiently strongly related to giving behavior to be included in this analysis. Most of the variables that are relatively strongly related to giving behavior are measures of either (a) participation and/or commitment to organizations and institutions that serve as channels for giving and volunteering or (b) informal activities that involve helping others. Eight of the 10 variables are associated with giving behavior in the expected direction (greater participation and/or greater opportunities for participation lead to larger percentages of income contributed). However, two are not: (1) households that allocate a fixed proportion of their income to donate to nonreligious organizations tend to allocate smaller proportions than those that do not structure their donations so formally; and (2) larger households (which presumably have more opportunities for participation because of the activities of their members) tend to give smaller proportions of their incomes than do smaller households. In this case, larger households may not have sufficient financial resources to support larger proportions of income contributed after meeting the needs of members, especially since larger households tend also to have lower incomes.

## Framework of Consciousness

Based on multiple regression analysis of the available information in the survey data, we found that strongly held frameworks of consciousness advance charitable giving. The set of six variables corresponding to relatively stable beliefs and motives for giving is significantly related to

---

[7] Unless otherwise noted, all multiple regressions reported in this chapter used the population weights developed by the Gallup organization; casewise deletion when any variable was missing data; and ordinary least squares estimation of the regression coefficients on the independent variables. The values of $R$-Squared reported are not adjusted for the number of independent variables in the analysis.

giving behavior at the .0001 level of statistical significance. The strength of the relationship as measured by $R$-Squared is .073, nearly double that of youthful experiences—indicating that even partial measures of one's current framework of consciousness are more strongly related to current giving behavior than are youthful experiences, which are more distant in time. The substance of the relationship is also rather interesting. Those who are motivated mainly either (1) to fulfill a business or community obligation or (2) to change the way society works, tend to give smaller percentages of their income than those who are motivated by (1) meeting religious beliefs or commitments, (2) enhancing the moral basis of society, (3) teaching people to be more self-sufficient, or (4) giving back to society some of the benefits it gave the respondent. This pattern is phenomenologically consistent with the definition of framework of consciousness.

## Direct Requests

Regression analysis of the relevant survey data indicates that the mode of petition affects the level of charitable response. The set of six variables corresponding to the direct invitation cluster is significant at the .0001 level; and its strength, measured as usual by $R$-Squared, is .052. However, only three of the variables indicate that direct invitation leads to higher percentages of income contributed while three others indicate that direct invitation is actually associated with lower, if any, percentage of income contributed (Q66b, Q66c, Q67j).

Closer inspection of each subset of three variables implies that the method of direct contact may be more important than just the contact itself. The three direct invitations that seem to lead to higher levels of contribution imply a personal contact by a previously known individual—a personal friend, business associate, or clergyperson. The three direct invitations that seem to lead to small if any contributions are associated with less intimate contact—phone call, someone coming to the door, or workplace-based encouragement by an employer.

## Discretionary Resources

Regression analysis shows that the set of seven variables corresponding to the discretionary resources cluster is significant at the .0001 level of statistical significance. The strength of the relationship, as measured by $R$-Squared, is .062. Variables that indicate increases in income or optimism concerning one's financial future are associated with higher percentages of income contributed.

Two variables that we associated with greater household resources, however, had signs that implied lower rather than higher percentages of income contributed. The first of these variables was the number of people employed in the household—the more people employed, according to this analysis, the lower the percentage of income contributed. One might speculate that households have a larger than average number of people employed because the household's income is not sufficient to meet the basic needs of the household and additional people have to work just to make ends meet—leaving very little left over for philanthropy. A more mean-spirited speculation would be that the members of some households are so materialistic and selfish that more of their members go to work and keep all of their increased earnings for themselves.

The second variable was gross household income, whose sign indicated lower percentages of income are contributed by households with higher gross incomes. This sign, however, makes some sense when one considers that another resource variable was the respondent's intentions to list charitable contributions as an itemized deduction. This variable would tend to pick up moderate and higher income households who made significant charitable contributions, leaving moderate and higher income households who made small or no charitable contributions to be reflected in the sign of the gross household income variable.

## Models and Experiences from One's Youth

Multiple regression analysis of the information available in the survey data indicates that youthful experiences are related to current giving behavior. The set of three variables corresponding to this cluster is significantly related to giving behavior at the .0001 level of statistical significance. Although significant, the strength of the relationship is relatively modest with an $R$-Squared of .038, but the coefficients of each of the three variables are associated with higher levels of household giving at the current time.

## Urgency and Effectiveness

Do the urgency of the cause and perception of the donation's effectiveness lead to *giving behavior?* Here, the answer is more ambiguous, and perhaps closer to "maybe." The set of eight variables corresponding to the urgency/effectiveness cluster is significant at the .045 level rather than the .0001 level as in the previous theoretical clusters. The strength of relationship is quite small at .0144, as measured by $R$-Squared. Of the eight variables, five have signs consistent with greater urgency and/or effectiveness being associated with larger proportions of income contributed; one is ambiguous (Q47b); and two are negative (Q47g, Q69h). Thus this cluster is less internally consistent than the other theoretical clusters, but once again there is evidence that confidence in charitable organizations is related to increased giving (Q47h).

## Demographic Characteristics

Multiple regression analysis shows that the set of eight demographic factors is significant at the .0001 level of statistical significance and the strength of relationship, as measured by $R$-Squared, is .064. These variables were the age of the respondent, the education of the chief wage earner, the retirement status of the chief wage earner, the race of the respondent, and religious affiliation (represented as four dummy variables). It should be noted that the first three of these demographic variables survived the variable reduction process while the last two were included because of the special interest of the researchers. Demographic characteristics that were related to giving behavior but were only weakly related when considered jointly with other demographic factors include marital status, presence of teens in the household, and Hispanic origin.

## FINDINGS FROM JOINT ANALYSIS OF VARIABLE CLUSTERS

The multiple regression analysis provides strong statistical evidence that five of the theoretical factors identified in the conceptual framework are, in some sequence and/or causal structure, related to giving behavior. The one theoretical factor, urgency/effectiveness, that emerged during the course of the analysis, in fact, seems also to be related to giving behavior. In this case, however, the empirical evidence is borderline at best. In view of the findings about the individual clusters, our second major question is *When the many factors relevant to the theory are taken into account simultaneously, which factors are most strongly related to giving behavior?* Multiple regression was again used to investigate this research question. As described earlier, variables from all clusters were entered into an initial analysis, which were then reduced to a smaller set of the 25 variables most relevant for the remaining research questions. As one would expect from the foregoing results, the reduced set of variables were significantly related to giving behavior at .0001 level of statistical significance (see Exhibit 8.3). The strength of the relationship, as measured by *R*-Squared, was .276,[8] which is in the moderate range for social science research based on survey data.

In this joint analysis, three of the five variables with the strongest relation to giving behavior, as measured by their standardized beta coefficients, are community of participation variables. All three are closely related to participation in institutions and organizations that already contain formal channels through which they may receive charitable contributions (Exhibit 8.3). One of the five is a resource variable and one is a demographic characteristic. Of the four remaining variables significant at the .05 level, two are general community of participation variables and the other two are invitation to participate variables. Thus of the nine variables significant at the .05 level, five are communities of participation variables, two are invitation to participate variables, one is a resource variable, and one is a demographic characteristic.

---

[8] This value is less than the value of .288 for the communities of participation analysis reported under question A3. However, the two analyses are not comparable in the strict mathematical sense: The first analysis included all participation variables that had survived the first stage of the variable reduction process resulting in a sample size of 1,099 cases, while the second analysis included a smaller subset of variables surviving the second stage of the data reduction process and is based on an expanded sample size of 1,375 cases.

**EXHIBIT 8.3. Joint Regression Analysis of All Clusters for Total Population**

| | N = 1375 | R-Squared* = 0.276 | | Significance Level = 0.0001 |
|---|---|---|---|---|

| | Variable Name | Non-Standardized Coefficient | Standardized Coefficient | Statistical Significance Level |
|---|---|---|---|---|
| | *Independent Variables with the Five Largest Standardized Coefficients* | | | |
| Rfix | Gives a fixed proportion of income to church, synagogue, or mosque | 2.865 | 0.289 | 0.0001 |
| Ngiv | The number of different types of organization to which the respondent's household makes a contribution in money and/or in kind | 0.361 | 0.193 | 0.0001 |
| Inc | Household gross income ($1000's) | −0.019 | −0.130 | 0.0001 |
| Q87 | Frequency of attending church or synagogue | 0.368 | 0.110 | 0.0001 |
| Hret | Retirement Status of Chief Wage Earner | 0.011 | 0.101 | 0.0002 |
| | *Other Independent Variables Significant at the .05 Level* | | | |
| Q27 | Length of time living in community | 0.238 | 0.066 | 0.0081 |
| Q67j | Being encouraged by an employer was motivation for charitable giving and volunteering time | −0.361 | −0.062 | 0.0150 |
| Q66c | Importance for charitable giving of someone coming to the door asking you to give | −0.264 | −0.059 | 0.0356 |
| Hvol | The number of hours per month that the respondent volunteers | 0.020 | 0.055 | 0.0282 |

* This value of R-Squared is based on all 25 independent variables in the analysis—in the interest of space only the values statistically significant at the .05 level or lower are presented in this exhibit; none of the variables excluded had standardized coefficients as large as .100.

The lack of variables from the youthful experiences, framework of consciousness, and effectiveness/urgency clusters means only that these clusters, as reflected in the variables contained in the Survey of Giving and Volunteering, are not strongly or consistently related to the percentage of income contributed once participation, resource, and demographic variables are taken into account. It does not necessarily mean that these clusters are only minor factors in giving behavior, indeed they may critical factors in causal sequences involved in giving behavior but they may be either (1) less proximate factors than participation, discretionary resources, and demographic factors or (2) more proximately related to giving behavior but only for selected segments of the population. Hypothetically, youthful experiences might influence framework of consciousness, and jointly they may influence the pattern and magnitude of community of participation so that the community of participation variable may already capture the effects of youthful experiences and framework of consciousness. This hypothetical sequence is one of many that are consistent with both the five-variable theory and the multivariate regression results.

## DISCUSSION

Reviewing these findings from the broad theoretical standpoint of identification theory, it appears that for the population as a whole, participation, especially participation that already embodies a commitment to philanthropy or to a philanthropic organization, is directly related to giving behavior. Within community of participation, religious commitment and participation in religious organizations have a strong influence on general giving behavior. Variables from other theoretical clusters do not have as central and consistent impact on giving behavior: Retirement status appears to influence the percentage of income contributed mainly through reductions in income that are proportionately much less than reductions in contributions; the impact of income appears to filter out those middle and higher income households that make relatively small contributions which they do not intend to deduct on their income taxes; the impact of direct invitations to participate appears to be to filter out those households contributing small percentages of their income who are prodded into making a small donation by door-to-door contact or a general contribution campaign (e.g., United Way) at their place of work.

The impact of household income (together with charitable deductions) seems less an indicator of discretionary resources than the delineator of higher income households making smaller donations; direct invitation variables seem less indicators of the impact of direct invitation to participate in the general population as delineators of households that are prodded into making a small contribution and are not in general internally motivated to give to charitable institutions; and the only demographic variable seems an indicator of reduced household income without commensurate reductions in the pattern of contribution.

The only variable in the empirical analysis that has theoretical significance is community of participation. To understand giving behavior in the total population, it turns out one should focus on understanding the community of participation, with special emphasis on the role of religious participation. A major task for future research on causal sequences affecting giving behavior should be the investigation of the relationship between communities of participation and the other theoretical clusters of variables in the five-variable theory—youthful experiences, frameworks of consciousness, discretionary resources, invitation to participate, and possibly urgency/effectiveness.

## SUMMARY OF FINDINGS

The findings can be summarized as follows:

- Each of the five theoretical variable clusters that could be operationalized within the limits of the data from the Survey of Giving and Volunteering (youthful experiences, framework of consciousness, communities of participation, invitation to participate, and discretionary resources) are significantly related to giving behavior.
- While there are variations in the strength of the relationships between each cluster and giving behavior, communities of participation is the cluster with the strongest and most consistent relationship to giving behavior.
- When considered jointly with other variable clusters, communities of participation is the only cluster that evinces a distinctive relationship to giving behavior.
- Two dimensions of communities of participation seem especially important for giving behavior: (1) a general level of participation and (2) religious participation and commitment.
- Two subgroups of higher income households (the retired and those intending to claim a charitable deduction at higher income levels) give a larger than average percentage of their incomes to charity.
- Participation and commitment, especially religious participation and commitment, are centrally and strongly related to giving behavior. Moreover, there is reason to believe that this cluster may operate, at least in part, as an intervening variable through which other clusters affect giving behavior.

## Research Agenda

The foregoing literature and multivariate analysis provide several significant empirical findings on the factors that induce charitable giving. Taken together, the findings about the impact of participation and frequency of participation, being asked, volunteering, generosity across income groups, and the fact that larger gifts are generated from those who have given large gifts—all indicate that charitable giving is largely a consequence of forging a connection between the existing inclinations and involvement of individuals and the needs of recipients. It is not the absence of self that must be generated but the presence of self-identification with others. This is what Thomas Aquinas teaches as the convergence of love of neighbor, love of self, and love of God. It is also, in its civic expression, what Tocqueville meant by self-interest properly understood. In this way, the inspiration for charitable giving is a function of the social-psychological processes of associational density, group incorporation, personal identification, and the satisfying experience of making an important difference.

Despite these solid initial findings, a weighty research agenda needs to be addressed—not simply because of the never-to-be-minimized vocation of intellectual discovery "for its own sake," but because there are important practical implications. In the study of charitable giving, there is a fortunate convergence between the discovery of the most technical detail and the invigoration of the equally honorable vocation of generosity and care.

The research agenda on the factors mobilizing charitable giving includes the following items.

## CONFIRMATORY POPULATION STUDIES

There must be continuing *confirmation and amendment* of existing findings, such as those generated in the foregoing analysis. This includes continued *application of multivariate statistical techniques* that enable researchers to distinguish between the more and less important determinants of charitable giving by measuring the relative effects of numerous variables simultaneously.

## SEGMENTATION ANALYSES

Researchers need to develop *separate analyses for differing segments* of the population. John Havens and I have undertaken (1994) such an analysis and have some preliminary findings to report. We hypothesized that the population of givers must reflect the national population in being segmented roughly along the lines of liberal and conservative policy orientations. Our major finding is that the seven-variable model explored in the previous section appears to be even more fully supported for each segment than it is for the population as a whole. That is, the impact of several mobilizing factors that tend to cancel out for the population as a whole are revealed when either of the segments is analyzed separately.

To discover an effective segmenting variable, we identified more than a dozen variables as potential components of sociopolitical ideological orientation. Originally, we anticipated developing a measure that would distinguish between "liberal" and "conservative" lifestyles and ideologies. A variety of indices were constructed using several methods. Cross-validation with other variables and descriptions of other behavior indicated that none of the indices adequately captured the essence of the "conservative" versus "liberal" dimension we had originally conceived.

One of the measures derived after item and item-index analysis appears to come as close to the desired categorization as any of the others and, empirically, leads to relatively more homogeneous giving behavior "within group" compared with "between groups" than did the other measures. We then used this measure to segment the sample in assessing whether the explanatory power of the seven-variable model increased when the two groups were analyzed separately.

The measure identifies one group as those households whose respondent indicated that "keeping taxes or other costs down" was a more major goal of their giving money and volunteering time than was the goal of "helping individuals meet their material needs." It identifies a second group as those households whose respondent indicated that "helping individuals meet their material needs" was a more major goal of their giving money and volunteering time than was the goal of "keeping taxes or other costs down." For convenience of presentation, we refer to the first group as "tax-motivated" and to the second group as "needs-motivated." We believe, however, that each group embodies a constellation of societal and political goals, motives, attitudes, and behavior that may not be appropriately captured by these convenient labels.[9]

For both tax-motivated and need-motivated households, the regression analyses reveal many elements that operate identically for each segment of households and for the population of all households. Communities of participation variables, with special emphasis on participation in and commitment to religious organizations, are the most prominent feature of the regression analysis among both tax-motivated households and the population of all households. A second common feature is that several of the variables seem not to operate on a broad theoretical basis but to delineate two of the same special groups: (1) households with moderate-to-high incomes that give relatively small proportions of their income to charity compared with households with similar incomes that give larger-than-average proportions of their income and expect to claim a charitable deduction, and (2) households whose chief wage earner is retired compared with other low-to-moderate-income households whose chief wage earner is not retired.

The regression analyses, however, do reveal important new features idiosyncratic to the way the theory manifests among each segment of households. Among the tax-motivated segment, three new groupings of variables are prominent on a broad theoretical basis: framework of consciousness, a

---

[9] We know that this grouping is empirically important, but we are not yet entirely confident that we understand the composition of the groups. Indeed, we believe that each group may actually be a combination of several other groups with similar giving behavior.

psychological continuum ranging from less to more generous, and (less prominently) youthful experiences. Among the needs-motivated segment, three groupings of variables are also prominent: framework of consciousness, youthful experiences, and (less prominently) invitation to participate.

There are differences between the way that common clusters of variables manifest themselves in the two segments:

- Among tax-motivated households, the important dimensions of framework of consciousness, in regard to different levels of giving behavior, are (1) a sense of social indebtedness expressed as variations in a desire to give back to society some of the beneficence received from society and (2) a consistency of the framework at either a psychological or behavioral level. Among need-motivated households, the important dimension of framework of consciousness is the degree to which religious commitment has been internalized.
- Among both tax-motivated and need-motivated households, the same youthful experience dimension is revealed as important— being helped when young, rather than youthful experiences helping others or the importance of philanthropically oriented role models when young. However, among tax-motivated households this dimension has a minor impact compared with its prominence among need-motivated households.
- Religious participation and commitment are important factors among both tax-motivated and need-motivated segments. Among tax-motivated households, religious behavior is the important facet of the dimension, but among need-motivated households both religious behavior and internalized commitment to religious principles are strongly related to giving behavior.

For each segment, there is also one cluster that is important for that segment but not the other:

- Among tax-motivated households, an important dimension related to giving behavior is the psychological continuum that we have labeled as the nongenerous/generous continuum. This dimension does not appear to affect the giving behavior of need-motivated households.[10]

---

[10] In a sense, the definition of the segments facilitates this finding for the tax-motivated households but does not facilitate the finding for need-motivated households. In this sense, the analysis is biased toward this finding among tax-motivated households—or, more correctly, biased against this finding among need-motivated households. It may still be the case that this dimension or its analog is important among need-motivated households but limited data does not adequately permit its measurement; consequently analysis cannot reveal its importance.

- Among need-motivated households, invitation to participate is an important dimension that identifies a subgroup that appears to be prodded to give a token contribution, much as this cluster operates in the population of all households. This variable is not at all prominent among tax-motivated households—it neither directly affects giving behavior nor delineates special groups.

These findings are preliminary in every sense with the exception that it is now clear that it is worth pursuing such segmented analyses. To do so we need to continue to explore what sociopolitical orientation scales should be included among the questions in the IS/Gallup surveys, and to pursue theoretical thinking and empirical analyses regarding relevant demarcations in the population.

## ANALYSES OF SECTORAL GIVING

An additional area for exploration is analyses of sectoral giving patterns. The major sectoral distinction is between religious (approximately 45%–50% of individual giving) and nonreligious giving. The explanatory determinants of religious giving need to be distinguished from the determinants of nonreligious giving in general, and specific areas of nonreligious giving, in particular. For example, it would be intellectually and practically important to carry out a multivariate analysis of the variables that predict level of giving to educational institutions.

## CAUSAL PATH ANALYSES

Virtually absent from the research literature, but implied in almost every conceptual depiction of the giving process is the notion that charitable giving is the outcome of a series of influences and forces. Two additional directions of causal analysis are warranted in addition to the determination of the factors that lead to levels of giving. The first is the development of a first-stage model that explains how people become givers in the first place. Although several variables that are significant determinants of giving in the analysis of individual clusters are not significant in the joint analysis, this does not mean that the specific variables in the cluster analyses are not important. Rather, we believe, the correct interpretation is that their impact is mediated by the participation cluster. That is, these apparently "insignificant" variables affect participation, which, in turn, affects giving behavior. For example, if volunteering and other variables associated with communities of participation induce giving, the next question becomes what factors induced volunteering and participation. Therefore, just because, as Havens and I found, most of the variables in the seven-variable model "dropped out" in favor of the communities of participation variable, these "dropped" variables probably remain extremely important for inducting people into communities of participation in the first place. The second venue for further causal analysis is to develop and test measures of the factors, such as intrinsic and extrinsic rewards and various forms of deeper personal engagement that lead to *increased* giving. The elaboration of such expanded causal pathways applies to each of the three foregoing research domains.

## ANALYSES OF GIVING PATTERNS BY INCOME AND WEALTH

It is of no surprise to anyone who has followed the research and popular literature on giving patterns by income and wealth that there remains much work to be done by way of settling the debate about the relative generosity of the rich and poor. My colleague, John Havens, and I have written several papers on this topic (Schervish & Havens 1995a, 1995b). In our recent paper, entitled "Wherewithal and Beneficence: Charitable Giving by Income and Wealth" (1995c), we extend the analysis of the upper income groups contained in the IS/Gallup studies to the very wealthy by analyzing the Survey of Consumer Finances that contains information on charitable giving of approximately 400 individuals at the upper extremes of income and wealth. In the income range up to $100,000, there is a relative equality of generosity measured by percentage of income contributed. Above $100,000, there is a dramatic increase in percentage of income contributed. Thus the popular notion of the generous poor and the stingy rich is simply incorrect. Our analysis of the Survey of Consumer Finances also enables us to conclude that virtually all the rich are contributors, that they donate very large amounts to charity, and that they give higher proportions of their income to charity than do the poor or affluent. That this pattern represents "generosity," however, is not for us to say. But it certainly contradicts the statistical portrait harbored by those who refer to the wealthy as "ungenerous" and "stingy" (Nielsen, 1992).

In view of these findings, I identify four specific research tasks:

1. Investment in acquiring larger and more detailed *datasets* on the charitable giving patterns of the individuals at the uppermost ends of wealth and income, the primary source of charitable contributions, especially nonreligious contributions.
2. Analysis of the *variation* of giving by income and wealth. Our preliminary research from the Survey of Consumer Finances and the IS/Gallup data confirm the earlier finding by Auten and Rudney (1990). While Auten and Rudney emphasized that only a small portion of the superwealthy are truly generous givers, we have found that in *every category* of income and wealth, there is a small proportion of extraordinary givers and that there is some evidence that among the highest income and wealth groups there may in fact be a greater proportion of such extraordinary givers.
3. Given our finding that income and wealth are not in themselves the source of generosity or stinginess, an important research

question is to determine *what other factors distinguish the extraordinary from ordinary givers* within each income and wealth group.

4. We have thus far found that it is possible to chart the relationship between percentage of income given and level of income, and percentage of income given and level of wealth. We have not yet discovered a pattern, however, when the dependent variable is *percentage of wealth given to charity*. We suspect this is because wealth is not a unidimensional resource. This implies a research effort to discern how the relative distribution of one's wealth into liquid and nonliquid assets as well as the period in one's business and investment life cycle are connected to one's timing and level of giving.

## CAPACITY TO GIVE

An important research effort that has been begun under the auspices of the Center on Philanthropy and in a different way by John Havens, Thomas Murphy, and me at Boston College (Murphy & Schervish 1996) is to derive micro- and macromeasures of the capacity to give. To date, the Center on Philanthropy has directed efforts to establish an aggregate figure of the capacity to give by compiling an aggregate measure of a modified notion of the discretionary income for the wealthy. The Boston College effort has focused instead on developing micromeasures of the capacity to give that focus on a combination of discretionary wealth and discretionary income as well as on the subjective orientations and tax policies that advance the psychological capacity to give.

## NEW HORIZONS OF TAX INCENTIVES

Perhaps the most neglected yet most consequential determinant of substantial giving among the upper income earners and wealth holders is the estate tax environment instituted by the Tax Reform Act of 1986. Much research has been conducted on the effect of marginal income tax rates and of the role of charitable deductions for the level of charitable giving. But in both of these cases, the question remains about the effect of such tax regulations on charitable contributions from income. Far more important, and therefore worthy of extensive research, is the consequence of existing and prospective federal and state estate taxes for charitable giving. The most neglected fact among researchers and commentators on charitable giving is something that is now patently obvious to financial planners, tax accountants, and increasing numbers of wealthy individuals (especially small business holders). This is that the 1986 tax code has dramatically increased the incentives of wealthy individuals to make substantial contributions to charity in lieu of paying an effective minimum wealth tax of at least 60%. Research would be very fruitfully directed toward studying the requirement embedded in the current estate tax laws for wealth holders to choose between dedicating their wealth (both while alive and at their death) to government uses or to charitable uses. As Richard Haas, an experienced financial planner, has put it, the only substantial tax shelter for the very wealthy is philanthropy. How to communicate to wealth holders this unanticipated and heretofore unappreciated convergence between a Republican tax reform and philanthropy is just one of several important research topics. Perhaps even more important will be research that helps us understand how to develop an entrepreneurial philanthropic agenda whereby the wealthy come to discern which socially beneficial projects they wish to undertake and how they wish to dedicate their wealth to such endeavors.

## Conclusion: Associational Density, Inclination, Obligation, and Invitation

The major implication of the foregoing is that much research has been initiated on the determinants of charitable giving, and that much more needs to be done. I would be pleased if the foregoing research agenda be viewed as more than just another of those self-serving global calls for more research that we have grown to expect at the end of research chapters. Rather, I believe the foregoing tenders a sensible, practical, and targeted research agenda that picks up where current research leaves off and has direct implications for advancing charitable giving. Current research offers many leads about what makes a difference in generating generosity. These leads, I am happy to note, are usually in concert with what fund raisers and donors know from their personal experience. However, the following four tasks require attention: (1) to draw together in a systematic manner those findings on which research and experience concur, (2) to examine in more detail the simultaneous interplay of factors so as to attribute fund raising successes and failures to their fundamental rather than apparent sources; (3) to explore the workings of new factors such as estate-tax changes introduced in the 1986 tax legislation; and (4) to correct downright mistakes and misconceptions about the determinants of charitable giving. As our current research has indicated, generosity is not a function of income but of the personal and social aspects of associational density, inclination, obligation, and invitation. Therefore, it is of great practical significance and, hence, a worthy investment of resources to improve our understanding of those determinants.

## Bibliography

Auten, Gerald, and Rudney, Gabriel. "The Variability of Individual Charitable Giving in the U.S." *Voluntas: International Journal of Voluntary and Nonprofit Organizations*, 1990, 1(2), 80–97.

Fischer, Rose Lucy, and Schaffer, Kay Banister. *Older Volunteers: A Guide to Research and Practice*. Newbury Park, CA: Sage, 1993.

Langdon, John P. *Capitalism and the Moral Life*. Forthcoming.

Martin, Mike W. *Virtuous Giving: Philanthropy, Voluntary Service, and Caring*. Bloomington: Indiana University Press, 1994.

Mixer, Joseph R. *Principles of Professional Fundraising: Useful Foundations for Successful Practice*. San Francisco: Jossey-Bass, 1993.

Murphy, Thomas B., and Schervish, Paul G. "The Dynamics of Wealth Transfer: Behavioral Implications of Tax Policy for the $10 Trillion Transfer." In *Nonprofit Organizations as Public Actors*. Eds. Astrid Merget, Ed Weaver, and Virginia H. Hodgkinson. San Francisco: Jossey-Bass, 1996.

Nielsen, W. A. "A Reason to Have Fund-Raisers: Our Stingy Rich People." *Chronicle of Philanthropy*, Oct. 6, 1992, 41.

Ostrander, Susan A., and Schervish, Paul G. "Giving and Getting: Philanthropy as a Social Relation." In *Critical Issues in American Philanthropy: Strengthening Theory and Practice*. Ed. Jon Van Til. San Francisco: Jossey-Bass, 1990.

Schervish, Paul G. "Gentle as Doves and Wise as Serpents: The Philosophy of Care and the Sociology of Transmission." In *Care and Community in Modern Society: Passing on the Tradition of Care to the Next Generation*. Eds. Paul G. Schervish, Virginia A. Hodgkinson, and Margaret Gates. San Francisco: Jossey-Bass, 1995.

Schervish, Paul G. *The Modern Medicis: Strategies of Philanthropy among the Wealthy*. San Francisco: Jossey-Bass: Forthcoming.

Schervish, Paul G., with Benz, Obie, Dulany, Peggy, Murphy Thomas B., and Salett, Stanley. *Taking Giving Seriously*. Indianapolis: Indiana University, Center on Philanthropy, 1993.

Schervish, Paul G., and Havens, John J. "Do the Poor Pay More? Is the U-shaped Curve Correct?" *Nonprofit and Voluntary Sector Quarterly*, 1995a, 24(1), 79–90.

Schervish, Paul G., and Havens, John J. "Explaining the U in the U-Shaped Curve." *Voluntas: International Journal of Voluntary and Nonprofit Organizations*, 1995b, 6(2), 202–225.

Schervish, Paul G., and Havens, John J. "Social Participation and Charitable Giving: A Multivariate Analysis." *Voluntas: International Journal of Voluntary and Nonprofit Organizations*, 8(1), Winter, 1997.

Schervish, Paul G., and Havens, John J. "Wherewithal and Beneficence: Charitable Giving by Income and Wealth." In *Cultures of Giving II: How Heritage, Gender, Wealth, and Values Influence Philanthropy*, Summer issue of *New Directions for Philanthropic Fundraising*. Eds. Charles H. Hamilton and Warren F. Ilchman, 1995c, 8, 81–109.

Schervish, Paul G., and Herman, Andrew. *Empowerment and Beneficence: Strategies of Living and Giving among the Wealthy*. Final Report: The Study on Wealth and Philanthropy. Presentation of findings from the Study on Wealth and Philanthropy submitted to the T. B. Murphy Foundation Charitable Trust. July 1988.

Smith, David Horton. "Determinants of Voluntary Association Participation and Volunteering: A Literature Review." *Nonprofit and Voluntary Sector Quarterly*, 1994, 23(3), 243–263.

Wolpert, Julian. "The Demographics of Giving Patterns." Draft chapter for the 1995 Think Tank on Fund-Raising Research, Indianapolis: Indiana University, Center on Philanthropy. 1995a.

Wolpert, Julian. "Fragmentation in America's Nonprofit Sector." In *Care and Community in Modern Society: Passing on the Tradition of Care to the Next Generation*. Eds. Paul G. Schervish, Virginia A. Hodgkinson, and Margaret Gates. San Francisco: Jossey-Bass, 1995b.

Wolpert, Julian. *Patterns of Generosity in America: Who's Holding the Safety Net?* New York: Twentieth Century Fund, 1994.

# From Motivation to Mutual Understanding

## Shifting the Domain of Donor Research

KATHLEEN S. KELLY, PhD, CFRE, APR, Fellow PRSA

*University of Southwestern Louisiana*

Answers to questions about "Who enacts a giving behavior, and why?" are important to fund raising. Yet donor motivation rarely has been studied as a fund raising problem by scholars engaged in ongoing research. What we currently know comes from two diverse sources: (1) full-time teacher-scholars who study donor motivation as a philanthropy problem, and (2) part-time student-practitioners who conduct one-shot dissertation studies. Neither source has provided fund raisers with what Lindblom and Cohen (1979) called *usable knowledge*.

Domain differences and presuppositions about fund raising clarify this major issue. As explained by philosophers of science, such as Laudan (1977), research domains are defined by the problems selected for study. Presuppositions are *"a priori* assumptions about the nature of truth, of society, of right or wrong, or simply of how things work in the world" (Grunig, 1992, p. 8). The presuppositions scholars bring to their work usually are unstated; yet they influence what problems are studied, how the problems are described, who is observed, and what the findings mean.

Research studies in the philanthropy domain, for example, are designed to address problems of voluntary action for the public good, including giving (Payton, 1988)—not fund raising. Studies on donor motivation deal with the *generic* act of giving and are from the perspective of donors. Little effort is made to understand the phenomenon of giving as perceived by those individuals responsible for managing an organization's relationships with donors. Philanthropy scholars assume that fund raising is something charitable organizations do, not a function carried out by trained practitioners. Research is limited to one donor type at a time because scholars assume there are few common factors in the giving of individual, corporate, and foundation dollars. Of particular concern, scholars usually equate fund raising to solicitation, only one part of the process through which gifts are raised.

I approach philanthropy as the larger research domain, which encompasses nonprofit management, of which fund raising is a part. Although certainly related, the domains are not synonymous; indeed, philanthropy and fund raising represent the two distinct sides of the philanthropic coin: voluntary giving and systematic *"getting"* of money. To gain a fuller understanding, donor research, which has concentrated on one-sided motivation, or the internal factors associated with giving, must be shifted to the fund raising domain.

This chapter promotes such efforts by examining factors affecting donor behavior from the perspective of fund raisers. It first presents the presuppositions that influence my thinking. Key concepts are defined, and two constructs from philanthropy—America's philanthropic tradition and the theory of the commons—are described to link my views to scholarship from the larger domain. The discussion then turns to the two sources responsible for most of the research on donor motivation and the difficulties associated with their work.

Giving must be studied in the context of relationships between donors and organizational recipients if research is to yield findings relevant to fund raising. To identify an appropriate framework, this chapter draws from time-tested principles of fund raisers that emphasize mutual understanding, rather than motivation. The principles are tied to a well-researched theory from public relations, which predicts that donor behavior is dependent on the three factors of involvement, problem recognition, and constraints. Combining practitioner wisdom with theories about relationship management provides a theoretical framework for studying giving and usable knowledge for practicing fund raising.

## Presuppositions

In previous work, I identified two categories of presuppositions about fund raising: asymmetrical and symmetrical (Kelly, 1991). Asymmetrical presuppositions assume that fund raising involves manipulating donors for their own good, as well as for the financial benefit of a good cause. When practitioners or others—including researchers—hold asymmetrical presuppositions, they assume that the organization knows best and that if potential donors "just understood" they would willingly give. This know-best assumption leads them to assume further that, because of the worthiness of the mission, donors benefit from giving primarily because the organization benefits (i.e., the donor benefits from "doing good"). Fund raising is competitive, and the more dollars raised, the more important and valuable the organization is. Fund raising is analogous to marketing; it is effective if it generates targeted amounts of revenue.

In contrast, symmetrical presuppositions assume fund raising is the means by which charitable organizations and donor publics interact in a pluralistic system to fulfill their interdependence for their benefit, as well as society's. Practitioners and others who hold such presuppositions support an "idealistic" approach to raising gifts. Donors give, not because they are persuaded, but because they have their own reasons for doing so. A decision to make a gift is based on mixed motives of interest in self and interest in a common good. Fund raising concentrates on the juncture where the interests of donors and the organization meet. Rather than generating revenue, its primary value to the organization is its management of relationships with donors. My scholarly work, which is informed by more than 17 years of fund raising experience, is based on symmetrical presuppositions. These fundamental assumptions are extended in the following definitions.

## DEFINITIONS

Fund raising is a management function unique to the not-for-profit sector. Specifically, the function belongs to the charitable subsector, or those not-for-profit organizations defined by Section 501(c)(3) of the Internal Revenue Code. Fund raising's evolution to managerial status is relatively recent.

Although charitable organizations have been raising funds throughout most of our nation's history, it has been only since the early 1900s that systematic efforts have been employed to bring about desired outcomes (Kelly, 1997). Until World War I, the fund raising function primarily consisted of part-time efforts by nonspecialists. Between World Wars I and II, fund raising consultants dominated the practice. Today, about 75,000 specialists are responsible for fund raising, and all but a few are *staff* fund raisers, or full-time employees of charitable organizations.

Given that 73 percent of all Section 501(c)(3) organizations have total revenues of less than $25,000 (Hodgkinson & Toppe, 1991), and that 23 percent of those with higher revenues are private foundations (Meckstroth, 1994), I estimated that fewer than 115,000 of the approximately 600,000 charitable organizations hire fund raisers—staff or consultants (Kelly, 1997). Furthermore, as only 4 percent of all U.S. charitable organizations have assets and expenditures of $1 million or more (Hodgkinson & Toppe, 1991), I concluded that the fund raising function as I define it is limited to somewhere around 25,000 organizations. Regardless of their minority representation, these organizations and their fund raising practitioners account for the majority of dollars raised each year.

Systems theory explains the relationships between charitable organizations and donors as environmental interdependencies (Kelly, 1991). Organizations succeed and survive depending on how well they manage interdependencies with numerous stakeholders, or those critical constituencies that can influence organizational goals. Donors are *enabling* stakeholders whose resources are needed to varying degrees by organizations, and donors look to recipients of their gifts for various returns (i.e., they engage in a social exchange). Fund raisers serve in a boundary role between the organization and its environment. They are responsible for reducing the uncertainty of private support by managing relationships with donors. In definitional terms, then:

**Fund raising is the management of relationships between a charitable organization and its donor publics.**

Individuals, corporations, and foundations constitute the three donor publics with which fund raising is concerned. They make two types of gifts: lower level and major. Adopting my parsimonious typology, lower level gifts are raised through the annual giving program and major gifts are raised through the major gifts program (Kelly, 1991). Definitional dollar amounts vary among organizations (e.g., $10,000 or $100,000 may divide the two types). Major gifts also are raised through planned giving efforts and capital campaigns, which actually are *strategies* that can be incorporated in the two primary programs. Annual gifts usually are unrestricted in purpose, whereas major gifts almost always are restricted. Although the techniques fund raisers use differ between the two gift types, there is little difference in the overall management of relationships with the three donor publics (i.e., the process is the same).

## THE FUND RAISING PROCESS

When fund raising is defined as simply seeking gifts for charitable organizations, anyone can do it—other managers, trustees, or volunteers. Fund raising, as I define it, encompasses much more. It involves a process that must continually be organized and managed, and responsibility for process management belongs to the trained practitioner, who attends to fund raising full-time and focuses the chief executive officer's (CEO) and others' attention on it at critical points in the process.

I conceptualized the process of fund raising and titled it **ROPES** (Kelly, 1997). As given in Exhibit 9.1, it consists of five steps: **R**esearch, **O**bjectives, **P**rogramming, **E**valuation, and **S**tewardship.

The process, which draws from a public relations model by Hendrix (1995), begins with research in three areas: (1) the organization, (2) the opportunity, and (3) the publics related to the organization and opportunity. The first step is the most important. Failure to conduct research dooms fund raising to sporadic results, with high costs, that contribute little to organizational effectiveness. The second step in the process is setting specific and measurable objectives. Fund raising objectives flow from the charitable organization's goals (i.e., their attainment directly supports organizational plans). The third step of programming consists of planning and implementing activities designed to bring about the outcomes stated in the objectives. These activities are grouped in two categories based on their desired effects: cultivation and solicitation.

Contrary to conventional wisdom, solicitation activities constitute a minority portion of the fund raising process and only part of the programming

## EXHIBIT 9.1. Fund Raising Process of ROPES

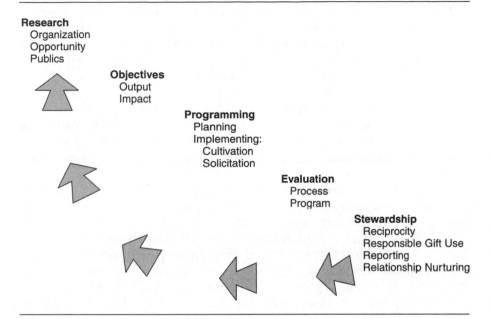

step. Practitioners spend much of their time and efforts on cultivation of donor prospects. Consultant Ernest Wood (1989) estimated that when raising major gifts, fund raisers spend 60 percent of their time on cultivation, 25 percent on research, 10 percent on stewardship, and only 5 percent on solicitation.

Evaluation is the fourth step in ROPES, whereby programming is monitored and adjusted (process evaluation) and results are measured and compared with the set objectives (program evaluation). Finally, stewardship completes the process and provides an essential loop back to the beginning of fund raising. Four elements are basic to stewardship: reciprocity (consisting of appreciation and recognition), responsible gift use, reporting, and relationship nurturing. ROPES provides practitioners with a strategic approach to raising gifts and ensures that donor relations are managed effectively and ethically.

## Domain Congruencies

### TRADITION OF PHILANTHROPY

Americans are generous. Throughout our country's history, they customarily have given away their money, as well as their time. Elizabeth Dole ("Fund-Raisers," 1993), president of the American Red Cross, explained,

"The idea of giving to others is ingrained in our nature, taught by our parents who were taught by theirs" (p. 8). Although other countries also have a philanthropic tradition, the pervasiveness and fundamentalism of American philanthropy make it unique in the world (Gurin & Van Til, 1990).

Donors gave an estimated $143.8 billion to charitable organizations in 1995, which was 10.8 percent more than the amount given in 1994 (American Association of Fund-Raising Counsel [AAFRC] Trust for Philanthropy, 1996). Gifts have increased every year since AAFRC began tracking them in 1959. According to INDEPENDENT SECTOR's (1994) recent biennial survey on giving and volunteering, 73 percent of all American households contribute to one or more charitable organizations each year. On average, individuals give away about 2 percent of their annual household income.

The percentage holds across all income groups. Debunking a popular myth that the wealthy give away a smaller proportion of their income than less affluent Americans, Schervish and Havens (1995) found from reanalyzing national data that the average household gives about 2 percent of its income, regardless of income level. The philanthropy scholars stated: "This result contradicts the imagery of the caring poor contributing more than the uncaring rich. Both groups appear equally caring" (p. 84).

Actually, individuals who have acquired wealth through our capitalistic system are held to a special philanthropic standard. Andrew Carnegie (1889/1983) set forth this standard in his essay, "The Gospel of Wealth," in which he said the duty of America's wealthy is to live unostentatiously, provide moderately for family, and consider all surplus revenues as trust funds that they have been called on to administer (i.e., give away). Carnegie, according to historian Peter Hall (1989), reasoned that if capitalism was to survive, it must be a self-renewing system, "and only by putting back into the social organism what they had taken out could its future be assured" (p. 183). Dramatically summarizing his gospel, Carnegie proclaimed, "He who dies rich dies disgraced" (p. 108).

The standard remains evident today. Billionaire Walter Annenberg (Greene, 1994)—who made a fortune from *TV Guide* and *Seventeen* magazines—gave $365 million in cash to three universities and one private school and pledged another $500 million to the nation's public schools, all in one year. He explained, "If you have been fortunate economically in life, I think you have a very important obligation to share and support others less fortunate than you" (p. 11). Echoing Carnegie, he added, "And if you don't understand that, you're a rather shabby citizen" (p. 11).

A standard of philanthropic behavior also exists among businesses. Corporations collectively give away about 2 percent of their pretax dollars every year. Galaskiewicz (1989) has advanced a theory of contributions used as social currency by those who head companies. Often referred to as "old boy network philanthropy," Galaskiewicz said the phenomenon "is better understood as status competition among very powerful actors within an economic elite" (p. 252). He concluded after numerous studies and a review of the literature that "giving is the norm in many business elite subcultures, and those who want to remain in the inner circles had best conform and make the appropriate contributions" (p. 252). A well-researched explanation of corporate philanthropy, then, is that American businesses make gifts because their senior managers are expected to do so by business peers.

Foundations, by legal definition, are required to behave philanthropically. Members of this third donor public currently are required to give away (and spend on administration) an amount equal to 5 percent of their assets each year. As Sheldon (1991) explained, their very purpose is "to provide support to charitable organizations through grants" (p. 243).

On a macro level, giving as a percentage of the United States' gross domestic product (GDP) is 2 percent, which has remained essentially the same for the past three decades (AAFRC Trust for Philanthropy, 1996). The amount of gifts as a percentage of national income—a statistic different from GDP—hovers around 2.5 percent (Hodgkinson, Weitzman, Toppe, & Noga, 1992). Similarly, the 2 percent of household income represented by gifts varies little from year to year. And the 2 percent of pretax dollars given by corporations has been consistent for 50 years, even though the allowable deduction was increased from 5 percent to 10 percent in 1981 (Bailey, 1994). In other words, about 2 percent of GDP, national income, household income, and corporate pretax dollars, as well as 5 percent of foundation assets, define the parameters of American philanthropy.

This is a critical point for understanding fund raising. Although percentages may fluctuate in the short term because of such factors as tax laws, the parameters appear invulnerable to efforts to substantially change them. In 1995, for example, INDEPENDENT SECTOR (IS) announced that it was phasing out its "Give Five" campaign to get people to volunteer five hours per week and donate 5 percent of their income ("New Drive," 1995). After conducting the public information campaign for more than eight years, "surveys of donors and volunteers [led] officials to concede that Americans do not—and may never—give five percent of their income away" (p. 16). Instead of trying to change donor behavior, IS launched a new campaign to reinforce giving, using the slogan: "Thanks for all you've given. Imagine what more could do" (p. 16).

The stable statistics defining the parameters of philanthropy support my approach to fund raising: Fund raisers affect not whether donors give, but to which specific organizations they give, the purposes of their gifts, and the gift amounts. At the 1993 International Conference of the National Society of Fund Raising Executives (NSFRE), consultant Bruce Flessner (H. Hall, 1993) argued that because giving as a percentage of GDP has not changed since the early 1960s, "when most nonprofits either had no fund raisers or only a very few," legitimate questions arise about whether practitioners have made any real difference (p. 24). In answer, fund raisers do make a difference, but not by *making* people give. Although the GDP statistic has not changed in more than 30 years, gift dollars have grown each year as the GDP has increased. Fund raisers' aggregate difference has been keeping private support steady as a percentage of GDP and other economic indicators (i.e., they reinforce giving behavior).

Individuals, corporations, and foundations in the United States traditionally give away money. They do so for many reasons, but the one reason fundamental to understanding fund raising is that donors make gifts because giving is a customary, admired, expected, and even legally required behavior in our society. Fund raising, therefore, is not about educating, persuading, or manipulating donors to give money because they already are predisposed to do so.

Schervish and Havens (1994) reached similar conclusions from their empirical study of wealthy individuals:

> First, fundraisers do not need to induce the financially well-off to become givers. . . . Nearly all upper income and all wealthy households are already participating in charitable giving and many from each group are substantial givers. Second, this means that much of the groundwork for fundraisers has already been done. (p. 30)

The primary task for practitioners, Schervish and Havens argued, "is to provide a *reason* for people who are already givers to focus on a particular cause" (pp. 30–31; italics added).

## THEORY OF THE COMMONS

Although generous, Americans do not give indiscriminately. Decisions to make a gift are dependent on the intended recipient. Using the metaphor of the commons, Lohmann (1992a, 1992b) provided an elegant theory of the not-for-profit sector that explains why people give to some organizations but not to others.

Lohmann's theory holds that a sector separate from business and government exists "to create a protected space for the collective expression of what people find most important in their lives" (Van Til, 1992, xi). Not-for-profit organizations—or commons—form to produce common goods, which Lohmann (1992a) defined as "desirable or preferred outcomes that are uncoerced, that are associated with shared purposes and pooled resources, and that engender a sense of . . . community and fairness" (p. 320). Differentiating among the three sectors, he stated, "Markets produce private goods, states produce public goods, and commons produce common goods" (p. 320). Whereas public goods produced by government are indivisible and uniformly available to all, common goods reflect the mutuality and meaning of distinct groups and are limited in access. Lohmann (1992b) commented, "Of course, nonprofits attempt to argue that their common goods are public goods, but they are being disingenuous" (p. 269).

Lohmann's distinction is critical in that common goods are desirable ends within a particular commons, but not necessarily beyond. Whereas terms such as *public good* imply that any gift contributes to the good of an abstract *general public*, Lohmann's theory helps us understand that a gift to one organization as opposed to another (e.g., prolife vs. prochoice) does not contribute to a public good, but rather to a good in which the donor and the recipient-organization share common interests. As Lohmann (1992a) said, "Outside a reference group, any common good may be a matter of indifference or may even be considered a 'bad'" (p. 320).

The distinction is congruent with the public relations concept of publics (plural) as opposed to *the* public. Grunig and Hunt (1984) explained: "A 'general public' is a logical impossibility. Publics are always specific; they always have some *common problem*. Thus, they cannot be general" (p. 138; italics added). Publics form around particular problems, which also are defined as issues or opportunities. Problems seldom affect everyone in the population (Grunig & Repper, 1992).

The social problems addressed by charitable organizations, whether cultural, educational, religious or other, are embedded in their missions. Translated from mission statement to the case for support, "Institutional needs are presented as opportunities for donors to invest in programs that are solving community *problems* effectively," explained fund raiser Kay Grace (1991, p. 189; italics added).

Lohmann (1992b) appropriately argued that his theory "resolves confusing and inconsistent applications of public goods to analysis of fund raising" (p. 321). Practitioners raise gifts in support of common goods, not goods that are desired by or available to all. Redefined by Lohmann's theory, philanthropy is voluntary action for particular common goods that, collectively, undergird our pluralistic democracy. Or as consultant Marianne Briscoe (1994) stated, "Donors give to organizations and causes like themselves. . . . Philanthropy enables people to make possible what they, individually, believe is important" (p. 11).

In other words, when we examine giving behavior from a fund-raising perspective, we are concerned with the donor's *interpretation* of what is in the best interest of society—an interpretation with which we may or may not agree. For example, based on the 1995 terrorist bombing in Oklahoma City, I may not believe that a gift to the National Rifle Association Foundation is in the best interest of society but other people obviously do. As Payton (1987) said, "It is very difficult to understand that one's own good cause isn't necessarily someone else's" (p. 44). Regardless, pluralism is essential to our democracy, and the collective common goods supported by philanthropy are essential to pluralism.

Vandeventer (1993) applied theories of the Chicago School of Social Thought to questions about donor motivation. Through qualitative methodology, including in-depth interviews with major donors to the University of Northern Iowa, she found evidence that philanthropy provides a sense of community in a disengaged and fragmented society. Giving allows people to go beyond majority rule (government) and consumer demand (business) to join with others who think and believe as they do.

Schervish and Havens (1997) reached compatible conclusions through extensive quantitative research on donor motivation, which involved multivariate analyses of 107 variables grouped in clusters. The variables, representing nearly all the factors suggested in the literature, were operationalized by matching them to national data collected through INDEPENDENT SECTOR's biennial surveys. The match resulted in five clusters, including "Community of Participation," which Schervish and Havens defined as "groups and organizations in which one participates."

The analyses showed that all five clusters are significantly related to giving but that Community of Participation "is the cluster with by far the strongest and most consistent relationship to giving behavior." Schervish and Havens concluded, "Charitable giving is largely a consequence of forging a *connection* between the existing inclinations and involvements of individuals and the needs of recipients" (italics added).

Fund raisers raise gifts in support of common goods, and their efforts are bounded by voluntary participation, shared purposes, mutuality, and fairness. There is no such thing as *the* public for the purposes of fund raising, rather there are numerous publics of which some share an interest in particular common goods, and some of those are donor publics. Fund raising, then, concentrates on the juncture where the interests of donors and the organization meet.

Tying this conclusion to previous discussions, fund raising practitioners are effective and ethical when they accept—but do not take for granted or abuse—America's philanthropic tradition and focus on the self-interest of donors. This other-directed mind-set demands that they rely on research, the first step in the fund raising process, to identify appropriate donor prospects. Bypassing research and assuming the organization knows best lead to unethical practice, as Lord (1983) warned: "We can easily get in trouble—for we may end up trying to coerce people. We may find ourselves trying to convince people how they *should* think and what they *should* do" (p. 11). Philosopher Mike Martin (1994) also condemned fund raising based on asymmetrical presuppositions: "We should renounce the heavy-handed moralizing that insists every caring person must give to this or that cause" (p. 93).

## Domain Differences

Theories and research on donor motivation from the philanthropy domain can help us understand fund raising. As just demonstrated, they are particularly valuable as scholarly "litmus tests" for theories conceptualized in the fund raising domain. A powerful synergy results when explanations from the two perspectives of donors and fund raisers compliment each other. Yet without the contributions of fund raising scholars, the philanthropy domain generates knowledge that is insufficient and only indirectly related to the practice of fund raising.

Paramount among the differences between the two domains is that philanthropy scholars study giving in isolation of the donor's relationship to specific organizations, whereas organizational relationships are fundamental to the study of fund raising. Stated another way, the philanthropy domain concerns itself with only one side in the two-way philanthropic exchange. Or as Ostrander and Schervish (1990) noted, most of the research on philanthropy conceptualizes and studies it as a world of donors. "An exclusive focus on donors runs the risk of obscuring issues that are of concern to recipients and therefore to philanthropy as a whole" (p. 67).

The importance of relationships to fund raising is well documented in the practitioner literature. For example, Howe (1991) stated, "The essence of raising money lies in the relationship of an organization to its support constituency" (p. 75). Nudd (1991) asserted, "Whether it is called development, advancement, attracting philanthropic resources, cultivating voluntary support, or friend raising, the key to fundraising success is *relationship building*" (p. 175). Grace (1991) simply said, "Fundraising is about relationships more than it is about money" (p. 185).

## GENERIC FINDINGS

Because of domain differences, philanthropy findings sometimes can be misleading for fund raising purposes. Studies, such as the IS (1994) biennial surveys, measure giving behavior as having made one or more gifts of any amount to any and all charitable organizations. This generic giving is not the same thing as making a gift to a specific organization (i.e., the dependent variables are different).

Illustrating potential problems with fund raising application, religious factors consistently emerge among the donor variables most strongly associated with giving. This does not mean that religiousness is a promising determinant of who will make a gift to a particular art museum or environmental group; the findings merely reflect the pervasiveness of religion in our society. When just one gift to any one organization, including a church, is defined as giving behavior, it is no wonder that religious factors are found significant because almost 50 percent of all gift dollars from individuals go to religion (AAFRC Trust for Philanthropy, 1996), and an amazing 89 percent of all household donors make at least one gift to a religious organization in a given year (IS, 1994).

Furthermore, most national studies examine giving behavior primarily as it relates to annual gifts; major donors, due to their smaller number, are not well represented. Of the contributing households sampled by IS (1994), 56 percent gave a total of $300 or less. Yet to be effective and efficient, fund raising depends on donors who make major gifts, which usually are defined as $10,000 or more.

## NEGLECT OF FUND RAISING

Fund raising is an honorable occupation that I and others, such as Carbone (1989), define as an emerging profession. To become a profession and, more importantly, to move the practice from systematic organization to effective management, fund raising requires theories grounded in research that explain the function, including theories on which practitioners can rely to predict donor behavior.

Fund raising has received little attention from those who build theory. According to Payton, Rosso, and Tempel (1991), "There is widespread academic bias against fundraising and fundraisers but very little solid argument to justify the prejudice" (p. 3). They charged, "Scholars, even those interested in philanthropy, have neglected fundraising" (p. 3).

Layton (1987) concluded from her compilation of the first comprehensive bibliography on philanthropy, "While there is an enormous practical literature on fund-raising [sic], there is almost nothing which examines the phenomenon of 'getting' with the same depth and comprehension that the phenomenon of giving has received" (p. xv). Whereas only slightly more than 1 percent of the works referenced by Layton dealt with fund raising, Brudney and Durden (1993) found that about 3 percent of the 472 articles published by philanthropy's leading academic journal, *Nonprofit and Voluntary Sector Quarterly*, during its first 20 years (1972–1992) dealt with fund/resource raising. Even this low proportion is inflated in that the scholars placed the broader topic of philanthropy—including gift giving—in their operational definition of fund/resource raising.

Lohmann (1992a) explained that whereas most of the major concepts in philanthropy began as subspecialities within existing academic frameworks, "Fund raising emerged entirely outside the organized knowledge industry of the universities, with its order of disciplines and sciences" (p. 309). The study of voluntary organizations grew out of sociology; charity and community organization came from researchers within social work; and nonprofit organization was the province of public administration. Historians have studied foundation giving, psychologists have studied individual giving, and sociologists have studied all three sources of gifts, including corporations. In contrast, the study of fund raising came from those practicing the function. No academic discipline claimed this organizational function until recently (Kelly, 1997). Therefore, it is not surprising that the void left by philanthropy scholars has been filled by practitioners, specifically, those pursing graduate degrees as part-time students. Most of their research has constituted a search for *magic buttons* that determine giving behavior.

## Theory of Magic Buttons

Donor motivation has captivated the attention of practitioners conducting research on fund raising almost to the exclusion of other equally or even more important problems. The search to identify cross-situational demographics, cognitions, and attitudes that underlie donor behavior has dominated research for decades and is largely responsible for the slow accumulation of a scholarly body of knowledge on fund raising.

Brittingham and Pezzullo (1990) explained student-practitioners' preoccupation, saying that such researchers "have naturally been drawn to studies of donors' behavior, just as practitioners have longed for a simple list of characteristics that could help them identify likely donors from longer lists" (p. 90). The authors concluded from their review of fund raising research, "The cumulative results of these studies have been somewhat disappointing, given their relatively high numbers" (p. 90).

The hundreds of practitioner studies designed to predict giving are based on what I call the *theory of magic buttons* (Kelly, 1991, 1997). The theory is not articulated by the researchers employing it, it is not grounded in any scholarly domain, and it is not espoused in the fund raising literature. In fact, the literature, consisting almost entirely of practitioner wisdom, provides little support for the theory (i.e., face validity). Regardless, searching for magic buttons arguably is the most popular theory guiding past and current fund raising research.

The theory of magic buttons is a product of asymmetrical presuppositions (e.g., practitioner-researchers assume that the purpose of fund raising is to generate targeted amounts of revenue). The theory holds that there is a causal linkage between giving behavior and donor demographics, cognitions, and attitudes, if just the right combination can be found. Based on this premise, it assumes that prospective donors are passive participants in the philanthropic exchange—that donor characteristics determine behavior. It assumes that some people have a natural inclination to give and others do not. Those that do, the theory presumes, can be manipulated to behave as the organization desires. Donor characteristics are assumed to be cross-situational and even cross-organizational (i.e., donors will enact a giving behavior regardless of the purpose for which the gift is made or its recipient). The theory is based on a powerful model of communication in that messages sent to the receiver, whether in person or through other channels, will result in the desired behavior. Paraphrasing the mystical voice in the 1989 movie, *Field of Dreams,* "If you find the right buttons, they will give."

## MAGIC BULLET THEORY

The theory corresponds to the *magic bullet theory* of mass communication. This first theory of media effects, as described by Lowery and DeFleur (1995), held that "a media message would reach every eye and ear in the same way, like a symbolic 'bullet,' immediately bringing about the same changes of thought and behavior in the entire audience" (pp. 13–14). Also known as the "hypodermic-needle theory," it assumed communication would have powerful effects on attitudes and behavior: the "injection of information into a population" would bring rapid and desired results (Simmons, 1990, p. 18).

Studies based on this theory viewed audiences as vulnerable to messages; they could be manipulated by those who controlled message design and delivery. Attesting to the theory's general acceptance, most people in the early twentieth century thought that the media were powerful, manipulative, and therefore dangerous.

Accumulated findings from studies starting in the 1940s discredited the magic bullet theory (e.g., Hyman & Sheatsley, 1947). By the early 1960s, researchers concluded that communication, especially mass communication, does not exert strong, direct and powerful effects on audiences (Dozier & Ehling, 1992). People are not passive receivers of messages, but active participants in the communication process. For example, the theory of selectivity explains that generally only people who already hold attitudes and beliefs similar to those expressed in the message will pay attention to that message. A corollary provided by the theory of cognitive dissonance is that people avoid information that is contrary to their views and seek information that is consonant (e.g., nonsmokers more so than smokers pay attention to antismoking messages). A more contemporary and elegant explanation is simply that people engage in communication when it is of relevance to them (Grunig & Hunt, 1984). Therefore, people cannot be easily manipulated by communication, and they resist unwanted persuasion.

Scholars further rejected the concept of a *general public*. Adding to the theoretical explanations already given, Cutlip, Center, and Broom (1994) stated, "Effective programs that communicate and build relationships call for specifically defined 'target publics'" (p. 245). The authors summarized findings of the communication research: "In short, the notion of a monolithic and passive mass audience does not describe reality. Rather, the more accurate description suggests selected active receivers processing messages designed for the few, not the masses" (p. 235).

## DOMINO MODEL

Despite the body of knowledge accumulated over 50 years, variations of the magic bullet theory still are accepted by many communication practitioners. The theory obviously is also accepted by fund raising researchers conducting studies on donor motivation. Grunig and Hunt (1984) presented their *domino model* to graphically illustrate the assumptions people hold about powerful communication effects.

The model consists of four dominos—message, knowledge, attitude, and behavior—toppling each other in line. As Dozier and Ehling (1992) described, "The domino model . . . implies strong causal linkage between communication (or messages) from an organization and direct, immediate impact on the knowledge, attitudes, and behavior of publics" (p. 163). In other words, some practitioners believe that communication increases knowledge, after which knowledge leads to a positive attitude, which results in a desired behavior—all in an inevitable progression.

Grunig and Hunt (1984) explained the fallacy of the model in that it assumes each domino affects subsequent dominos in the progression and that effects only occur in the sequence given. Furthermore, they stated, "There is little evidence that the knowledgeable person's attitude or behavior will consistently be that advocated by the organization communicating a particular message" (p. 125). Whereas some studies have shown that knowledge does at times lead to favorable attitudes, other studies have shown that the most knowledgeable people often have the most negative attitudes—when negative means those people oppose the organization's point of view. Grunig and Hunt further pointed out that not everyone to whom a message is directed will choose to pay attention to the message, and not everyone who pays attention will remember it. The scholars summarized, "The dominos may fall, but only rarely do they fall in a line and topple each other" (p. 125).

Based on Grunig and Hunt's work, Dozier and Ehling (1992) calculated the probabilities associated with the domino model, which are presented in Exhibit 9.2.

Drawing from their collective observations, the authors assigned a 40 percent chance that members of a targeted public actually are exposed to a communicated message (e.g., they may choose to throw away a piece of mail). They argued that there is only a 50 percent chance that the members reached by the message actually will learn the key message points communicated (i.e., retain, understand, or know). There is only a 20 percent chance that those who learn the key message points actually will adopt an attitude consistent with the intention of the message. Finally, only 10 percent of those holding a desired attitude will behave in a manner consistent with that attitude. As given in Exhibit 9.2, multiplying these probabilities shows that there is only a 0.4 percent, or 4 in 1,000, chance of achieving a desired behavior with any particular member of the targeted public.

Patrick Jackson ("Opinion," 1993), a well-known public relations consultant, said that anyone who still believes information alone affects behavior should examine the AIDS epidemic, one of the most publicized phenomenons in history. Public information campaigns, research has shown, result in *awareness*, but do not have significant impact on behavior. Jackson said the most noticeable outcome of publicity on AIDS is that people wear red ribbons; the objective was to get them to wear condoms.

The fund raising literature generally advocates principles supported by communication research. Unfortunately, it also contains evidence that

## EXHIBIT 9.2. Probabilities of Powerful Effects Assumptions

| Message | | Knowledge | | Attitude | | Behavior | | |
|---|---|---|---|---|---|---|---|---|
| 40% | × | 50% | × | 20% | × | 10% | = | 0.4% |

Adapted from Dozier & Ehling (1992).

many practitioners accept the domino model. Grace (1991), for example, argued that "education" is required to bring donors to a giving behavior, which she called "maturation of the prospect" (p. 185). She explained, "Constituents must be moved from awareness, to understanding, to involvement and, finally, to commitment if they are to become stakeholders" (p. 185). Similarly, Howe (1991) declared, "The interrelation of an organization with its supporters is a progression: first an awareness, then a familiarity and emerging interest, in turn an involvement, all leading to a contribution" (p. 75). The "Cultivation Cycle," developed by G. T. (Buck) Smith (1977), is widely recognized as the standard formula for raising major gifts. Also known as the "Five I's of Fund Raising," the popular formula is simply the domino model expressed in five steps: (1) identification, (2) information, (3) interest, (4) involvement, and (5) investment.

Donors are not passive participants that can be programmed to give, nor are they a predictable homogeneous group. As Steele and Elder (1992) warned, fund raisers must resist "the tendency to view people (and to treat them) as so many objects gliding along on a conveyor belt toward solicitation" (p. 22).

More serious is evidence that fund raisers utilize the domino model to justify asymmetrical practice, such as viewing all people as prospective donors. For example, Howe (1991) asserted, "The potential for support is as wide as the number of people who can be reached by mail and as high as the largest gift of the most generous donor" (p. xvii). In a study of NSFRE members, I found high agreement with the statement: "The more people who know about our cause, the more dollars we will raise" (Kelly, 1995). Mean scores on this item, which measured asymmetrical practice, were the second highest of 16 items measured: 11.33 ($SD = 3.57$) for the annual giving program and 10.81 ($SD = 4.36$) for the major gifts program, when 10 represented the typical response. Such views, considered in isolation, bode poorly for effective and ethical fund raising; however, practitioners also espouse principles based on symmetrical presuppositions.

## Situational Theory of Publics

I believe an appropriate framework for fund raising research can be found in public relations. Specific to this chapter, James Grunig's (e.g., Grunig & Hunt, 1984) situational theory of publics offers a symmetrical approach to understanding donor behavior that is validated by principles of fund raising practitioners. The principles emphasize mutual understanding, rather than internal motivation.

### PRACTITIONER PREDICTORS

A time-tested principle handed down from veteran fund raisers is *Separate prospects from suspects*. Rosso (1991) presented the Linkage-Ability-Interest

(L-A-I) formula to guide practitioners. According to the formula, prospects are separated from suspects by three factors: (1) linkage to the organization, (2) ability to give, and (3) interest in the organization's mission, goals, and priorities. All three factors, Rosso warned, must apply; elimination of just one invalidates the process and reduces the "gift candidate" from prospect to suspect (p. 29). Wood (1989) illustrated, "Asking someone who has a lot of money—but no relationship with your organization—to make a major gift is like asking an attractive stranger to marry you just because you think they're eligible" (p. 1).

Another principle endorsed in the literature is *Those closest to the organization are the best prospects.* A third is *Belief in mission is the strongest reason for giving.*

Steele and Elder (1992) graphically portrayed the closeness principle with three concentric circles, or rings, which defined stakeholders most likely, less likely, and least likely to give to annual giving and major gifts programs. They placed previous donors and people with "strong ties" to the organization in the center ring (p. 29). Such groups as clients and employees were in the second ring, and national foundations and corporations were in the third. Moving from the center outward, they warned, "You are not looking to make a convert out of a nonbeliever—someone in the outer ring. . . . You are mainly looking for people who already believe in your cause on some level" (p. 28).

They applied the principle to annual giving donors, who throw away a good deal of direct mail without even opening it, "but every so often a piece will arrive that coincides with some feelings you have about a given issue, whether it is handgun control, civil rights, or an environmental concern. Whatever it is, you decide you must support that cause, and you write a check" (p. 30).

Regarding the major gifts program, Steele and Elder (1992) advised fund raisers, "The vast majority of major gifts will come from a relatively small number of prospects, most of whom will already be known to you" (p. 3). They added, "The simplicity of this idea belies its importance" (pp. 27–28). Broce (1986) elaborated:

> Most major donors are close friends of the institution or have logical reasons to give to it. That is why prospect research and evaluation are so important. They are the processes by which we identify the legitimate prospects: which ones will give; how much they might give; [and] what programs they will likely support. (p. 177)

Evidence suggests that people's identification with the mission of the organization is paramount to giving. Panas (1984), for example, concluded from his interviews with donors of $1 million or more that their chief motivation was "belief in the mission of the institution" (p. 227). There was not a close second reason. File, Prince, and Cermak (1994) reported a similar finding from their study of 476 individuals who established a charitable remainder trust of $1 million or more: "In our sample, the motivation to donate to a *specific* nonprofit was driven by a *perceived similarity* between the donor's goals and those of the nonprofit (86 percent said that this rationale was very important)" (p. 275; italics added).

Summarizing this collective wisdom, practitioners rely on three important factors to identify donors of both annual and major gifts: (1) closeness or the degree to which prospects are connected to the organization and its work, which can be defined as *involvement*; (2) belief or interest in the organization's mission, goals, and priorities, which can be defined as identification with a *problem*; and (3) ability or capacity to give, which can be defined as financial *constraints*.

## THEORETICAL PREDICTORS

The three factors on which practitioners rely correspond to the three predictor variables incorporated in Grunig's (e.g., Grunig & Hunt, 1984) situational theory of publics: (1) level of involvement, (2) problem recognition, and (3) constraint recognition. *Level of involvement* is the degree to which members of a population feel *connected* to a problem, issue, or opportunity involving an organization. *Problem recognition* is the degree to which population members think the problem is important. *Constraint recognition* is the degree to which the members believe they can personally do something to affect the problem.

In the late 1970s, Grunig theorized that the three variables explain why people engage in a behavior and communicate in the process of planning that behavior. Extensive empirical research since has shown that the variables successfully segment stakeholders into publics by "the extent to which the members passively or actively communicate about an issue and the extent to which they behave in a way that supports or constrains the organization's pursuit of its mission" (Grunig & Repper, 1992, p. 125).

All combinations of the three variables generate eight possible publics, but Grunig (Grunig & Repper, 1992) has collapsed these to four: (1) *active public*, which has high level of involvement and high problem recognition and does not feel constrained in doing something about the problem; (2) *aware public*, which has high problem recognition, but varies on involvement and beliefs about constraints; (3) *latent public*, which is low in problem recognition and involvement and has not thought about constraints; and (4) *nonpublic*, or everyone else, with no involvement and no recognition of the problem.

The situational theory, as its name indicates, holds that *how* people perceive a situation determines whether they will enact a behavior relevant to that situation (i.e., people respond differently to different situations); general attitudes and personal characteristics explain little variance in people's views of a given situation. Practitioners are advised to concentrate their attention and resources on the first two publics, active and aware.

Members of the latent public should be monitored and selected for communication only when resources allow. Those constituting the nonpublic should be dismissed—"they are of no concern to an organization" (Grunig & Repper, 1992, p. 125).

The theory predicts that members of the nonpublic will not communicate (will not pay attention to messages). Members of the latent public will passively process information. Active and aware publics, on the other hand, will actively seek information. As Grunig and Hunt (1984) emphasized, information actively sought has greater impact on cognitions, attitudes, and behavior than information processed or ignored altogether.

## APPLICATION TO FUND RAISING

The situational theory of publics offers a powerful theoretical guide for the study and practice of fund raising. It explains how fund raisers effectively identify those donor publics with the highest probability of giving. Equally important, it reinforces practitioners' assertions that people who are not involved with the organization, do not care about its mission and program services, and do not have discretionary income or assets to give away, are of no concern to fund raising efforts—they constitute a nonpublic.

The theory instructs fund raisers to spend their time and resources on active and aware publics, those with high levels of involvement and problem recognition and low constraints. Latent publics may be targeted for programming, but only when resources are not needed for the first two publics and can be expended at a higher cost ratio.

Level of involvement is the most critical variable affecting decisions to give. The variable is key, according to Grunig (1989), because it has been shown to result from people's perceptions that a problem affects their self-interest.

Involvement is differentiated by its two dimensions of cognitive and physical (Grunig & Repper, 1992). The first can only be determined by directly measuring the connection a person perceives between him-or herself and the charitable organization and its work. Physical involvement can be identified by affiliation; for example, such stakeholders may be clients or volunteers. Attesting to the variable's explanatory power as it relates to volunteering in general, IS (1994) reported that its biennial surveys have consistently documented that "volunteers give more than nonvolunteers, and contributing households with a volunteer give a much higher percentage of their household income than contributing households which do not have a volunteer" (p. 91). In 1993, 90 percent of all volunteers made gifts, compared with only 59 percent of nonvolunteers, and the average amount volunteers gave was more than four times higher.

Problem recognition discriminates those individuals, corporations, and foundations that believe a charitable organization's program services are important and needed from donor suspects who do not. When the social problem addressed by an organization has salience for prospects, they are more likely to become donors, whereby they express their interpretation of what is best for society. Perceptions of importance, not positive attitudes, are the determining factor. Culbertson, Jeffers, Stone, and Terrell (1993) explained: "People may feel the American Cancer Society is very commendable as gauged by rating scales or agree-disagree items. Yet they may consider it less important than supporting research on AIDS" (p. 45).

Although constraint recognition encompasses physical, social, economic, or political obstacles to taking actions, those dealing with economics logically have great impact on behavior that entails giving away money. Providing empirical evidence, IS (1994) reported that its surveys "have consistently shown that respondents who worried about having enough money in the future gave less as a percentage of household income than those who did not worry" (p. 93). In 1993, the average percentage of household income contributed by people who worried about money was 50 percent less than the average contributed by people who were not worried. The level of income contributed declined as the level of worry increased (e.g., people who worried a little gave 2 percent on average, whereas those who worried a lot gave only 1.2 percent).

Grunig and Hunt (1984) summarized this discussion with their simple but theoretically sound advice, "To raise funds, identify, cultivate, and solicit publics that have money to give and take interest in your organization" (p. 366).

## Conclusion

Answers to questions about "Who enacts a giving behavior, and why?" are important to fund raising. Theories dealing with magic buttons, bullets, and dominos, however, seek simplistic solutions and fail to acknowledge the subject's complexity. All the social and behavioral sciences are concerned with the same fundamental question: "Why do people behave as they do?" (Grunig & Repper, 1992). Pat answers should not be expected.

Philanthropy scholars have ignored fund raising and concentrated on only the donors' side of the relationship between charitable organizations and the individuals, corporations, and foundations that make gifts to them. If philanthropy is a social exchange, then as prescribed by that theory, giving behavior must be analyzed within the context of organizational relationships. A widely endorsed fund raising principle is *Match the organization's needs to donors' needs*. Tempel (1991) posed the symmetrical principle as a question that fund raisers must continually ask themselves: "What are the philanthropic interests and needs of the prospective contributor? This knowledge serves as the basis for a meaningful exchange of values between the asking organization and the potential gift source" (p. 25).

This chapter draws from the discipline of public relations to provide a theoretical framework for studying donor behavior and usable knowledge for practicing fund raising. My selection should not be interpreted as a blatant assertion that other disciplines do not offer theories of equal explanatory power. Rather than making a case for public relations, the thrust of the chapter is that fund raising can no longer be ignored. Problems related to donor behavior must be defined and studied by researchers interested in and knowledgeable about the management function. As prescribed by symmetrical principles of practitioners, future research should focus on mutual understanding, not one-sided motivation.

## Bibliography

American Association of Fund-Raising Counsel (AAFRC) Trust for Philanthropy. *Giving USA: The Annual Report on Philanthropy for the Year 1995.* New York: Author, 1996.

Bailey, A. L. "Corporate Giving Loses Ground to Inflation Despite an Increase in Pre-Tax Profits." *The Chronicle of Philanthropy,* Sept. 20, 1994, 7, 10.

Briscoe, M. G. "Is an Endowment Justified?" *The NonProfit Times,* March 1994, 10–11.

Brittingham, B. E., and Pezzullo, T. R. *The Campus Green: Fund Raising in Higher Education,* ASHE-ERIC Higher Education Report No. 1. Washington, DC: George Washington University, School of Education and Human Development.

Broce, T. E. *Fund Raising: The Guide to Raising Money from Private Sources* (2nd ed.). Norman: University of Oklahoma Press, 1986.

Brudney, J. L., and Durden, T. K. "Twenty Years of the *Journal of Voluntary Action Research/Nonprofit and Voluntary Sector Quarterly:* An Assessment of Past Trends and Future Directions." *Nonprofit and Voluntary Sector Quarterly,* 22(3), 207–218, 1993.

Carbone, R. F. *Fund Raising as a Profession* (Monograph No. 3). College Park. University of Maryland, Clearinghouse for Research on Fund Raising, 1989.

Carnegie, A. "The Gospel of Wealth." In *America's Voluntary Spirit* Ed. B. O'Connell. New York: Foundation Center, 1983, 97–108. (Original work published 1889)

Culbertson, H. M., Jeffers, D. W., Stone, D. B., and Terrell, M. *Social, Political, and Economic Contexts in Public Relations: Theory and Cases.* Hillsdale, NJ: Lawrence Erlbaum, 1993.

Cutlip, S. M., Center, A. H., and Broom, G. M. *Effective Public Relations* (7th ed.). Englewood Cliffs, NJ: Prentice-Hall, 1994.

Dozier, D. M., and Ehling, W. P. "Evaluation of Public Relations Programs: What the Literature Tells Us about Their Effects." In *Excellence in Public Relations and Communication Management* (159–184). Ed. J. E. Grunig. Hillsdale, NJ: Lawrence Erlbaum, 1992.

File, K. M., Prince, R. A., and Cermak, D. S. P. "Creating Trust with Major Donors: The Service Encounter Model." *Nonprofit Management & Leadership,* 1994, 4(3), 269–283.

"Fund-Raisers Integral to America's Social Contract." *NSFRE News,* April 1993, p. 8.

Galaskiewicz, J. "Corporate Contributions to Charity: Nothing More than a Marketing Strategy?" In *Philanthropic Giving: Studies in Varieties and Goals* Ed. R. Margat. New York: Oxford University Press, 1989, 246–260.

Grace, K. S. "Can We Throw Away the Tin Cup?" In *Taking fund raising seriously: Advancing the profession and practice of raising money* Eds. D. F. Burlingame & L. J. Hulse. San Francisco: Jossey-Bass, 1991, 184–199.

Greene, E. "Walter Annenberg's Aim: Give It All Away." *The Chronicle of Philanthropy,* Jan. 11, 1994, 1, 10–11.

Grunig, J. E. "Communication, Public Relations, and Effective Organizations: An Overview of the Book." In *Excellence in Public Relations and Communication Management.* Ed. J. E. Grunig. Hillsdale, NJ: Lawrence Erlbaum, 1992, 1–28.

Grunig, J. E. "Sierra Club Study Shows Who Become Activists." *Public Relations Review,* 1989, 15(3), 3–24.

Grunig, J. E., and Hunt, T. *Managing Public Relations.* New York: Holt, Rinehart & Winston, 1984.

Grunig, J. E., and Repper, F. C. "Strategic Management, Publics, and Issues." In *Excellence in Public Relations and Communication Management.* Ed. J. E. Grunig. Hillsdale, NJ: Lawrence Erlbaum, 1992, 117–157.

Gurin, M. G., and Van Til, J. "Philanthropy in its Historical Context. In *Critical Issues in American Philanthropy: Strengthening Theory and Practice.* Eds. J. Van Til et al. San Francisco: Jossey-Bass, 1990, 3–18.

Hall, H. "Many Boards Are Said to Be Unhappy over Fund-Raising Costs." *The Chronicle of Philanthropy,* 24–25, March 9, 1993.

Hall, P. D. "Business Giving and Social Investment in the United States." In *Philanthropic Giving: Studies in Varieties and Goals.* Ed. P. Magat. New York: Oxford University Press, 1989, 221–245.

Hendrix, J. A. *Public Relations Cases* (3rd ed.). Belmont, CA: Wadsworth, 1995.

Hodgkinson, V. A., and Toppe, C. "A New Research and Planning Tool for Managers: The National Taxonomy of Exempt Entities." *Nonprofit Management & Leadership,* 1991, 1(4), 403–414.

Hodgkinson, V. A., Weitzman, M. S., Toppe, C. M., and Noga, S. M. *Nonprofit Almanac 1992–1993: Dimensions of the INDEPENDENT SECTOR.* San Francisco: INDEPENDENT SECTOR and Jossey-Bass, 1992.

Howe, F. *The Board Member's Guide to Fund Raising: What Every Trustee Needs to Know about Raising Money.* San Francisco: Jossey-Bass, 1991.

Hyman, H. H., and Sheatsley, P. B. "Some Reasons Why Information Campaigns Fail." *Public Opinion Quarterly,* 11(3), 1947, 412–423.

INDEPENDENT SECTOR. *Giving and Volunteering in the United States: Findings from a National Survey, 1994 Volume I.* Washington, DC: Author, 1994.

Kelly, K. S. *Effective Fund-Raising Management.* Mahwah, NJ: Lawrence Erlbaum, 1997.

Kelly, K. S. *Fund Raising and Public Relations: A Critical Analysis.* Hillsdale, NJ: Lawrence Erlbaum, 1991.

Kelly, K. S. "Utilizing Public Relations Theory to Conceptualize and Test Models of Fund Raising." *Journalism & Mass Communication Quarterly,* 1995, 72(1), 106–127.

Laudan, L. *Progress and Its Problems.* Berkeley, CA: University of California Press, 1977.

Layton, D. N. *Philanthropy and Voluntarism: An Annotated Bibliography.* New York: Foundation Center, 1987.

Lindblom, C. E., and Cohen, D. K. *Usable Knowledge: Social Science and Social Problem Solving.* New Haven, CT: Yale University Press, 1979.

Lohmann, R. A. "The Commons: A Multidisciplinary Approach to Nonprofit Organization, Voluntary Action, and Philanthropy." *Nonprofit and Voluntary Sector Quarterly,* 1992a, 21(3), 309–324.

Lohmann, R. A. *The Commons: New Perspectives on Nonprofit Organizations and Voluntary Action.* San Francisco: Jossey-Bass, 1992b.

Lord, J. G. *The Raising of Money: Thirty-Five Essentials Every Trustee Should Know.* Cleveland, OH: Third Sector Press, 1983.

Lowery, S. A., and DeFleur, M. L. *Milestones in Mass Communication Research: Media Effects* (3rd ed.). White Plains, NY: Longman, 1995.

Martin, M. W. *Virtuous Giving: Philanthropy, Voluntary Service, and Caring.* Bloomington: Indiana University Press, 1994.

Meckstroth, A. "Nonprofit Organizations and Charitable Giving, 1986–1992: A Compendium of Statistical Information and Analyses." *Nonprofit Management & Leadership,* 1994, 4(3), 359–364.

"New Drive to Spur Gifts to Charity." *The Chronicle of Philanthropy,* April 20, 1995, 16.

Nudd, S. P. "Thinking Strategically about Information." In *Achieving Excellence in Fund Raising: A Comprehensive Guide to Principles, Strategies, and Methods.* Eds. H. A. Rosso et al. San Francisco: Jossey-Bass, 1991, 174–189.

"Opinion, Timing—Not Info—Triggers Human Behavior, Says Consultant." *PR News,* Nov. 22, 1993. 8.

Ostrander, S. A., and Schervish, P. G. "Giving and Getting: Philanthropy as a Social Relation." In *Critical Issues in American Philanthropy: Strengthening Theory and Practice.* Eds. J. Van Til et al. San Francisco: Jossey-Bass, 1990, 67–98.

Panas, J. *Megagifts: Who Gives Them, Who Gets Them.* Chicago: Pluribus Press. 1984.

Payton, R. L. "Philanthropic Values." In *Philanthropy: Private Means, Public Ends.* Ed. K. W. Thompson. Lanham, MD: University Press of America. 1987.

Payton, R. L. *Philanthropy: Voluntary Action for the Public Good.* New York: American Council on Education-Macmillan, 1988.

Payton, R. L., Rosso, H. A., and Tempel, E. R. "Toward a Philosophy of Fund Raising." In *Taking Fund Raising Seriously: Advancing the Profession and Practice of Raising Money.* Eds. D. F. Burlingame & L. J. Hulse. San Francisco: Jossey-Bass, 1991, 3–17.

Rosso, H. A. "Developing a Constituency: Where Fund Raising Begins." In *Achieving Excellence in Fund Raising: A Comprehensive Guide to Principles, Strategies, and Methods.* Eds. H. A. Rosso et al. San Francisco: Jossey-Bass, 1991, 28–38.

Schervish, P. G., and Havens, J. J. "Do the Poor Pay More? Is the U-Shaped Curve Correct?" *Nonprofit and Voluntary Sector Quarterly,* 24(1), 1995, 79–90.

Schervish, P. G., and Havens, J. J. "Social Participation and Charitable Giving: A Multivariate Analysis." *Nonprofit and Voluntary Sector Quarterly,* 26, (2), 1997.

Schervish, P. G., and Havens, J. J. *Wherewithal and Beneficence: Charitable Giving by Income and Wealth.* Paper presented at the Indiana University Center on Philanthropy Seventh Annual Symposium on Taking Fund Raising Seriously, Indianapolis, IN, Aug. 1994.

Sheldon, K. S. "Foundations as a Source of Support." In *Achieving Excellence in Fund Raising: A Comprehensive Guide to Principles, Strategies, and Methods.* Eds. H. A. Rosso et al. San Francisco: Jossey-Bass, 1991, 243–260.

Simmons, R. E. *Communication Campaign Management: A Systems Approach.* White Plains, NY: Longman, 1990.

Smith, G. T. "The Development Program." In *Handbook of Institutional Advancement.* Ed. A. W. Rowland. San Francisco: Jossey-Bass, 1977, 142–151.

Steele, V., and Elder, S. D. *Becoming a Fundraiser: The Principles and Practice of Library Development.* Chicago, IL: American Library Association, 1992.

Tempel, E. R. "Assessing Organizational Strengths and Vulnerabilities." In *Achieving Excellence in Fund Raising: A Comprehensive Guide to Principles, Strategies, and Methods.* Eds. H. A. Rosso et al. San Francisco: Jossey-Bass, 1991, 19–27.

Vandeventer, D. J. *The Phenomenon of American Philanthropy: A Parallel to the Theories of the Chicago School of Social Thought.* Unpublished master's thesis, University of Northern Iowa, Cedar Falls, IA, 1993.

Van Til, J. Foreword. *The Commons: New Perspectives on Nonprofit Organizations and Voluntary Action.* R. A. Lohmann. San Francisco: Jossey-Bass, 1992, xi–xiii.

Wood, E. W. "The Four R's of Major Gift Solicitation. *Reid Report,* 1989, (141), 1, 6. (Available from Russ Reid Company, 2 North Lake Avenue, Pasadena, CA 91101.)

# Financial and Management Performance

# Costs and Performance Measurements

JAMES M. GREENFIELD, ACFRE, FAHP

*Hoag Memorial Hospital Presbyterian*

Fund raising continues to lack uniform methods to budget, evaluate, and report its results. As a consequence, performance measurements are incomplete, misinterpreted, and undependable. Nonprofit organizations and their professional fund raising executives are challenged to defend their performance against an unknown and undocumented standard. It is hard to answer the complaint that "costs are too high" when nonprofit organizations do not count and compare their results with consistent data elements. Board members and management favor a simple "bottom line" cost-to-gift figure, which can be misleading and is frequently misunderstood, but it is used as a near-infallible assessment of performance.

To permit any level of credible cost-benefit analysis, the budget and expense for *each* fund raising activity must first be captured with consistency. Details about how each solicitation method performs is quite valuable to the fund development manager who must supervise a budget for improved results. Published reports of fund raising performance are likely to achieve higher credibility after uniform data are available and in widespread use.

Performance analysis is an underutilized management tool in fund raising. It can and should be applied in annual budget preparation; in assessing performance of new and renewed donors and their giving levels; in comparing expenses against budget estimates; in analyzing gift income for each solicitation activity; and in measuring the performance of volunteers and staff as well as the solicitation method they collaborated on.

Performance measurement also gives fund raisers the ability to forecast future gift income with reliability, a benefit to fiscal planning for nonprofit organizations. Board members and executive directors are now becoming convinced that "cost-effectiveness analysis is a clear necessity for responsible nonprofit management" and "that the rigor involved will improve the organization's internal effectiveness and efficiency and will enhance the organization's external image" (Schmaedick, 1993, p. 3).

Despite these convictions, a lack of consensus exists on how fund raising performance measurements ought to be done. What measurement tools should be used? Is a uniform reporting model available? Against what standards are these results to be compared?

No comprehensive set of financial standards exists for measurement of fund raising practice as there are standards in the for-profit business sector. Further, "there are no measures comparable to net income or return on investment to assess the efficiency and effectiveness of not-for-profit accomplishments" (Harr et al., 1991, p. 1). Certainly the figures and the data behind them are present within nonprofit institutions and agencies. Is their nonuse due to a lack of willingness to dig them out, to a fear of accountability, or to the effort required to educate board members and administrative staff on how to interpret the results?

Some reasonable cost guidelines based on the experience of the most common solicitation activities have been developed. Performance measurement is the basis for taking action. If one fund raising activity yields a large number of donors and high average gifts, it should be used again provided the costs also were reasonable. However, when someone questions any one or all three of the following basic figures—number of donors, average gift size, and reasonable cost—how are their results to be interpreted? A frequent target is direct mail acquisition, which can cost as much as $1.25 to $1.50 to raise $1.00. Acquisition is an investment in constituency building and may not be fund raising, per se. Renewing these and other prior donors by mail *is* fund raising and is capable of achieving a retention rate of 50 percent or better with higher levels of giving, and at a cost of $0.20 to $0.25 to raise $1.00. Because both are important to evaluate, their performance in combination represents the overall effectiveness of the use of mail for solicitation purposes.

Board members and executive managers are often frustrated by the reluctance of fund development professionals to be evaluated on total dollars raised. What if boards and managers were focused on the cost-effectiveness of each method or its efficiency in producing a larger number of donors willing to continue to give more each year? Or on success in recruiting and training more volunteers? Total dollars raised is no test of the potential for efficiency and effectiveness of the methods and techniques being used.

This chapter outlines a uniform method of investing (budgeting) for each solicitation activity. It also offers measurement tools to assess the ability of each activity to increase numbers of donors *and* their dollars as a total return on investment. And, it proposes to provide a reliable forecasting model to predict future returns and to set standards for continued performance measurement.

## Program Budgeting

Every solicitation activity is a separate fiscal event within the overall fund development program. Each has an estimated budget, actual expenses, measurable results, a cost-benefit ratio, and a return on investment. Each these factors can be measured to demonstrate the profit potential for the activity. In preparing a budget for each fund raising activity, it is necessary to define each of its direct, indirect, and overhead expense areas (see Exhibit 10.1). compared against expenses that follow, reliable measurements can be taken and the results interpreted with accuracy and understanding.

Budgets are investments. Fund raising budgets should produce profits from each solicitation activity, but each will not perform at the same level. Maximum returns result from a closely integrated array of activities. By

## EXHIBIT 10.1. Sample Budget Preparation Worksheet for Solicitation Activity[1]

|  | | Activity #1 | Activity #2 | Activity #3 | Total |
|---|---|---|---|---|---|
| **A. Labor Costs (Salaries and Benefits)** | | | | | |
| 25 | Compensation | $ | $ | $ | $ |
| 26 | Others salaries/wages | | | | |
| 27 | Pension plan contributions | | | | |
| 28 | Other benefits | | | | |
| 29 | Payroll taxes | ____ | ____ | ____ | ____ |
| | Sub-Totals: | $ | $ | $ | $ |
| **B. Non-Labor Costs (Office Operations)** | | | | | |
| 30 | Professional fees | $ | $ | $ | $ |
| 31 | Accounting fees | | | | |
| 32 | Legal fees | | | | |
| 33 | Supplies | | | | |
| 34 | Telephone | | | | |
| 35 | Postage/shipping | | | | |
| 36 | Occupancy/rent | | | | |
| 37 | Equipment rental/maintenance | | | | |
| 38 | Printing/publications | | | | |
| 39 | Travel | | | | |
| 40 | Conferences/meetings | | | | |
| 41 | Interest | | | | |
| 42 | Depreciation | | | | |
| 43 | Other expenses | | | | |
| 43a | _____ | | | | |
| 43b | _____ | | | | |
| | Sub-Totals: | $ | $ | $ | $ |
| 44 | Grand Totals:<br>(A + B) | $ | $ | $ | $ |

[1] Internal Revenue Service Form 990, Part II, Column D, Lines 25–44.

Source: Fund-Raising Cost Effectiveness: A Self-Assessment Workbook, James Greenfield. © 1996. Reprinted by permission of John Wiley & Sons, Inc.

adding good analysis, nonprofit organizations can target limited budget dollars for their "most likely to succeed" solicitation activities to achieve larger numbers of donors, more frequent and larger gifts, and higher net revenue at lower costs. To count only gross revenue, total costs, and net proceeds is inadequate and incomplete.

Consider the example of a major benefit event, a once-a-year fund raising activity for most nonprofit organizations. A benefit is the result of months of planning, volumes of volunteer and staff hours, widespread promotion, and more. Success can be measured in at least 16 different ways: (1) by the comments of satisfied customers (donors) who attended, (2) by how many people attended, (3) by the amount of media coverage achieved, (4) by the number and size of sponsor and underwriting contributions, (5) by keeping expenses low with donated services and in-kind donations. A vast array of data demonstrate the success of benefits in addition to attendance, a "good time," newsprint, donations, and net proceeds. Comparative analysis can link (6) ticket pricing to cost of production, (7) promotion efforts and costs to media coverage, (8) direct ticket sales to sponsor and underwriting gifts. Benefit events are also opportunities to achieve other measurable objectives, such as (9) major donor cultivation, (10) recognition of donors and volunteers, and (11) communicating important information to the audience. Finally, critical details that must be examined include (12) contracts and negotiations for cost of facilities, entertainment, meals, decorations, printing, and so on, (13) attendance and customer satisfaction, (14) gross revenue and total costs (direct, indirect, and overhead), (15) volunteer leadership and committee members performance, and (16) net proceeds available for charitable purposes.

## Performance Measurement

A comprehensive group of measurement criteria appropriate to each solicitation method can and should be defined. The results and their performance analysis also should be shared with others including the public. What is most often reported, however, is only one figure—how much was raised—without any distinction whether this figure is gross revenue or net proceeds. What was the relationship between gross revenue, total costs, and net proceeds? Is $30,000 in net proceeds a "success" if gross revenue for the event was $100,000 (a $0.70 to raise $1.00 cost-benefit ratio)? Yes, if it is a first-ever event. No, if the event is in its third year of operation.

Performance measurements should be applied uniformly to each and every fund raising program, not just to benefit events. Assessment criteria can be defined to fit each solicitation activity and to measure each against its prior performance to document where progress has been made and where additional improvements may lie. Performance measurement has a higher purpose, to help define the capacity to achieve optimum potential.

## PERFORMANCE MEASUREMENT TOOLS

Nine measurement criteria can be applied uniformly to every fund raising program. These criteria demonstrate effectiveness, efficiency, productivity, and profitability. They illustrate how expenses (budgets) are applied to raise money successfully, which solicitation activities are working to increase the number of donors and commitment to continue giving and volunteering, and demonstrate potential for more frequent contributions. This nine-step performance index (see Exhibit 10.2) should be used as comparative analysis within each fund raising method but not between solicitation methods. Each index factor is an indicator of success; in combination, they report the details required to make decisions about the future use of each solicitation activity. They also contain details for public reporting on results. A brief explanation of each element follows:

1. *Participants.* The number of donors responding illustrates whether those groups solicited were the best ones to ask, how effective this method was in its appeal to each audience, and whether more potential may exist among those who did not reply. Because success in each solicitation activity depends on requests that stimulate replies, understanding each prospect and donor audience is critical for planning future appeals.

2. *Income Received.* Every appeal will receive some revenue. Gross contributions are often reported as the contributions amount received, before

---

## EXHIBIT 10.2. Nine-Step Performance Index

1. Participants = Number of donors responding with gifts.
2. Income Received = Gross contributions.
3. Expenses = Fund raising costs.
4. Percent Participation:
     Divide participants by total solicitations made.
5. Average Gift Size:
     Divide income received by participants.
6. Net Income:
     Subtract expenses from income received.
7. Average Cost per Gift:
     Divide expenses by participants.
8. Cost of Fund raising:
     Divide expenses by income received; multiply by 100.
9. Return:
     Divide net income by expenses; multiply by 100.

Source: Fund-Raising Cost Effectiveness: A Self-Assessment Workbook, James Greenfield. © 1996. Reprinted by permission of John Wiley & Sons, Inc.

expenses. Type of revenue is important to classify (e.g., cash, pledge, stock, real estate, in-kind donation, planned gift, bequest) along with the correct contribution value as allowed by the Internal Revenue Service. Each gift ought to be recorded (a) by its source, (b) by the donor's purpose or specified use of the funds, and (c) by the solicitation activity that successfully stimulated a response.

3. *Expense.* The budget or cost of fund raising required to stimulate the income received must be recorded against the solicitation activity that brought in the gift. Budgets control how much effort can be given each solicitation; spending options vary within each fund raising activity. For example, a one-ounce first-class letter will cost 32 cents per letter; mailing 200 or more letters first class using the 9-digit (ZIP + 4) presort will cost 26.7 cents per letter. Choosing to use the nonprofit bulk rate privilege, the same contents sent via third class, 9-digit presort (under 3 ounces) will cost 10.3 cents per letter. The decision is to write fewer people or more people, based on cost. The response rate will be higher using first class but three times as many people will be contacted using third class.

4. *Percent Participation.* The number of replies reflects a percentage of those invited to give. Because rate of return varies for each solicitation method, it is important to understand that a one percent performance for new donor acquisition is as valid a measurement of success as is a 50 percent renewal rate for prior mail donors, or a 20 percent response rate from proposals submitted to corporations or foundations. All are also mail solicitations. Percent participation reflects how well the solicitation was planned in terms of selecting the most receptive audiences invited by mail to make a gift.

5. *Average Gift Size.* How much a donor gives is a financial indicator of how motivated they were to give when solicited. It also demonstrates the amount of spendable cash available, and reflects prior giving history or habits. Gift size also indicates whether the amount requested was well chosen, how effective the solicitor was, level of acceptance of the solicitation method, and how appealing and worthwhile the project was.

6. *Net Income.* Net income is the amount of actual cash available for charitable purposes after expenses; this is the ultimate goal. Net income describes productivity along with efficiency of the solicitation method. The keys to increasing net income are many, beginning with accurate and complete expense tracking that includes indirect and overhead costs attributed to each solicitation, along with its direct costs.

7. *Average Cost per Gift.* Average cost per gift along with average gift size are indicators of program progress and performance, not only profitability. Can more money be raised from current donors? If the average gift for a membership or donor club program can be increased, will average gift size increase and average cost per gift decrease? If so, a higher level of net income will be achieved from the same donor audience.

8. *Cost of Fund Raising.* Cost-benefit analysis performed on each fund raising activity measures their separate rates of efficiency and productivity.

## EXHIBIT 10.3. Reasonable Cost Guidelines

| Solicitation Activity | Cost Guideline |
|---|---|
| Direct mail acquisition | $1.25 to $1.50 per $1.00 raised |
| Direct mail renewal | $0.20 to $0.25 per $1.00 raised |
| Benefit events | $0.50 per $1.00 raised of gross revenue* (direct costs only) |
| Corporations and foundations | $0.20 per $1.00 raised |
| Planned giving | $0.20 to $0.30 per $1.00 raised |
| Capital campaigns | $0.10 to $0.20 per $1.00 raised |

\* Benefit Event Cost Allocations.

   To calculate bottom line net proceeds from a benefit event, add the internal and overhead support expenses to direct costs and subtract from gross revenue.

   Performance measurement of benefit events must also include assessments of added value received in the following areas: Marketing, media relations, community relations, major gift cultivation, donor relations, image building, and influence on other external affairs constituents.

Source: Fund-Raising Cost Effectiveness: A Self-Assessment Workbook, James Greenfield. © 1996. Reprinted by permission of John Wiley & Sons, Inc.

This bottom line for each activity is helpful as a performance guideline and especially valid when measured against prior experience. It is less valid when measured against the bottom line results of all the other solicitation activities performed by the organization. And, it is quite invalid when compared against a similar form of solicitation activity at other nonprofit organizations. Several cost-benefit criteria have begun to be accepted as reasonable guidelines (see Exhibit 10.3), although the Philanthropic Advisory Service of the Council of Better Business Bureaus and the National Charities Information Bureau continue to advocate a single bottom line percentage no greater than 35 percent as acceptable.

   9. *Return.* Budget dollars invested in each fund raising activity provide a positive return on these investments. Each solicitation should demonstrate improved results (higher return) from continued use based on performance analysis to understand its potential for increased effectiveness and efficiency. This final bottom line figure also translates a cost of fund raising of $0.20 to raise $1.00 into a 400 percent return. Fund raising should be given due consideration as a profit center, not as just another cost center in a nonprofit organization.

## FORECASTING SOLICITATION RESULTS

After a solicitation activity is concluded and its results measured by the nine performance indicators and reasonable cost guidelines, these assessments are likely to illustrate several areas of potential for improved results. Lessons learned relate to audience selection, responsiveness to the "case" for support, average gift size, total expenses required, and other criteria. Used together, this combination of performance measurements provides adequate data to begin to forecast future results.

Forecasting becomes more reliable after a solicitation activity has been used three or more times and the nine-step data analysis has been performed. Based on this amount of data, board members and administration, donors and volunteers are more likely to begin to accept these results. Future budget decisions should continue (and increase) the amount invested where solicitation results demonstrate the reliability that further investments will continue to produce a constant or increasing level of net profits from each solicitation activity.

Areas of likely improvement should be linked to requests for added budget when expected "profits" can be shown. If more budget dollars are made available, where should they be invested? In acquiring more donors? In raising more money from current donors? In recruiting and training more volunteers? In hiring more staff to supervise more solicitation activity? Answers vary depending on several factors such as individual program growth, likely potential to be realized, strategic development in numbers of renewing and upgraded donors, priority of need and pressure for cash from the nonprofit organization, present staff capability to increase workload, changing economic trends in the community, and competition for funds from other nonprofit organizations. Increasing budget without evidence of improved return based on performance measurement is as unwise as it will be unproductive.

## PERFORMANCE STANDARDS

After three years of experience, it is possible to establish performance standards for each solicitation activity. Experience also provides sufficient data for estimating reasonable expectations (see Exhibits 10.4 and 10.5). Each addition from solicitation activity adds more data to performance maturity, increasing its reliability in predicting continued gift revenues. When major gift or capital campaign needs arise, a solid base of experience is available to assess potential for meeting higher goals. Between major campaigns, a return to routine annual giving activities can be expected to perform at new levels of efficiency and effectiveness to meet demands for higher amounts of annual support.

## Conclusion

The benefits of performance measurements include an improved understanding of current results and how to apply existing budgets for maximum

## EXHIBIT 10.4 Multiyear Summary Results with One-Year Forecast Including Cost of Fund-Raising and Return Percentages

|  | | Year 1 | Year 2 | Year 3 | Est. Year 4 |
|---|---|---|---|---|---|
| A. Annual Giving Programs | | | | | |
| Direct mail (acquisition) | | $27,550 | $31,250 | $35,500 | $42,000 |
| Direct mail (renewal) | | 55,880 | 69,500 | 76,500 | 85,000 |
| Membership dues | | 40,400 | 44,000 | 48,500 | 55,000 |
| Benefit events (3) | | 45,500 | 53,400 | 59,600 | 68,000 |
| Volunteer-led solicitations | | 58,500 | 65,500 | 82,000 | 90,000 |
| | Subtotal | $227,830 | $263,650 | $302,100 | $340,000 |
| B. Major Gifts Programs | | | | | |
| Corporations | | $13,500 | $28,000 | $45,500 | $55,000 |
| Foundations | | 8,000 | 35,500 | 65,000 | 80,000 |
| Individuals | | 35,000 | 78,000 | 145,500 | 160,000 |
| Bequests received | | 5,000 | 26,000 | 45,000 | 25,000 |
| | Subtotal | $61,500 | $167,500 | $301,000 | $320,000 |
| | Total | $289,330 | $431,150 | $603,100 | $660,000 |
| C. Expense Summary | | | | | |
| Labor/payroll | | $68,015 | $72,100 | $79,800 | $85,000 |
| Nonpayroll costs (Includes indirect costs and overhead) | | 39,550 | 46,225 | 51,315 | 50,000 |
| | Subtotal | $107,565 | $118,325 | $131,115 | $135,000 |
| | Net Income | $181,765 | $312,825 | $471,985 | $525,000 |
| Cost of fund-raising | | 37% | 27% | 22% | 20% |
| Return | | 169% | 264% | 360% | 389% |

Source: Fund-Raising Cost Effectiveness: A Self-Assessment Workbook, James Greenfield. © 1996. Reprinted by permission of John Wiley & Sons, Inc.

return. With accurate data, it is also possible to estimate future performance with reliability. To achieve these dual benefits, uniform budget practices are required, along with consistent measurement tools. When performance measurements become common practice, comparative analysis between nonprofit organizations may be possible. Until then, the best comparisons today and in the future will continue to come from analysis of prior performance yielding reliable expectations and cost-effective solicitation practices.

## EXHIBIT 10.5 Illustration of Multiyear Summary Results with One-Year Forecast

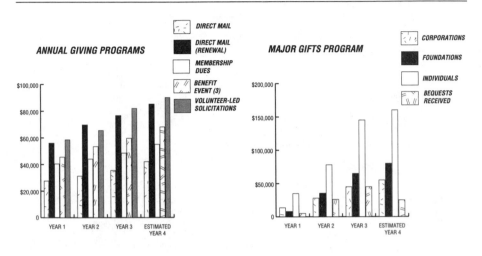

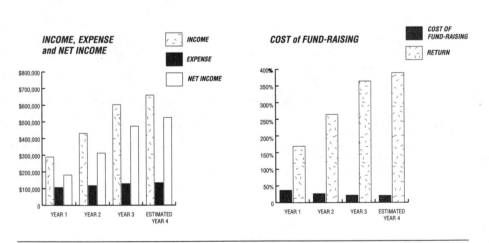

Source: Fund-Raising Cost Effectiveness: A Self-Assessment Workbook, James Green-field. © 1996. Reprinted by permission of John Wiley & Sons, Inc.

# Bibliography

Blazek, Jody. *Tax and Financial Planning for Tax-Exempt Organizations.* New York: John Wiley & Sons, 1990.

Bradford, David L., and Cohen, Allan R. *Managing for Excellence: The Guide to Developing High Performance in Contemporary Organizations.* New York: John Wiley & Sons, 1984.

Collier, Arthur S. "Criteria for Audits and Measurements for Demonstrating Fundraising Success," In *Financial Practices for Effective Fundraising.* Ed. James M. Greenfield, *New Directions for Philanthropic Fundraising.* San Francisco: Jossey-Bass, 3, Spring 1994, 49–76.

Costa, Nick B. "Measuring Progress and Success in Fund Raising: How to Use Comparative Statistics to Prove Your Effectiveness." *Association for Healthcare Philanthropy.* Falls Church, VA, 1991.

Council of Better Business Bureaus. *Standards for Charitable Solicitations.* Arlington, VA, 1982.

Drucker, Peter F. *The Drucker Foundation Self-Assessment Tool for Nonprofit Organizations,* Peter F. Drucker Foundation for Nonprofit Management. San Francisco: Jossey-Bass, 1993.

Fink, Norman S., and Metzler, Howard C. *The Costs and Benefits of Deferred Giving.* New York: Columbia University Press, 1982.

Grace, Kay Sprinkel. "Managing for Results." In *Achieving Excellence in Fund Raising.* Henry A. Rosso et al., San Francisco: Jossey-Bass, 1991.

Gray, Sandra T. *A Vision for Evaluation.* Washington, DC: INDEPENDENT SECTOR, 1993.

Greenfield, James M. "Accountability, Program Performance, and Profitability." Part I: "How to Assess Fund-Raising Program Performance." *AHP Journal,* Spring 1994. Part II: "Comparative Analysis, Profitability, and Forecasting," *AHP Journal,* Fall, 1994.

Greenfield, James M. *Fund-Raising Cost Effectiveness: A Self-Assessment Work Book.* New York: John Wiley & Sons, 1996.

Greenfield, James M. *Fund-Raising: Evaluating and Managing the Fund Development Program.* New York: John Wiley & Sons, 1991.

Greenfield, James M. *Fund-Raising Fundamentals: A Guide to Annual Giving for Professionals and Volunteers.* New York: John Wiley & Sons, 1994.

Greenfield, James M., and Dreves, John P. "Fund-Raising Assessment." In *The Nonprofit Management Handbook: Operating Policies and Procedures.* Ed. Tracy Daniel Connors, New York: John Wiley & Sons, 1993, 647–693.

Gross, Malvern J., Jr., Warshauer, William, Jr., and Larkin, Richard F. *Financial and Accounting Guide for Not-for-Profit Organizations* (4th ed.). New York: John Wiley & Sons, 1991.

Harr, David J., Godfrey, James T., and Frank, Robert H. "Are Volunteers Worth Their Weight in Gold; But Not in Dollars?" *Philanthropy Monthly.* Sept. 1992, 19–27.

Harr, David J., Godfrey, James T., and Frank, Robert H. *Common Costs and Fund-Raising Appeals: A Guide to Joint Cost Allocation in Not-for-Profit Organizations*. Landover, MD: Nonprofit Mailers Federation and Frank & Company, p.c., 1991.

Herman, Robert D. et al. *The Jossey-Bass Handbook of Nonprofit Leadership and Management*. San Francisco: Jossey-Bass, 1994.

Hopkins, Bruce R. *A Legal Guide to Starting and Managing a Nonprofit Organization*. (2nd ed.). New York: John Wiley & Sons, 1993.

Hopkins, Bruce R. "Tax Exempt Status Threatened by Fund-Raising." *Fund Raising Management*. October, 1983.

Jacobson, Harvey J. "15 Ways to Measure Fund Raising Program Effectiveness." *Fund Raising Management*, Dec. 1982, 24–28.

Lane, Frederick S. "Enhancing the Quality of Public Reporting by Nonprofit Organizations." *The Philanthropy Monthly*, July 1991.

Larkin, Richard F. "Accounting Issues Relating to Fundraising." In *Financial Practices for Effective Fundraising*. Ed. James M. Greenfield, *New Directions for Philanthropic Fundraising*, San Francisco: Jossey-Bass, 3, Spring 1994, 27–48.

Levis, Wilson C., and New, Anne. "The Average Gift Size and Cost per Gift: New Valuation Tools for Grantmakers." *Foundation News*. Sept./Oct. 1982.

Lindahl, Wesley E. "Multiyear Evaluation of Fundraising Performance." In *Financial Practices for Effective Fundraising*. Ed. James M. Greenfield, *New Directions for Philanthropic Fundraising*, San Francisco: Jossey-Bass, 3, Spring 1994, 77–93.

Lindahl, Wesley E. *Strategic Planning for Fund Raising: How to Bring In More Money Using Strategic Resource Allocation*. San Francisco: Jossey-Bass, 1992.

Lindahl, Wesley E., and Winship, Christopher. "Predictive Models for Annual Fundraising and Major Gift Fundraising." In *Nonprofit Management and Leadership*. Ed. Dennis R. Young. San Francisco: Jossey-Bass, Fall 1992, 3, 1.

Logan, Timothy D., "Forecasting Fund-Raising Income: Managing the Telemarketing Process." *Fund Raising Management*, April 1995.

Martin, Del. "The Development Audit: Providing the Blue Print for a Better Fund-Raising Program." *NSFRE Journal*. Autumn 1990.

Merlyn, Vaughan and Parkinson, John. *Developing Effectiveness: Strategies for IS Organizational Transition. The Ernst & Young Information Management Series*. New York: John Wiley & Sons, 1994.

Mixer, Joseph R. *Principles of Professional Fundraising: Useful Foundations for Successful Practice*. San Francisco: Jossey-Bass, 1993.

Murray, Dennis J. *Evaluation of Fund Raising Programs: A Management Audit Approach*. Boston, MA: American Institute of Management, 1983.

Murray, Dennis J. *The Guaranteed Fund-Raising System: A Systems Approach to Planning and Controlling Fund Raising* (2nd ed.). Poughkeepsie, NY: American Institute of Management, 1994.

National Charities Information Bureau. *Standards in Philanthropy.* New York: 1988.

New, Anne L. with Wilson C. Levis. *Raise More Money for Your Nonprofit Organization.* New York: Foundation Center, 1991.

Schmaedick, Gerald L. *Cost-Effectiveness in the Nonprofit Sector.* London, CT: Quorum Books, 1993.

Smith, Bucklin & Associates. *The Complete Guide to Nonprofit Management.* Eds. Robert H. Wilbur, Susan Kudla Finn, and Carolyn M. Freeland. New York: John Wiley & Sons, 1994.

Tracey, John A. *How to Read a Financial Report: Wringing Vital Signs out of the Numbers* (4th ed.). New York: John Wiley & Sons, 1994.

Tobin, Gary A. "Effects of Administrative Cost Perceptions in Major-Gift Decisions." In *Financial Practices for Effective Fundraising.* Ed. James M. Greenfield, *New Directions in Philanthropic Fundraising.* San Francisco: Jossey-Bass, 3, Spring 1994, 95–113.

Weinstein, Stanley. "Time Management and the Development Professional." *NSFRE Journal,* Winter 1991, 42–53.

Wholey, Joseph S., Hatry, Harry P., and Newcomer, Kathryn E. (Eds.). *Handbook of Practice Program Evaluation.* San Francisco: Jossey-Bass, 1994.

# 11 ▼ A Horse of a Different Color

## Management and Financial Implications of Nonformula Fund Raising

MARJORIE A. WINKLER, ACFRE

*Neighborhood Reinvestment Corporation*

A standard formula for conducting successful fund raising campaigns has never been officially declared. A body of knowledge drawn from the experience of early practitioners in the field, however, has become, de facto, a standard formula. This formula is being put forward in educational seminars all across the country as a guide for those entering the profession and those who are seeking to be more effective. In this chapter, that de facto formula will be identified as the *classic fund raising formula,* and institutions that can successfully apply that formula will be called *classic formula organizations.*

In the past couple of decades, and particularly since government began getting out of the business of funding not-for-profits in the 1980s, thousands of organizations have entered the private sector fund raising arena for the first time, or have been expanding their efforts to capture a larger share of that market. With so many new and different kinds of not-for-profits attempting to do organized fund raising, it is becoming apparent that there are many for whom the classic fund raising formula does not work well. They will be identified as *nonformula organizations.*

Not surprisingly, many fund raising professionals, schooled in the classic formula, are at a loss when confronted with raising money for a nonformula organization. Fund raising failure is often blamed on the organization itself—ineffective board members, inadequate participation by top staff, unrealistic expectations—the list goes on. Neither organizations nor fund raisers recognize that they may be dealing with a horse of a different color; that perhaps a different sort of fund raising formula is called for.

# Classic Fund Raising Formula

The classic fund raising formula was developed and continues to work most successfully in an environment that is quite different from that within which nonformula organizations must function. Early fund raising practitioners worked mostly for large, visible, credible institutions in urban areas. These organizations had established reputations, with boards composed primarily wealthy community leaders who could dedicate resources and staff to the fund raising function, and service users who were a major source of significant prospective donors. The profile of organizations that most successfully raise money using the classic fund raising formula is still the same today.

The classic fund raising formula incorporates principles that must be used and conditions that must be met to achieve a successful fund raising campaign.

## COMPONENTS OF CLASSIC FUND RAISING FORMULA

### Top Down—Inside Out
Fund raising is most effective if large gifts are secured first, as they influence subsequent giving, and because that is the way wealth is distributed in this country; in 1989, 10 percent of the people owned 84 percent of the net assets in the United States, a figure probably little changed today (Baker, 1996). "Inside out" means that money must be raised starting with the organization's closest constituencies and then expanding methodically outward in seeking donors (Seymour, 1966).

### Board Giving = 15–30 Percent of Goal
Board members are an organization's closest constituency, and should lead the giving by 100 percent participation and by contributing 15 to 30 percent of the goal if a campaign is to succeed (Seymour, 1966).

### Peer Principle
People give to people, and the best person to do the asking is a donor who is a peer in influence, affluence, prestige, and power (Mixer, 1993).

### Leadership Imperative
The campaign leader must be a major donor, preferably the lead donor, if the goal is to be met, because that gift sets the example for all that follow (Marts & Lundy, 1983).

### Lead Gift = 5–10 Percent of Goal
Depending on the type and size of campaign, the lead gift should be 10 percent (Dove, 1988), or two 5 percent gifts (Klein, 1994).

## Domino Theory

Successive major donors will use the lead donor's gift as a standard of comparison and will make a decision to give and to scale their own gifts proportionately. The right lead gift causes all the rest to fall in line like dominos (Marts & Lundy, 1983).

## Advance Gifts = 40 Percent

This is to assure a reasonable likelihood of success before public announcement of the campaign goal (Broce, 1986).

## A Prospect

This person has the money that is needed, has an interest in the solicitor or institution, and can be accessed by the organization (Seymour, 1966).

## Annual Attrition Rate = 15–20 Percent

This is the average amount of funding that must be replaced each year just to stay even because of nonrenewals (Greenfield, 1995).

## Rule of Thirds

In a successful campaign, ⅓ of the gifts will come from the top 10 donors (or a small number), ⅓ from 10 times that number, and ⅓ from all others (Lord, 1987). Recently those percentages have shifted closer to 40/40/20.

## GIFT TABLE

Based on the preceding information, an accurate projection can be made of the numbers and levels of gifts needed to reach any given goal, using a mathematical formula in which each successive gift after the lead gift is ½ the previous one, while each successive donor number is doubled (Dove, 1988). This forms what is called a "gift table," or "standards of giving table."

A gift table can also be used to calculate how many prospects and campaign solicitors will be needed (see Exhibits 11.1 and 11.2). Since the average refusal rate is 4 out of 5, but some prospects will give at lower levels, multiply the number of gifts by 4 for total prospects needed at each level (Rosso, 1991). Then divide that number by 5 to get the number of workers needed to reach the goal (Seymour, 1966).

To successfully implement the classic fund-raising formula, an organization must function in an environment that closely resembles that out of which the formula evolved, which will be called the *classic formula environment*. Expanding on a format developed to determine reasonable fund raising costs (Greenfield, 1994), Exhibit 11.3 is a rating chart of environmental factors common to classic formula organizations, with some additional factors that are common to nonformula organizations. Each factor should be rated according to its value to successful fund raising. Classic

**EXHIBIT 11.1. Classic Fund Raising Formula—Sample Gift Table $1 Million Goal**

| No. of Gifts | Amount | Total Gifts | Cumulative Amount | Cumulative % of Goal |
|---|---|---|---|---|
| | | **Major Gifts** | | |
| 1 | $100,000 | $100,000 | $ 100,000 | 10% |
| 2 | 50,000 | 100,000 | 200,000 | 20 |
| 4 | 25,000 | 100,000 | 300,000 | 30 |
| | | **Special Gifts** | | |
| 8 | $ 2,500 | $100,000 | $ 400,000 | 40% |
| 16 | 6,250 | 100,000 | 500,000 | 50 |
| 32 | 3,125 | 100,000 | 600,000 | 60 |
| 64 | 1,560 | 99,840 | 699,840 | 70 |
| | | **General Gifts** | | |
| Many | Less than 1,500 | $300,160 | $1,000,000 | 100% |

**EXHIBIT 11.2. Classic Fund Raising Formula Sample Gift Table $100,000 Goal**

| No. of Gifts | Amount | Total Gifts | Cumulative Amount | Cumulative % of Goal |
|---|---|---|---|---|
| | | **Major Gifts** | | |
| 2 | $5,000 | $10,000 | $ 10,000 | 10% |
| 4 | 2,500 | 10,000 | 20,000 | 20 |
| 10 | 1,000 | 10,000 | 30,000 | 30 |
| | | **Special Gifts** | | |
| 20 | $ 500 | $10,000 | $ 40,000 | 40% |
| 80 | 250 | 20,000 | 60,000 | 60 |
| 250 | 100 | 25,000 | 85,000 | 85 |
| | | **General Gifts** | | |
| Many | less than $100 | $15,000 | $100,000 | 100% |

**EXHIBIT 11.3. Classic Fund Raising Formula Environmental Factors Rating Chart**

| Factor | Low | Medium | High | Can It Be Changed? | Compensated For? |
|---|---|---|---|---|---|
| Prosperous geographic area | | | X | | |
| Size of population | | | X | | |
| Corporate funding base | | | X | | |
| Foundation funding base | | | X | | |
| Wealthy individuals | | | X | | |
| Community power structure | | | X | | |
| Popularity of organization/cause | | | X | | |
| History of committed donors | | | X | | |
| Donor/client base | | | X | | |
| Range of funding options available | | | X | | |
| Reputation for dedicated board leadership | | | X | | |
| Wealth & influence of board | | | X | | |
| Track record of completed programs | | | X | | |
| Reputation for professional management | | | X | | |
| Donor/volunteer involvement opportunities | | | X | | |

*NONFORMULA ENVIRONMENTAL FACTORS*

| Factor | Low | Medium | High | Can It Be Changed? | Compensated For? |
|---|---|---|---|---|---|
| Culture Diversity | | | ? | | |
| Ethnic Values | | | X | | |
| Isolation factor—Geography | | | X | | |
| Isolation factor—Economics | | | X | | |
| Isolation factor—Fear | | | X | | |
| Government factor | | | ? | | |

formula organizations would rate "high" on most of those in the first section, but might rate low on those in the second section.

## CLASSIC FORMULA ENVIRONMENTAL FACTORS

### Prosperous Geographic Area
Clearly an advantage to fund raising, a prosperous geographic area at least means that money is there to be sought.

### Size of Population
The greater the population, the larger the possible prospect pool, the smaller the population, the smaller the pool. The amount of money it is possible to raise can be limited by population size unless an organization has a client/donor base that extends outside its population base, as is the case with universities.

Depending on the cause, however, a small population base can have certain advantages: greater visibility and recognition, easy access to top decision makers, more entre to the media, easier access to volunteers, and more participation by individual donors.

### Corporate Funding Base
The larger the number of corporate headquarters or regional offices and plants, the greater the corporate prospect pool, as well as the prospective solicitor pool. Even with geographic prosperity and population size rated favorably, if a city's employment base is dominated by one entity, such as government or universities, fund raising possibilities and leadership choices will probably be affected by that circumstance.

### Foundation Funding Base
It is fortunate indeed to be located in a city like Minneapolis, where state laws have long encouraged the formation of hundreds of foundations. But in a state like Montana, significant foundations can just about be counted on two hands, and are unlikely to ever be a sizable source of funding.

### Wealthy Individuals
Since nearly 90 percent of all private contributions are given by individuals, the existence of wealthy individuals and access to them are important factors in most successful fund raising. Certain causes, however, do not seem to be particularly attractive to individual donors. For them, access to wealthy individuals is important for influence leveraging, but not for personal contributions.

### Access to Community Power Structure
Every community has a power structure made up of movers and shakers, the people who make things happen. An organization's ability to identify and build access to that power structure will affect its fund raising potential.

Sometimes there are separate political and economic power structures, but usually they are intertwined to varying degrees.

## Popularity of Organization or Cause

Fund raising will be affected by an organization's public popularity and visibility, or lack thereof. If a cause is controversial, it may limit donor appeal, but it may also engender strong loyalties and committed donors and volunteers (e.g., an organization for conscientious objectors). An organization may be popular, but with only a specific segment of the population, which would limit its donor universe (e.g., Italian American Community Services).

## History of Committed Donors

Past contributors are the most likely source of future funding, and having a relatively stable, committed cadre of donors over time gives an organization great credibility with prospective donors. In addition, people dislike traveling the philanthropic road alone (Seymour, 1966). This desire of donors not to be out there alone has particular significance for start-up organizations, for organizations attempting to establish a private funding base for the first time, and for organizations with small numbers of donors.

## Donor/Client Base

The users of an organization's services, such as alumni, concert-goers, or patients, are its natural potential donor constituency. An organization is at a great disadvantage if its client base is not a significant potential donor base. Rather than being connected to the organization through use of its services, it becomes difficult for a donor to determine the quality of the services provided, because the organization stands between the donor and the service user (Gronbjerg, 1993).

## Range of Funding Options Available

The range of funding options available to an organization is related to which of the five donor markets it is able to access: individuals, corporations, foundations, associations, and government (Mixer, 1993). An option like planned giving, for example, is utilized primarily by individuals. That positions organizations whose missions do not easily attract individual donors very unfavorably; this most profitable of the private donor markets is largely inaccessible to them.

Consequently, planned giving, a fast-growing donor option, is also largely unusable; thus building an endowment is unlikely too, since endowments are funded primarily by individuals who make planned gifts (Mixer, 1993). Since direct mail is a primary means both for soliciting individual gifts and for acquiring new donors, this major fund raising strategy may be unproductive for these organizations as well.

## Reputation for Dedicated Board Leadership

Many organizations, particularly smaller ones, have extremely dedicated board members, but no one outside the organization knows it. With no reputation in the community, an advantage is lost.

## Wealth and Influence of Board

There is a good reason why people of wealth and influence make up the great majority of board members for classic formula organizations: it is a very effective means of institutionalizing the donor relationship, thereby assuring a stable pool of major contributors and fund raising volunteers (Gronbjerg, 1993). Many boards are composed mostly of parents, social workers, musicians, or the like, few of whom are apt to possess abundant wealth or influence. Since a classic formula board is expected to give 15 to 30 percent of the goal and to be the core of the major gift solicitors, this is an enormously important missing piece for which nonformula organizations must somehow compensate.

## Track Record of Completed Programs

An organization's potential will be judged by its past performance in advancing its mission and in funding it.

## Reputation for Professional Management

Never mind that some of the most blatant violations are committed by the most professionally managed not-for-profits, the all-volunteer or smaller organization is usually at a perceived disadvantage here. Since sophisticated and highly complex management skills are usually required of organizations receiving government grants and contracts, they are likely to have a competitive advantage on this factor.

## Donor and Volunteer Involvement Opportunities

Volunteering is a major catalyst for giving. Actual participation in an organization's programs creates a pride of association that makes for committed donors (Panas, 1984). If an organization must limit direct volunteer involvement because of confidentiality or safety requirements, (e.g., a battered women's shelter), that will be a hindrance to its fund raising efforts.

# NONFORMULA ENVIRONMENTAL FACTORS

## Cultural Diversity

When the classic formula was developed, cultural diversity was neither an issue nor a factor to be considered, but cultural diversity in an organization and on its board is now an asset in the eyes of most institutional funders. Cultural diversity is not, however, synonymous with "minority" or "people of color." It means having a variety of people represented, rather than all of any one kind.

## Ethnic Values

The classic fund raising formula was developed and generally operates using the values of the "white, Anglo-Saxon male network" (Burlingame & Hulse, 1991), whose members are still the CEOs and board members of most of the corporate world and many other funding sources. Fund raisers and organizations who share those same ethnic values are at an advantage when trying to access funding markets compared with, for example, a Native American whose culture teaches that it is impolite to look another person directly in the eye, that it is important to give but unacceptable to ask, and that one must never put one's self ahead of another person. It may be extremely difficult for an African American who grew up in constant fear of violence under unjust segregation laws to seek funding from a source that was once viewed as oppressive.

A diversity of ethnic values in an organization may result in many inclusive and creative innovations, but it can also cause a certain amount of tension, misunderstanding, and sometimes ethical confusion that must be resolved promptly and sensitively.

## Isolation Factors

There are different causes of isolation, all of which can make fund raising more difficult and affect outcomes:

- *Geography.* Sinte Gleske Tribal College on the Rosebud Sioux Indian Reservation in South Dakota is over five hours from an airport. There are no hotels, restaurants, banks, or supermarkets there. Many Alaskan towns and cities, including the state capital, can be reached only by air or water. Rural or small-town not-for-profits are often located hours away from any major potential funders. Since face-to-face solicitation is by far the most profitable and cost-effective fund raising strategy (Warner, 1975), geographic isolation can be a negative factor in fund raising. An organization in a small city which is a satellite to a much larger city can be so overshadowed by its neighbor, both in visibility and in perceived need, that it acts as an isolating factor, making fund raising particularly arduous.
- *Economics.* Most Indian reservations are further isolated by poor economics: a dearth of viable employers, poor healthcare, limited educational opportunities, and unemployment rates of up to 65 percent. Many urban neighborhoods in this country are isolated by miles of deteriorated and abandoned buildings, by poor public transportation and services, and the few viable businesses within their boundaries, such as liquor stores, often contribute to the problem (Gronbjerg, 1993). Many of these neighborhoods don't have hotels, restaurants, supermarkets, or banks either.
- *Fear.* In many urban neighborhoods, fear is an isolating factor: fear of having one's car broken into while attending a meeting, fear of

drug-dealing, fear of theft or vandalism, fear of being accosted by street people, fear of drive-by shootings. An organization's mission itself can engender fear, as was the case for AIDS causes in the early days of the AIDS crisis, and is the case with battered women's shelters where secrecy is a requirement for safety.

*Government Factor*
The classic fund raising formula applies only to private sector fund raising. The influence of successful government grant-seeking on private sector fund raising, either positive or negative, is not recognized or acknowledged in the formula. Government funding bestows on not-for-profits a certain amount of public credibility and provides legitimate access to the political arena (Gronbjerg, 1993). The not-for-profit can often leverage its government relationships and influence with the private sector, and in reverse can leverage its private sector relationships and influence with government. There is evidence that public funding may also increase agency effectiveness (Krashinsky, 1990).

An organization receiving government funding risks incurring hidden and often unrecognized transaction costs and co-optation by government. Interfacing occurs primarily with an agency's staff, often relegating its board to the status of resource-dependent bystanders (Young, 1993). An organization's structure and goals may be altered and its mission distorted to obtain the resources it needs. The organization must also establish and monitor key relationships with constantly changing actors, and anticipate future policy directions that could alter its environment or funding level (Gronbjerg, 1993).

## Nonformula Fund Raising Research

Most fund raising research has been conducted with classic formula organizations. They are far easier to survey than nonformula organizations, who tend to have less standardized outputs, often have no professional fund raising staff, and may not track fund raising results or costs uniformly or consistently. If the classic formula does not work for some organizations, how are they to determine what will work? Can they all use a similar formula or must each custom design its own individual formula? Might one formula be developed that would work at least for all organizations engaged in similar work?

Using the premise that a nonformula organization has a substantially different profile and fund raising environment than a classic formula organization, six community development organizations will be examined to determine if they fit the nonformula description, and whether they reveal a commonality of environment and formula. The organizations selected represent a cross-section based on population, size, geographic location, age, and degree of sophistication in fund raising.

The organizations surveyed are all affiliated with the national Neigh-borWorks® network of 173 independent, community-based development organizations that collectively make up the nation's largest system for restoring neighborhoods in decline. Developed by the congressionally chartered Neighborhood Reinvestment Corporation, NeighborWorks organizations rehabilitate or build some 7,000 homes and leverage over $340 million in direct reinvestment/service delivery annually in 44 states, the District of Columbia and Puerto Rico.

Each organization is a partnership of government, business, and residents of the low-income neighborhoods they serve. Each is required by charter to have a board composition that represents the partnership, with 51 percent being residents. Each organization has a revolving loan fund, usually capitalized by local government and corporate investors, from which it makes flexible loans to residents or potential homeowners who are not bankable.

## SINGLE ORGANIZATION—MULTIYEAR SURVEY

### Sacramento Neighborhood Housing Services

Exhibit 11.4 shows an eight-year giving history of one organization, Sacramento Neighborhood Housing Services (NHS), starting with 1987, the year it began operations. The high percentage of contributions from corporations and corporate foundations is typical of these organizations, because certain corporations are a natural constituency of low-income housing and community development: lenders, insurance companies, the real estate industry, and some utilities.

Over the eight years of this survey, lead gift size fell by one-third, while numbers of lead gifts rose from three to as high as eight, compensating for the drop in size. The lead gift for 1988 was a one-time occurrence—the profit from a new home donated by a builder. These results differ considerably from the classic formula expectation of one 10 percent gift or two 5 percent lead gifts.

The top 10 donors contributed from 55 to 92 percent of the total, compared with ⅓ expected in the classic formula. The top 12 donors contributed from 62 to 94 percent of the total, while the classic formula calls for the next 33 percent of contributions to come from the next 100 donors. Individual giving ranged from 1 to 6 percent, while the classic formula is based primarily on individual giving.

The annual attrition rate for nonrenewals was 33 to 54 percent, compared to 15 to 20 percent expected for the classic formula. The higher rate reflects the consolidations and bankruptcies in the lending industry, the volatility of the real estate industry, and the impact that losing even one major gift has with such a narrow donor base.

Actual gift tables for Sacramento NHS presented in Exhibits 11.5 and 11.6 further demonstrate how this organization's funding pattern differed

**EXHIBIT 11.4. Sacramento Neighborhood Housing Services—Multiyear Private Contributions Survey**

| Year | 1987 | 1988 | 1989 | 1990 | 1993 | 1994 |
|---|---|---|---|---|---|---|
| Private Donations to Operating Budget* | $105,400 | $109,344 | $114,670 | $131,770 | $128,384 | $133,193 |
| Lead Gift | $ 15,000 (x3) | $ 40,000 | $ 15,000 (x4) | $ 10,000 (x5) | $ 10,000 (x8) | $ 10,000 (x4) |
| % of Total Raised | 14% | 37% | 13% | 8% | 8% | 8% |
| % from Corporations, Foundations | 99% | 96% | 96% | 97% | 98% | 94% |
| % from Individuals | 1% | 4% | 4% | 2% | 2% | 6% |
| % from Top 10 Donors | 80% | 92% | 62% | 69% | 71% | 55% |
| % from Top 12 Donors | 86% | 94% | 77% | 76% | 77% | 62% |
| Total Number of Gifts Made | 49 | 57 | 87 | 74 | 63 | 89 |
| Dollar Attrition Rate (from previous years) | 38% | 38% | 47% | 54% | N/A | 33% |

* This survey does not include private funds raised for capital purposes or loan pools, nor does it include in-kind gifts, interest forgone or any type of financing mechanisms.

**EXHIBIT 11.5. Sacramento Neighborhood Housing Services—1987 Gift Table—$100,000 Goal (Actual)**

| No. of Gifts | Amount | Total Gifts | Cumulative Amount | Cumulative % of Goal |
|---|---|---|---|---|
| | | **Corporate Gifts** | | |
| 3 | $15,000 | $45,000 | $ 45,000 | 45% |
| 1 | 10,000 | 10,000 | 55,000 | 55 |
| 5 | 5,000 | 25,000 | 80,000 | 80 |
| 4 | 2,500 | 13,600 | 93,600 | 93.6 |
| 9 | 1,000 up | 10,200 | 103,800 | 103.8 |
| 1 | 500 | 500 | 104,300 | 104.3 |
| | | **Individual Gifts** | | |
| 26 | Various | $ 1,100 | $105,000 | 105.4% |

Lead Gift = 14% of total raised      Corporate = 99% of total raised
Top 10    = 80% of total raised      Individual =  1% of total raised
Top 12    = 86% of total raised

**EXHIBIT 11.6. Sacramento Neighborhood Housing Services—1994 Gift Table—$130,000 Goal (Actual)**

| No. of Gifts | Amount | Total Gifts | Cumulative Amount | Cumulative % of Goal |
|---|---|---|---|---|
| | | **Corporate Gifts** | | |
| 4 | $10,000 | $40,000 | $ 40,000 | 31% |
| 1 | 8,000 | 8,000 | 48,000 | 37 |
| 7 | 5,000 | 35,000 | 83,000 | 64 |
| 4 | 2,500 up | 12,500 | 95,500 | 74 |
| 5 | 2,000 | 10,000 | 105,500 | 82 |
| 7 | 1,000 | 17,000 | 122,500 | 95 |
| | | **Individual Gifts** | | |
| 51 | Various | $10,693 | $133,193 | 103% |

Lead Gift =  8% of total raised      Corporate = 92% of total raised
Top 10    = 55% of total raised      Individua l =  8% of total raised
Top 12    = 62% of total raised

from the classic formula over time. In the span of eight years, 94 to 99 percent of contributions came from fewer than 30 donors annually.

## MULTIPLE ORGANIZATIONS—SINGLE YEAR SURVEY

Exhibit 11.7 is an analysis of private operating contributions made to six NeighborWorks organizations in their most recent fiscal years. Until the 1980s, when the lending industry was deregulated and many institutions failed, operating budgets of NeighborWorks organizations were funded almost totally by banks and thrifts, and rehabilitation lending was the core service offered. Since the erosion of that donor base began, most NeighborWorks organizations have been scrambling to secure additional sources of scarce operating dollars from other kinds of contributors, as well as from earned income: fees for services, real estate development fees, income from joint ventures with for-profits, property management fees, and so on. There have been enormous management implications with that shift in funding sources, and a much higher level of complex skills and technical knowledge in real estate development, finance, lending, community organizing and fund raising is required of both staff and boards.

### Chicago Neighborhood Housing Services
One of the first organizations developed by Neighborhood Reinvestment, Chicago Neighborhood Housing Services (NHS) is also the largest and has the most sophisticated fund raising operation in the network. It serves eight neighborhoods (having completed work in seven others) and has two subsidiaries: NHS Redevelopment Corporation and Neighborhood Lending Services, which is the third largest rehab lender to low- and moderate-income homeowners in the city of Chicago. A resource development staff of five is responsible for both fund raising and public relations and raises private contributions for both operating and capital purposes. Chicago NHS spends less than 10 percent of its operating budget on fund raising and public relations combined, which amounts to about 20 percent of operating funds raised. If private funds raised for capital were factored in, that percentage would be lower.

### Los Angeles
Los Angeles NHS experienced sudden major growth after the 1992 riots in its south central neighborhood. It has had a full-time development director for only two years and is still building its fund raising capacity. Operating in four widely separated neighborhoods, this organization also raises over $300,000 a year in private funds for capital projects.

### Sacramento
SNHS has a part-time development director who also does public relations. In spite of California's recent recession, which decimated the organization's primary funding base of real estate developers, fund raising results

**EXHIBIT 11.7. Neighborworks® Network—Neighborhood Housing Services (NHS)—Private Contributions Survey**

| Organization | Chicago, IL NHS | Los Angeles, CA NHS | Sacramento, CA NHS | Inglewood, CA NHS | Great Falls, MT NHS | Ithaca, NY NHS |
|---|---|---|---|---|---|---|
| Year | 1994/95 | 1994 | 1994 | 1994 | 1994 | 1994 |
| Population | 3.4 Million | 3.5 Million | 469,365 | 113,000 | 60,000 | 40,000 |
| Organization Age | 20 Years | 11 Years | 8 Years | 16 Years | 15 Years | 18 Years |
| Characteristics | All | All | Government | Satellite to L.A. | Agriculture | Universities |
| Fund raising Staff | 5* | 1 | .5* | Exec. Dir. | Ass't. Dir. | .5 |
| Operating Budget | $4,327,000 | $1,200,000 | $400,000 | $262,000 | $163,415 | $289,684 |
| Private Donations to Operating | $1,610,446 | $374,241 | $133,193 | $90,054 | $72,535 | $83,684 |
| % of Budget | 37% | 31% | 33% | 35% | 44% | 29% |
| Total Number of Gifts | 395 | 91 | 89 | 18 | 557 | 389 |
| Lead Gift | $250,000 | $40,000 | $10,000 (x4) | $10,000 | $8,000 | $10,000 |
| % of Total Given | 15.5% | 11% | 8% | 11% | 11% | 12% |
| Corporations/ Corp. Foundations | 77% | 88.5% | 87% | 78% | 80% | 41% |
| Foundations | 20% | 10.7% | 8% | 22% | 2% | 21% |
| Individuals | 3% | .8% | 6% | 0% | 18% | 37% |
| Annual Attrition Rate | 6% | 30% | 33% | 20% | N/A | 11% |

* Fund-raising staff does both fund raising and public relations

This survey does not include private funds raised for capital (housing) purposes, including loan pools. It does not include in-kind gifts, interest deferred or foregone, below market financing, sale of tax credits, government funds through intermediaries, investment income, fees for services, etc.

have slowly grown. In 1994, fund raising and public relations costs combined amounted to less than 20 percent of total operating contributions received. The percentage would be even lower if private capital funding were included in total contributions.

### Inglewood (CA)
Inglewood is a satellite city to Los Angeles, and most major businesses operating there have their primary units in Los Angeles, making fund raising more difficult than if the city were geographically more separate. Even the riots of 1992, which involved substantial damage in Inglewood, brought little extra attention or funding. Inglewood NHS fund raising has been managed in the past primarily by its executive director, which is typical of most NeighborWorks organizations. However, since taking over the city's entire rehabilitation loan program, Inglewood NHS has hired a staffperson to do fund raising half-time and marketing half-time.

### Great Falls (MT)
Since the NHS was formed in 1980, Great Falls, a relatively small, isolated city, has experienced several serious economic downturns as major employers, including the military, have cut back or pulled out altogether. The original NHS operating budget of $60,000 was funded by about 25 corporate donors, mostly lending institutions. Since then they have had to aggressively seek funding from a larger segment of the community, including individuals and small businesses. Their newsletter goes out to 6,000 residents, and they have 557 donors to their annual fund campaign. The individual giving picture is somewhat skewed by one $6,900 repeating gift. Fund raising is managed by the organization's computer specialist.

### Ithaca (NY)
Located in the smallest city surveyed, Ithaca NHS has nevertheless been one of the most successful programs in the NeighborWorks network. Their outstanding track record and high visibility in a small but highly educated community has made it possible for them to raise money from individuals far in excess of any other NeighborWorks organization; the total raised, however, is somewhat unbalanced by one $5,000 gift which has been renewed annually for a number of years. They too, must seek funds from a large number of donors, but their annual attrition rate is quite low.

## National Research

National research of private sector contributions to all NeighborWorks organizations in the country over a 15-year period closely parallels the information given by those surveyed for this chapter (Neighborhood Reinvestment Corporation, 1995). Corporate contributions equaled 98.2 percent

**EXHIBIT 11.8. Private Sector Contributions—NeighborWorks® Organizations 1979–1993**

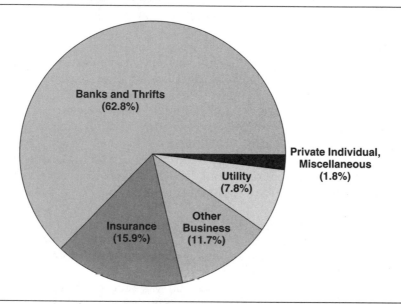

Source: Esmail Baku, Neighborhood Reinvestment Corp. Research and Information Services Annual Surveys, 1979–1993.

of the total, with individual and miscellaneous giving making up the remainder (see Exhibit 11.8).

## Comparative Environmental Rating

These surveys indicate that corporations supply almost all the private sector operating support to these community development organizations, with individual contributions significant only in small communities. Whether that anomality is due to external environmental factors or to greater effort expended to offset the organizations' reduced options can not be determined without more extensive research. Most NeighborWorks organizations have only recently begun asking for contributions from their board members, and have not yet even attempted to raise funds from other individuals.

Based on this research, a composite NeighborWorks organization is rated in Exhibit 11.9 using the fund-raising environmental factors chart previously shown (Exhibit 11.3). A classic formula organization would rate "high" on almost all factors listed. A composite NeighborWorks organization would rate "high" on only 20 percent of the classic formula

## EXHIBIT 11.9. Classic Fund Raising Formula—Environmental Factors Rating Chart

| Factor | Low | Medium | High | Can It Be Changed? | Compensated For? |
|--------|-----|--------|------|--------------------|--------------------|
| Prosperous geographic area | X | | | NO | Limited |
| Size of population | | X | | NO | Limited |
| Corporate funding base | X | | | NO | Limited |
| Foundation funding base | X | | | NO | Limited |
| Wealthy individuals | X | | | NO | Limited |
| Community power structure | | | X | | |
| Popularity of organization/cause | | X | | YES | |
| History of committed donors | | X | | YES | |
| Donor/client base | X | | | NO | Limited |
| Range of funding options available | X | | | Maybe | Limited |
| Reputation for dedicated board leadership | | X | | YES | |
| Wealth & influence of board | X | | | NO | YES |
| Track record of completed programs | | X | | YES | |
| Reputation for professional management | | | X | | |
| Donor/volunteer involvement opportunities | | X | | YES | |

### NONFORMULA ENVIRONMENTAL FACTORS

| Factor | Low | Medium | High | Can It Be Changed? | Compensated For? |
|--------|-----|--------|------|--------------------|--------------------|
| Culture Diversity | | | X | | |
| Ethnic Values | | | X | | |
| Isolation factor—Geography | X | | | NO | Limited |
| Isolation factor—Economics | X | | | NO | Limited |
| Isolation factor—Fear | X | | | Limited | YES |
| Government factor | | | X | | |

environmental factors, indicating that its fund raising environment is substantially different from that in which classic formula organizations function.

## Comparative Formula Rating

Using information from the composite environmental factors rating chart (Exhibit 11.9), the composite ratings in Exhibit 11.10 illustrate how the fund-raising formula for these organizations diverges substantially from the classic fund-raising formula.

## Financial and Management Implications

Nonformula fund raising is required of organizations whose profiles and fund-raising environments differ substantially from organizations that successfully raise funds using the widely accepted classic fund raising formula (Exhibit 11.10).

Environmental factors that are the most serious barriers to fund raising are those that preclude or significantly diminish the probability of an or-

**EXHIBIT 11.10. Classic Fund Raising Formula Rating Chart**

| | Low | Medium | High | Can It Be Changed? | Compensated For? |
|---|---|---|---|---|---|
| ▶ Top Down—Inside Out | Inside Out | | Top Down | | Limited |
| ▶ Peer Principle | | X | | | YES |
| ▶ Board Gives 15% of Goal | X | | | | With 100% Board Giving |
| ▶ Leadership Imperative | | | X | | |
| ▶ Lead Gift = 5%–10% of Goal | X | | | | 15%/20% or Several |
| ▶ Domino Theory | | X | | | |
| ▶ Advance Gifts = 40% | X | | | | 65%/80% |
| ▶ Attrition Rate = 15%–20% | X | | | | 30% Average |
| ▶ Rule of Thirds | X | | | | 70%/80% From Top 12 Donors |
| ▶ Scale of Gifts | X | | | | Revise |

ganization attracting individual gifts. Individual giving is by far the largest and most important private donor market to access. The inability to attract individual gifts excludes the use of planned giving as an option, which in turn makes establishing an endowment unlikely. An organization has few other effective means of assuring its long-term financial stability and viability.

Lack of a client/donor base and a wealthy, influential board of directors are probably the two greatest barriers to individual giving. It is very difficult to overcome the circumstance of clients who are unable to be significant donors by appealing to others outside the organization's sphere of operations for contributions. If the organization's mission is not one that easily generates individual giving, the problem is compounded. Without a wealthy, influential board of directors, an organization has to go further afield to draw in major donors and fund raising leadership. The commitment of such funders is likely to be more tenuous, and the difficulty of attracting enough of them usually means that much of the prospective donor pool is never approached at all, or must be solicited by staff.

Nonformula fund raising is not for beginners. Partly for lack of funds and partly out of ignorance of what is involved, it is often a beginner who is hired. This practice may account for much of the "revolving door" syndrome in the profession. Experience-based knowledge and judgment are required to accurately assess and rate relevant factors in the fund raising environment and devise a fund raising formula that will work. A high degree of creativity and innovation is needed to figure out how to compensate for low-rated or missing environmental factors. Superior donor cultivation and satisfaction must be achieved to hold down attrition rates, and new ways to institutionalize donor relationships must be explored if private gifts are ever to be a significant and stable income stream.

## Implications for Funders

The expectation of many in government that not-for-profit organizations can raise private funding to make up for rescissions and budget cuts made by them is naive in the extreme for nonformula organizations. Government representatives at every level must be helped to understand that environmental barriers limit the ability of a nonformula organization to raise private sector funds.

Foundations and corporations too must face the reality that nonformula organizations may have extremely limited options for raising operating funds, and that project-designated or time-limited grants do not serve them or their constituents well. The assumption that these organizations can somehow raise the level of operating funding they need from some other source is simply not realistic.

# Bibliography

Baker, Dean. Telephone conversation with Mr. Baker of the Economic Policy Institute, Washington, DC. 1996.

Broce, Thomas E. *Fund Raising, The Guide to Raising Money from Private Sources.* (2nd ed.), Norman: University of Oklahoma Press, 1986.

Burlingame, Dwight E., and Hulse, L. J. *Taking Fund Raising Seriously.* San Francisco: Jossey-Bass, 1991.

Dove, Kent E. *Conducting a Successful Capital Campaign.* San Francisco: Jossey-Bass, 1988.

Greenfield, James M. *Accountability, Performance Measurement, and Profitability.* AHP Region X/XI Joint Conference, 1994.

Greenfield, James M. *Fund-Raising, Evaluating and Managing the Fund Development Process.* New York: John Wiley & Sons, 1991.

Greenfield, James M. *Memorandum Regarding Attrition Rates.* Newport Beach, CA: 1995.

Gronbjerg, Kirsten A. *Understanding Nonprofit Funding.* San Francisco: Jossey-Bass, 1993.

Klein, Kim. *Fundraising for Social Change.* Inverness, CA: Chardon Press, 1994.

Krashinsky, Michael. "Management Implications of Government Funding of Nonprofit Organizations: Views from the United States and Canada." *Nonprofit Management & Leadership,* I, I. San Francisco: Jossey-Bass, 1990.

Lord, James G. *The Raising of Money.* Cleveland, OH: Third Sector Press, 1987.

Marts & Lundy, *Fund-Raising Guide.* Oakland: NHSA, 1983.

Mixer, Joseph R. *Principles of Professional Fundraising.* San Francisco: Jossey-Bass, 1993.

Neighborhood Reinvestment Corporation, Research & Information Services *Annual Survey 1979–1993.* Washington, DC, 1995.

NeighborWorks® Network *Annual fund-raising surveys.* Chicago NHS, Casey Hoffman, Development Director; Los Angeles NHS, Teri Zambon, Development Director; Sacramento NHS, Robert Ballou CFRE, Development Director; Inglewood NHS, Martina Guilfoil, Executive Director; Great Falls NHS, Jane Roberts, Computer Specialist; Ithaca NHS, Sue Perlgut, Development Coordinator.

Panas, Jerold. *Mega Gifts.* Chicago, IL: Pluribus Press, 1984.

Rosso, Henry A. *Achieving Excellence in Fund Raising.* San Francisco: Jossey-Bass, 1991.

Seymour, Harold J. *Designs for Fund-Raising, Principles, Patterns, Techniques.* New York; McGraw Hill, 1966.

Warner, Irving R. *The Art of Fund Raising.* New York: Bantam Books, 1975.

Young, Dennis R. *Governing, Leading, and Managing Nonprofit Organizations.* San Francisco: Jossey-Bass, 1993.

# U.S. Models and International Dimensions of Philanthropic Fund Raising

LILYA WAGNER, EdD, CFRE

*Indiana University Center on Philanthropy*

How appropriate are U.S. models for philanthropic fund raising in other countries? What lessons can we learn from activities in other cultures and nations? While considering those important questions in a period of world history that has experienced an extraordinary shift in social and political geography, I'm reminded of an incident I witnessed during my growing-up years in South America.

An American preacher spoke through an interpreter to a large Aymara Indian audience in the Altiplano of Bolivia. His proficiency of that unique Indian language was deficient; he could understand just enough to know what was being said but could not preach in it. Therefore, he preached in Spanish and used an interpreter. As he got caught up in his message, he was only vaguely aware of his interpreter's words. Soon, however, he began to use those pauses to listen more carefully. "That wasn't what I said," he thought, and promptly interrupted the interpreter. "You aren't telling them what I'm preaching," he remonstrated. The interpreter gave him a long and discerning look before answering, "Es verdad. Pero yo se que la gente necesita" (It's true, but I know what the people need).

There's a lesson to be learned through this homely illustration. While well-intentioned and superbly equipped to share fund raising knowledge around the world community, we Americans sometimes impose our own experiences and views on peoples and nations that are hardly equipped or inclined to function or think in the same way. The corporate sector is well aware of missteps and misunderstandings that plague the world traveler. Protocol, customs, etiquette, hand gestures, body language, gift giving and receiving are all topics on which the international businessperson receives some training, either self-imposed or corporation-induced. Non-profit personnel, especially those who travel abroad as consultants, can hardly ignore such important information about the global community.

The purpose of this chapter is to develop a conceptual framework to understand cultural diversity and pluralism as it relates to nongovernmental organizations (NGOs) around the globe, and to consider the pitfalls and cautions, outline basic differences, and make recommendations that can guide individual thinking in selective situations. Although I will draw examples from various parts of the world in developing the points made in this chapter, I will concentrate on the Baltic nation of Estonia. There are two reasons for this focus. First, I am Estonian-born, a refugee who eagerly and earnestly embraced all that is American yet one who has rediscovered a nation of origin. Therefore I have become knowledgeable about one redeveloping nation in a unique way. Second, Estonia is currently the most advanced of the newly independent states (NIS) in politics, economy, cultural development, and nonprofit emphasis. As a result, the third sector has experienced rapid growth in a rather salubrious climate.

There are many perils in making international generalizations. A book that has caused much comment and discussion is Robert S. McNamara's *In Retrospect* (1995). After years of silence, McNamara, the architect of the Vietnam war, outlines the mistakes made by people in the Kennedy and Johnson administrations who participated in the decisions. Whatever one's view of that whole debacle, the point is made when McNamara writes, "When it came to Vietnam, we found ourselves setting policy for a region that was terra incognita." Fund raising professionals working abroad may well be in *terra incognita* themselves unless they keep in mind the dangers of generalizing across nationalities and cultures, and fail to focus on the individual and unique context of each nation.

A foundation executive made the comment, "We're better off empowering NGO leadership in other nations rather than imposing U.S. views and practices. Too often we're alarmingly unaware of vast cultural and economic differences to facilitate a transfer of knowledge." *Do's and Taboos Around the World,* a delightful book on protocol, customs and etiquette, puts it this way, "If only the world's Customs inspectors could train their German shepherds to sniff out the invisible baggage we all manage to slip with us into foreign countries. They are like secret little land mines of the mind" (Axtell, 1993).

Making generalizations across cultures and nations can lead to erroneous assumptions and advice. For example, Estonia, Latvia, and Lithuania, are small Baltic nations that share boundaries. Yet there is no similarity among their languages. Their predominant religious orientation varies. Their cultural practices differ. Lumping these three NIS into one perspective certainly leads to less than intelligent views.

The average American has been known to say, "Southeast Asians all look alike to me." While no intelligent and educated individual would verbalize such a notion, we often use the same approach for Japanese professionals as for the Thais. Yet the two nations, both part of a same region, have enormous differences in historical context, nonverbal language, social relationships, and other factors that influence fund raising.

One also has to consider the homogeneity versus heterogeneity of a population group. India, which has a heterogeneous population, is more hospitable to nongovernmental organizations than is Sweden. With our preconceived notions about advanced civilizations, we might find this surprising. However, in Sweden, government is assigned the task of social responsibility, not the nonprofit sector.

Western views and practices do not always have a receptive audience in some nations. Although the "Yankee Go Home" mentality is not as prevalent as it was perhaps two decades ago, some of our ways of doing things are a threat if not an actual menace in some cultures. Our rich and healthy tradition of philanthropy and the nonprofit sector has caught on in much of the global community, or has been strengthened in nations that had some semblance of philanthropic and nonprofit practice and outlook. However, in much of the world it's still a foreign concept laden with suspicion, or worse yet, perceived as a menace. For example, in Bangladesh there is a backlash against NGOs. According to a powerful Bangladeshi politician, "These NGOs have challenged the most basic traditions of Islam" (Klein, 1995).

While we attempt to boost giving to the U.S. nonprofit sector each year, and find ourselves in greater need of philanthropic aid than ever before (partially due to cutbacks in government funding), we must remember that the funding situation is even more crucial and critical in much of the world community. How does one promote and engender a philanthropic attitude if there is no such tradition in a particular country? How can individuals be urged to give to others if their own needs are not yet met? Maslow's hierarchy of needs certainly comes into focus when such questions are asked.

In Estonia, for example, voluntarism surged into action at the same time nationalism became a predominant preoccupation of citizens, in approximately the 1860s. During the freedom years, between World Wars I and II, Estonia experienced tremendous economic, cultural, and educational growth, and thereby was hospitable to voluntary action for the public good. Then for nearly 50 years, foremost in citizens' minds was the danger of losing one's life in an instant and at the whim of the occupying forces. Concern about food, housing, heating, clothing and other basic necessities were paramount. Now that the country is making progress at the lower levels of Maslow's hierarchy, the mood and attention of citizens is moving closer to civic responsibility and philanthropy. This step, however, could not be hastened. The basic needs had to be met before attention could be focused on progressing up the hierarchy.

Generosity exists in the global community. Common themes that shape innate generosity are:

- Government's role in encouraging, limiting, or enhancing voluntarism and philanthropy.
- Ethical values.
- Religious and/or cultural values that influence giving.

- Traditions that include or do not include philanthropic attitudes.
- Differences among developing nations and developed nations that have gained freedom in the last half-decade and are once again gaining ground on the economic, political, cultural, and educational scene.
- Accountability issues—why funds are raised and what will be done with those funds.
- Technical aspects and fund raising strategies.

Within these themes there is much variation. Virtually the only safe generalization is that while nonprofit or nongovernmental organizations differ among nations, they have some characteristics in common: "They are organizations formed to serve the public good, and income (or profits) from these organizations are not distributed to members or owners" (McCarthy et al., 1992). For the most part, their role is to serve the underserved or neglected, to empower citizens, and to advocate social change.

The context of philanthropic tradition, voluntary action, and nongovernmental organizations is vital to keep in mind when focusing on actual fund raising practice. The two aspects cannot be separated. In short, we cannot operate the same way in different parts of the world:

- Elias finds it difficult to raise funds for the Deaf-Blind Center because the organization is new and unique, catering to multiple-handicapped individuals. He's trying to raise funds in Israel, a nation that is moving away from its status as a social welfare state.
- Sylvia is concerned that her volunteer-driven organization can't motivate its board to seek financial resources. Sylvia's situation is common in many countries where boards are truly just high-ranking names listed on stationery. They are not expected to raise funds; such activity is unthinkable.
- Miguel is worried about his board's ability to influence major donors among the corporate community in his city. Corporate giving varies in the global community, particularly if corporations are government controlled and therefore do not have a philanthropic budget.
- Daphne wants to mobilize an alumni relations program, intending to build alumni loyalty and subsequently converting alumni into donors. Alumni loyalty, and therefore philanthropy, is a new concept in many developed nations, including England.
- Arieh wants to learn about fund raising, since his university is just beginning a fund raising program. He's not even sure he wants to be involved in what he considers "begging," a common attitude in many parts of the world.
- Vladimir is concerned about finding funds to supplant those that the government no longer provides. In Ukraine, as in many of the NIS, this is a serious problem.

In numerous countries, the issues of fund raising are new and crucial. Nonprofit or nongovernmental personnel want to find new means of raising funds and new donor markets—or simply want to know what fund raising is all about. These professionals often look to U.S. organizations and personnel in their search for anything from philosophy to techniques.

The following information is perhaps the beginning of a dialogue that can take place often as we share our wealth of experience and knowledge about fund raising with those who are just venturing into this exciting endeavor.

## Philanthropic Tradition

In the United States, we are fortunate to build resource development on a strong philanthropic base and outlook. This type of tradition does not exist in many nations.

In Ukraine, for example, the population has long relied on governmental agencies to address society's problems. Now that a change in government has taken place, and government funds no longer exist or are rechanneled, nongovernment organizations must develop support from individuals and tap into their generous spirit. The habit of giving has not been developed over time, and fund raising is difficult. Red Cross officials who depended on a "tax" levied by the government on each citizen now find it necessary to approach individuals and corporations themselves and appeal to a charitable instinct. Consequently, fund raising must begin at an earlier point than in the United States. When involved in fund raising counsel or activity in other nations, we must help professionals tap into attitudes and philosophies that lend themselves to philanthropy, while the concept itself may not exist.

In Estonia, thousands of voluntary organizations were organized during the independence period of 1920–1940. The independence movement during the years 1987–1991 saw a redevelopment of civil society, and once again nonprofit organizations, especially in the cultural and social welfare spheres, emerged with rapidity until their number now approximately equals that of pre-Soviet occupation times. However, the majority of the population is concerned with day-to-day subsistence, while a few have accumulated riches with capitalistic ventures. Therefore a philanthropic attitude has been difficult to foster. In addition, there is little experience in managing such organizations; currently, advice in nonprofit management is being sought from the United States.

## Taxes as an Incentive to Giving

Even though a tax advantage is not the primary or even secondary reason for giving in the United States, at least we have a tax system that promotes charitable involvement. The same is not true in many other countries. In Israel, for example, there are slight tax advantages for making charitable gifts but not many donors know about them nor do they take advantage of them. The sophisticated planned gift vehicles we employ in America to secure larger gifts have no tax-favored or recognized status in most nations.

The tax incentive for giving is not universal. Before providing advice to professionals from other nationalities and cultures, it's wise to check on the taxation system. It does make a difference in giving in the United States, and that difference should be understood.

## Motivations for Giving

Although some motivations for charitable giving cross cultural and national lines, important differences exist. Certainly in many countries, there are individuals who are moved by compassion, or the desire to make a difference. However, sometimes even a simple concept can take on a different interpretation.

For example, when asked "Why do people give," professionals attending a fund raising workshop in Israel identified the primary motivation as "guilt." In the United States, we're taught that guilt is not a strong enough motivator, and will not provide long-term support. In Israel's culture, however, if an individual lives in another country, there is the guilt of not building up the homeland of Israel. If armed service is avoided by living elsewhere, there is inherent guilt. Another aspect of guilt is related to having survived the Holocaust while so many did not. Fund raising executives must explore donor motivations that are unique to a culture and tradition, as well as those which are universal, and apply them in making their appeals.

## Fund Raising Is Begging, or Worse

Although we haven't totally conquered the "tin cup mentality" in the United States, at least resource development has achieved some respectability and acceptance (even if we have to hide behind euphemisms such as advancement or resource development at times). In some nations, fund raising still has the image of begging or groveling for aid. Professionals in Israel joke about being a "shnorrer," which means professional beggar. In other nations, fund raising has the same image. The act of asking for money is a long way from respectability. Fund raisers are considered moochers and panhandlers.

In many nations, there are the "haves" and the "have nots," and they generally don't give to each other. Disparity between social groups is strong and doesn't cross over boundaries; philanthropic action is rare. This is true in nations such as Bolivia and Thailand.

However, experienced and emerging professionals in many nations are optimistic that a change in attitude will lend credibility to their activity and eventually accomplish philanthropic behavior. As in the United States, nonprofit leaders are at the forefront of replacing apology for fund raising with pride.

## Impact of the Economy

This point is so well understood that it hardly needs to be referenced. However, great differences exist on how a nation's economic situation affects nongovernmental organizations. Consider the impact of the economy in the NIS. In Estonia, the average salary is the equivalent of $36 to $100 per month. The free market economy is making strides, but some portions of the population still suffer, such as the pensioners. Those who have tapped into moneymaking ventures may not be likely to share their good fortune, given the deprivation they've experienced in the past 50 years. Time will tell. Economic impact should be studied before any fund raising advice or plan is shared between U.S. professionals and those from other countries.

## Board Roles and Involvement

In most countries, there are no expectations for board involvement in fund raising—if, indeed, boards exist as we know them in the United States. In Israel, members are selected, for the most part, for name value only. In Belarus, where nonprofits are just emerging, boards are forming with undefined and unclear roles. Mobilizing boards to secure financial resources for their organizations will take considerable time and training.

## Accountability

The issue of accountability has surfaced in the past two years with tremendous impact on the U.S. nonprofit sector. Our donors want more information on the effect of their donations, government is considering regulations and measures that would vastly affect our profession, and boards are looking over our shoulders with increasing intensity.

Imagine the questions being asked in nations where fund raising has not achieved the status of a legitimate activity or profession. Prior to addressing accountability issues, fund raising personnel must answer even more basic questions, including, "Why are you asking me?" "Why do you need money now?" and the like. The matter of reporting to government and donors varies greatly among nations that have NGOs or an emerging nonprofit sector. Governmental controls may prohibit certain activities, and impede even the most basic asking process. Without an awareness of accountability as unique to a situation, a fund raising professional may run afoul of government and other powerful entities.

## Fund Raising Techniques

The average fund raiser in the United States has a wealth of techniques available, ranging from special events to one-on-one solicitation of major donors. We have the resources to support such endeavors—telephone and mail systems that are usually efficient, easy means of travel, computer support, and other technological advances.

In some countries, phone service is feeble and in some cultures it's downright rude to call without notice. Mail delivery is undependable and difficult in some countries and regions. Many contacts have to take place person-to-person, an effort made even more difficult by inefficiency in the transportation system—or perhaps even lack of transportation. Often there is no such thing as electronic transfer of funds, or a PBS appeal for TV programming. Alumni loyalty and therefore support is virtually non-existent in most of the world. For all these reasons, fund raisers must be selective and discreet, innovative yet practical in seeking resources.

For example, direct mail has been very successful in Asia, partly because there isn't much junk mail. A direct-mail appeal in Hong Kong yielded a 50 percent response rate. Also, the United States could learn something from Australia, where electronic transfer of funds is commonplace, and Australian fund raisers use the banking systems for maximum benefit. The standard and accepted U.S. fund raising techniques must be adapted to suit each situation, or may not work at all. While many nations are making great strides, some traditional U.S. techniques may not be possible, feasible, or even desirable.

## Corporate and Foundation Fund Raising

Two markets we almost take for granted in the United States are corporations and foundations. Although we lament about foundations not giving enough of their assets, and decry seeming corporate stinginess, at least we have those markets accessible to us.

Many corporations in the NIS or other countries are foreign-held. In Ukraine, Johnson & Johnson is trying to make inroads in the developing economy. Mexico has a number of U.S.-held corporations. The Japanese have entered markets in a number of countries. The appeal to these corporations must differ from what we're used to in the United States. Why should a foreign-held company care about services for the local population? That's a difficult question to answer, and therefore a difficult appeal to make.

Ways of requesting corporate funds differ. In Japan, one needs persistence when approaching a corporation. Frequent visits and calls, to the extent that U.S. corporate executives would find annoying, are the accepted norm. However, it's not polite to set an actual figure for the donation; one should suggest units within which the donor may be comfortable.

## Prospect Research

In recent years, the issue of donor privacy has surfaced in the United States. For example, the Ohio Supreme Court ruled in January 1993 that a Toledo newspaper had the right to review donor records of the University of Toledo Foundation. However, while confidentiality of donor information may be at stake, generally we can compile prospect information to any extent that is practical and ethical, and we have relatively unlimited resources for doing so.

Contrast that with the situation in the Baltic States, where the KGB is a vivid and frightening memory. Learning about potential donors may not even be allowed by governments in some countries. Resources such as indexes or Who's who directories do not exist in many nations. Donor research is highly restricted by cultural mores in some areas. As a result, rapid, effective donor research cannot take place as in the United States, and the donor base takes longer to broaden, or even define.

## Donor Recognition

Recognition, such as awards and visibility at special events, can be embarrassing in countries such as Holland. However, although recognition isn't welcome, praying with the donor is. In Belgium, corporate recognition is not desirable; executives prefer to give anonymously. In Bolivia, gifts are opened after the giver has left; public recognition would be difficult for the recipient to handle. In Japan, the recipient of a gift is expected to reciprocate immediately. If recognition is unexpected, the donor may be in a quandary. In Estonia, where the northern European reserve is endemic, undue publicity may bias the donor negatively.

Many other issues could and should be addressed:

- Male/female dynamics and appropriateness in developing philanthropic relationships (in Latin American nations women are accepted as professionals, as they are in Africa, but in Muslim or Buddhist countries they might find themselves placed with the businessmen's wives, having tea and discussing children).

- Business done over lunch or dinner (Japanese have been known to ponder how Americans can eat and do business at the same time).
- Timing and timeliness (Thais wonder why Americans can't sit around and socialize, as is the custom, and have to hurry all the time; in other cultures being on time is either a compulsion or something to be ignored).
- Body language (does one touch, shake hands, or kiss, or neither or all of the above?).
- Dress (women in business suits that are totally appropriate in the U.S. culture might be totally out of place in a country where a suit is considered manly).
- Use of language (in Japan *membership* is offensive, while *supporter* is a comfortable term).

The list could go on; the topic is far from exhausted. What is evident is that fund raising principles are often adaptable, but none of us would be naive enough to think that what works in one place can be equally effective or possible in another. What's important, however, is to remember the principles of philanthropic fund raising and determine how they can be useful in a particular setting.

As we try to help our international colleagues, whether on our turf or theirs, we must keep in mind that situations vary greatly, while at the same time our basics of fund raising can be tools of teaching and learning.

We do live in a global village. We can apply our knowledge and experience in helping solve new problems, and we can have the fascinating and marvelous opportunity of learning how fund raising can work elsewhere. Unlike the missionary who returns with pictures of ditches used as open sewers and stories of beggar children, we can look at what's positive and put it into perspective—although not necessarily our perspective. We can make the fund raising community a truly global one by sharing our expertise and information, and doing so wisely in different cultural, national, and traditional settings.

## Bibliography

Axtell, Roger E., ed. *Do's and Taboos Around the World.* New York: John Wiley & Sons, 1993.

Klein, Joe, "Mothers vs. Mullahs," *Newsweek,* April 17, 1995.

McCarthy, Kathleen D., Hodgkinson, Virginia A., and Sumariwalla, Russy D. et al. *The Nonprofit Sector in the Global Community.* San Francisco: Jossey-Bass, 1992.

McNamara, Robert. *In Retrospect.* New York: Times Books, 1995.

# PART V

## Regulation

# 13 Government Regulation and Charitable Fund Raising

## Worthwhile Protection or Unreasonable Burden?

Bruce R. Hopkins, JD, LLM

*Polsinelli, White, Vardeman, & Shalton, PC*

## Some Introductory Thoughts

As a lawyer representing charitable organizations for over 25 years, I have specialized in tax and corporate law matters that apply to nonprofit organizations. But a lawyer with this specialty cannot long avoid close entanglement in the federal and state laws pertaining to fund raising by charities. Thus, it is not surprising that the law of fund raising became a significant component of my law practice in its early years.

When I started to familiarize myself with this field of law over 20 years ago, federal law on the point did not exist. The first of the Supreme Court decisions that would so dramatically shape this area was years away. What fund raising regulation there was thus was at the state, and sometimes local, level. At that time, however, much of the state law we have today did not exist. Enforcement of these statutes and ordinances was, at best, casual; punitive action was rare.

State law expansion came about because of occasional abuses that attracted the regulators' (and sometimes the public's) attention. As the climate became more consumer oriented, the few well-publicized fund raising misdeeds fed the states' appetite for regulation. Today, only three states lack statutory law on the subject; a large number of them have massive charitable solicitation acts. No letup is in sight on this front. States continue to write and rewrite charitable solicitation acts.

The federal government was slow to join this march of intensifying regulation but has made up for its initial years of inattentiveness. The Internal Revenue Service (IRS) has led the way in this regard, intensifying its adventuresomeness in the realm of charitable fund raising by, among other approaches, formulating regulations in the field of donor recognition and sponsorship programs, and trying to make the extent of fund raising costs an element of eligibility for tax-exempt status (the latter effort, attempted in court, being abandoned . . . for now). Other agencies are playing an increasing role, most notably the U.S. Postal Service and the Federal Trade Commission. Congress significantly added to the federal law of fund raising with tax legislation in 1993 (chiefly, the substantiation and quid pro quo contribution rules) and has just enacted additional rules, with heavy emphasis on disclosure. A perusal of the Clinton Administration's budget for fiscal year 1996 finds that it "supports and wants to work with Congress" on "disclosure requirements to improve public charities' compliance with the requirements for tax-exempt status."[1] Enacted in 1996 are rules levying "intermediate sanctions" and requiring important expansions of the annual information return.[2] Thus, there will be more federal fund raising law.

Opinions on the subject from federal and state courts reflect no cessation in the creation of fund raising law by the judiciary.

A student of the development of the law of fund raising must be puzzled in two respects. One is: Why did the state law blossom like it did and what fuels the ongoing ferment? The other is: Why do the members of the professional fund raising community so passively accept what the federal and state—particularly the state—forces are doing to them?

Taking the first of these puzzlements first, an explanation has yet to be found. The extent of abuses does not seem to warrant the crush of legislation that has been generated. Clearly, some of this law development has been swept along as part of the consumer protection movement. Many politicians have used this area as a basis for posturing. Regulation does breed regulation; some of the state regulatory offices seem to have grown in accordance with the principle that nature abhors a vacuum. While all of this law is good news for those who publish and speak on the subject, practice law or accounting in the field, or are part of the regulatory system, this question must be seriously asked: Is all of this regulation worth the effort? One has to wonder how the philanthropic world manages to do what it does while laboring under the burden of these laws.

This leads to the second of the puzzlements. The fund-raising community is generally into classic denial in relation to government regulation of its practices. This is understandable—few like to be regulated by the hand of government—but not realistic, given the volume of the regulation with which the professional fund raiser (employee or consultant) and the

---

[1] "Analytical Perspectives," Budget of the United States Government, Fiscal Year 1996, "Federal Receipts and Collections" at 27 (Government Printing Office, 1995).

[2] The essence of intermediate sanctions is to impose taxes on those who engage in excess benefit transactions (essentially, those entailing private inurement) with public charities (IRC § 4958). In general, see Hopkins and Tesdahl, *Intermediate Sanctions: Curbing Nonprofits' Abuse* (New York: John Wiley & Sons, 1997).

soliciting charitable organizations are required to cope. Sixteen years ago, I wrote a book describing the regulatory picture of charitable fund raising at the time.[3] The volume of fund raising regulation was striking then; the intervening one and one-half decades has seen this regulatory explosion balloon to a mind-numbing extent.[4] State law enforcement in this field has become a major regulatory force and federal regulation on a massive scale has arrived—and few seem to understand or even care.

The fact that this onslaught of regulation and expansion of enforcement has not attracted nearly the general attention and concern that is warranted is partially explicable because of its insidious nature. That is, the philanthropic community can be forgiven some impassivity because it has become conditioned to receiving its jolts of new regulation by enactment of federal legislation, usually tax acts. However, fund raising regulation has not come upon the voluntary sector by means of a single law but is instead an amalgam of slowly building and encompassing local, state, and federal legislation and administrative regulation. It is hard to fend off these forces—they are many and powerful.

The few abuses that have occurred have been well publicized. The realm of organized charity is under scrutiny and attack from a host of quarters. Part of this is due to the pressure on governments for additional tax revenue. It is reported that there is a new level of distrust of charitable institutions. The public appears supportive of the intense regulation of charitable fund raising, and there is demand—often encouraged by the prospective regulators—for more. These developments have combined to heighten the awareness of and sophistication about the methods and results of charitable giving on the part of federal and state regulators, the media, the watchdog groups, and donors and grantors.

The range of problems caused by the state charitable solicitation acts is considerable. Consider the charitable organization that raises its funds by direct mail in every state. Such an organization is confronted with a bewildering array of differing legal requirements, forms, due dates, bonds, accounting principles, and more. All too frequently, the organization "solves" this problem by registering in only a few states—or, perhaps in none at all.

Direct mail users are not the only types of charitable organization facing regulation. These laws directly apply to organizations that acquire funds pursuant to capital campaigns, planned giving programs, special events, annual giving solicitations and bequest programs. The regulatory requirements apply (with exceptions) to churches and other religious organizations; schools, colleges, and universities; hospitals and other healthcare

---

[3] Hopkins, *Charity Under Siege: Government Regulation of Fund-Raising* (New York: John Wiley & Sons, 1980).

[4] See Hopkins, *The Law of Fund-Raising* (2nd ed.) (New York: John Wiley & Sons, 1996). One measure of the growth of government regulation: *Charity Under Siege* consists of 274 pages, while *The Law of Fund-Raising* weighs in at 762 pages.

institutions; assorted related "foundations"; publicly supported charities; civic and patriotic groups; those seeking foundation and government grants, and corporate gifts; and many other types of nonprofit organizations seeking contributions. These bodies of law equally affect both old and new entities, those that are established as well as those that are unpopular or controversial, and those with an existing constituency and those building a donor base.

Many managers of charitable organizations and their consultants—fund raisers, lawyers, accountants, and the like—are not aware of the many difficulties, including the immense cost of compliance, imposed by the burgeoning number of laws regulating charitable fund raising. Thus, they require background information and a general understanding about the various charitable solicitation acts and their applicability to multitudinous philanthropic institutions.

Many organizations and their fund raisers are willing to make a reasonable effort to comply with these laws but do not know where to begin. There needs to be a means by which charitable organizations and their fund raising executives can rationally approach these laws and develop a procedure for effective compliance with them. Likewise, some organizations are in basic adherence with some of the applicable laws but need guidance as to what to do when their registration is being evaluated and perhaps threatened. This chapter includes a description of the process for keeping an organization in—or bringing one back into—compliance with these laws.

A number of legal problems are inherent in the administration and enforcement of these laws. They raise fundamental constitutional, administrative, tax, and other law issues, some of them very thorny and as yet unresolved.

State and federal regulation in the field of charitable fund raising is growing, as is the role of the "voluntary" standards agencies. In general, all of this is substantial overkill. Helmer Ekstrom, president of the American Association of Fund Raising Counsel once suggested it is like trying to kill a fly with an elephant gun; the extent of these laws is repressive, suffocating, unreasonable, and unnecessary.[5] There are problems in this field, to be sure, but nothing to warrant the volume of law crashing down on the nation's charitable organizations, which, after all, are working for the benefit of society and are a core component of our national decision-making and problem-solving structure. Fighting the underbelly of philanthropy is not worth maiming the entire body.

The fund raising community has yet to launch a coordinated, frontal attack on this exploding mass of regulation. From the fund raisers' standpoint, apparently, matters will have to get worse before getting better.

---

[5] Remarks on Oct. 26, 1994, at the third annual conference on "Fund-Raising and the Law," presented by the Georgetown University Law Center in cooperation with the National Society of Fund-Raising Executives. These remarks are summarized at 2 *Fund-Raising Regulation Report* (No. 1) 8 (Jan./Feb. 1995).

Hope remains that the charitable fund raising world will mobilize and successfully fight and squelch this rapacious regulatory impulse.

Before discussing the merits of the existing mass of government regulation of charitable fund raising, it is necessary first to summarize it.

The process of raising funds for charitable purposes, despite protection under constitutional law, is heavily regulated by the federal and state governments. Federal regulation is largely through the tax system. Nearly all of the states have some form of charitable solicitation act; 35 of them have comprehensive statutes in this area.

## Overview of Governmental Regulation

### FEDERAL GOVERNMENTAL REGULATION

Despite the absence of a federal charitable solicitation law akin to the broad statutes in effect in many states, regulation of the process of raising funds for charitable purposes at the federal level is immense, and constantly growing. Nearly all of this form of regulation is administered by the IRS.

The IRS regulates the practice of fund raising for charitable purposes in the following ways:

- It is engaged in an ongoing program of education and examination of charitable organizations that engage in fund raising.
- It is amplifying and enforcing the rules by which charitable organizations must substantiate contributions made to them.
- It is amplifying and enforcing the rules concerning quid pro quo contributions.
- It applies the unrelated business income rules in a variety of ways, to cause certain "fund raising" practices to be characterized as unrelated businesses.
- It requires a charitable organization to summarize its fund raising program at the time it applies for recognition of tax-exempt status.
- It requires an organization to report the receipts of its fund raising activities, and to report its fund raising expenses, on an annual basis.
- It applies the rules concerning private inurement in such a fashion as to discourage fund raising compensation arrangements that are based on percentages or otherwise involve commissions.
- It applies the rules embodying limitations on lobbying by, and calculation of the public support of, public charities in a way that defines and encourages certain forms of fund raising.
- It "regulates" the fund raising process by its interpretations and enforcement of the rules involving deductible charitable contributions.

There is also some regulation at the hands of the U.S. Postal Service, through its monitoring of use of the special bulk third-class mailing rates, and the Federal Trade Commission, particularly as it regulates telemarketing. The antitrust and securities laws have some applicability in this context as well.

## STATE GOVERNMENTAL REGULATION

All but three states have some form of statutory law governing the solicitation of charitable gifts. (The states that lack any such law are Montana, Texas, and Wyoming.) Thirty-five states have formal, comprehensive *charitable solicitation acts*, and the elements of these laws are discussed in this chapter. Also, the attorney general of a state has inherent authority to oversee charities; this authority is known as *parens patriae*.

Moreover, the states have laws concerning availability of tax exemptions, the deductibility of charitable gifts, the offering of securities, the sale of insurance programs, unfair trade practices, misleading advertising, and fraud—each of which can be applied in the realm of charitable fund raising.

## CONSTITUTIONALITY OF THESE STATE LAWS

In general, these laws are constitutional. Fund raising for charitable purposes is one of the highest forms of free speech. This means that governments can regulate it only by the narrowest of means.[6] The outer reaches of this doctrine are still being explored.[7]

Consequently, some features of state and local charitable solicitation acts have been struck down. The most infamous of them are limitations on the fund raising costs of charitable entities or on the levels of compensation paid to professional solicitors. Certain forced disclosures are also banned. However, the overall charitable solicitation acts themselves have been upheld, in the face of claims that they wrongfully hamper free speech or unduly burden interstate commerce.

State and local governments possess the *police power*. This is the authority to protect their citizens from harm such as fraud and other forms of misrepresentation. Thus, the police power can be used to shield persons from fraudulent and otherwise abusive fund raising practices. This police power directly clashes with the free speech rights of charities and their fund raisers. To date, this tension has been modulated by the courts, with the consensus being that the police power allows for the general application

---

[6] *Village of Schaumburg* v. *Citizens for a Better Environment,* 444 U.S. 620 (1980); *Secretary of State of Maryland* v. *Joseph H. Munson Co., Inc.,* 467 U.S. 947 (1984); *Riley* v. *National Federation of the Blind of North Carolina, Inc.,* 487 U.S. 781 (1984).

[7] E.g., *There to Care, Inc.* v. *Commissioner, Indiana Department of Revenue,* 19 F.3d 1165 (7th Cir. 1994).

of the charitable solicitation laws, while constitutional law principles force governments to regulate in this area by narrow means.

## Federal Law Requirements

As noted, most of the federal law pertaining to fund raising regulation is in the tax setting. Much of this law is attributable to IRS initiatives, although in recent years Congress has stepped up its legislating in this field.

### IRS AUDIT PRACTICES

The IRS has specific concerns about charitable organizations[8] that are engaged in charitable solicitation; these concerns are reflected in IRS audit guidelines promulgated for its examining agents. There are two sets of guidelines with which charitable entities should be particularly familiar.

The first of these is a set of audit guidelines formulated by the IRS in 1989–1990. These guidelines in turn led to the development of a "checksheet" used by agents in auditing the fund raising programs of charitable organizations. This checksheet, containing 83 questions of direct pertinence to a wide variety of fund raising practices, is termed the "Exempt Organizations Charitable Solicitations Compliance Improvement Program Study Checksheet" (Form 9215).

The second of these is the guidelines published by the IRS in 1994 for its agents to use during examinations of colleges and universities.[9] While technically these guidelines are applicable only in the context of higher education, they describe in considerable detail how the agent is to conduct the fund raising audit. The IRS will endeavor to identify each individual responsible for soliciting and accounting for charitable contributions, obtain lists of contributors, explore property valuations, determine compliance with the substantiation and quid pro quo contribution rules, analyze compliance with the appraisal requirements, review the information returns for gift properties sold, and examine the organization's agreements with the financial institutions that manage its funds.[10]

There should be no doubt that an audit of any charitable organization, from the standpoint of its fund raising practices, would be conducted in a manner close to that summarized in these guidelines.

---

[8] The term *charitable,* as used in the federal tax setting, means all organizations that are described in IRC § 501(c)(3).

[9] These guidelines are part of the *Internal Revenue Manual (Exempt Organizations Examination Guidelines Handbook* 7(10)69) and were published for public dissemination in Ann. 94-112, 1994-37 I.R.B. 36.

[10] In general, see "Fund-Raisers: Prepare for IRS Audits," I *Fund-Raising Regulation Report* (No. 3)1 (Nov./Dec. 1994).

## CHARITABLE GIVING RULES

The charitable giving rules apply in many ways, as they govern the deductibility of charitable gifts for federal tax purposes. The facets of this include the definitions of *charitable* and *gift*, the percentage limitations, the rules concerning the use of fair market value in computing deductions for gifts of property, the deduction reduction rules, and the rules concerning partial interests, including planned giving.

There are, however, three bodies of charitable giving law that have particular relevance in the realm of fund raising regulation. They are the charitable gift substantiation requirements, the quid pro quo contribution rules, and the appraisal rules.

The charitable gift substantiation rules generally deny a charitable contribution deduction for any charitable gift of $250 or more unless the donor has contemporaneous written substantiation from the donee charitable organization.[11] The quid pro quo contribution rules stipulate that a charitable organization must provide a written disclosure statement to donors who make a payment in excess of $75 which is partly a contribution and partly for goods or services provided to the donor by the charitable organization.[12] The appraisal rules generally deny a charitable contribution deduction for a gift of property in excess of $5,000 where the gift is not the subject of a qualifying appraisal.[13]

## NEW CHARITABLE ORGANIZATIONS

Nearly every organization that wants to be tax-exempt as a charitable entity must give notice to the IRS to that effect by filing an application for recognition of tax exemption.[14] That application requests certain information about the fund raising program of the organization.

These items of information include a description of the organization's fund raising program (actual and planned), details as to fund raising activities (such as formation of fund raising committees, use of professional fund raisers, and selective mailings), copies of solicitation materials, and a multiyear analysis as to fund raising expenditures.

## REPORTING RULES

Nearly every charitable organization must file an annual information return (usually, Form 990) with the IRS.[15] (The most notable exception is the

---

[11] IRC § 170(f)(8).

[12] IRC § 6115.

[13] Reg. § 1.170A-13(c).

[14] IRC § 508(a). The application form is Form 1023.

[15] IRC § 6033(b).

one for churches and their integrated auxiliaries.) This return requests certain information pertaining to the organization's fund raising program.

These items of information for the year include the amounts of direct and indirect public support, revenue from special events, fund raising expenses (including professional fund raising fees), allocations of costs between program and fund raising, the value of donated services and/or of the use of material or property, analysis of income-producing activities (including those leading to grant and/or contract revenue), and a summary of the organization's support (including contributions and grants).

## UNRELATED BUSINESS INCOME RULES

Several types of fund raising events or activities—sometimes known as *special events*—are technically *businesses* for federal income tax purposes. Thus, were it not for certain provisions in the federal tax law pertaining to unrelated businesses, some or all of the net income from these events would be taxable.

Some of this revenue is sheltered from taxation on the rationale that the activity is not *regularly carried on*.[16] This pertains to activities that are only conducted once each year, such as a dinner dance, a theater outing, or an auction. However, if the event is a seasonal one, such as the selling of holiday cards, the season is the measuring period, not a full year.

Some revenue-raising activities are considered related businesses. These include sales of various items in gift shops maintained by hospitals and museums, as well as in college and university bookstores. Other sales in these shops and stores may be nontaxable by operation of the *convenience doctrine*. This doctrine, available to charitable organizations, exempts from taxation a business that is carried on primarily for the convenience of the organization's members, students, officers, or employees.[17]

Still other fund raising practices are protected against taxation by specific statutory exceptions. Some fund raising events are run entirely by volunteers; businesses that are conducted substantially by individuals who are unpaid for their services are not taxed.[18] However, it does not take much for a court to conclude, for purposes of this exception, that someone is compensated. In one case, involving a gambling operation conducted weekly by a tax-exempt organization, individuals who were otherwise volunteers were found to be paid because they received tips from patrons.[19]

Another exception is for businesses that sell items that were contributed to the organization.[20] While this rule was created for the benefit of thrift

---

[16] IRC § 512(a)(1).

[17] IRC § 513(a)(2).

[18] IRC § 513(a)(1).

[19] *Executive Network Club, Inc.* v. *Commissioner*, 69 T.C.M. 1680 (1995).

[20] IRC § 513 (a)(3).

stores operated by nonprofit organizations, it can also be applicable in the case of frequent auctions.

Still another exception that can protect fund raising revenue is the one for *royalties*.[21] In one instance, an organization is attempting to use this exception to immunize income from an affinity card program from tax.[22] Earlier, this same organization was able to use the exception to protect revenue from the sale and rental of its mailing lists.[23]

## OTHER FEDERAL LAW REQUIREMENTS

Another application of the federal income tax rules are those pertaining to publicly supported charitable organizations that have that status by virtue of the facts and circumstances test. Under this test, the IRS determines whether a charitable organization is being operated so as to attract new and additional public and/or governmental support on a continuous basis. An organization is considered to be meeting this requirement if it maintains a continuous and bona fide program for the solicitation of funds from the general public, community, or membership group involved, or if it is attempting to attract support from governmental units or publicly supported charitable organizations. The IRS will evaluate whether the scope of the charity's fund raising activities is reasonable in light of its charitable activities.[24]

The U.S. Postal Service regulates some aspects of charitable fund raising by means of the postal laws. Qualified organizations (including charities) that have received specific authorization may mail eligible matter at special, reduced bulk third-class rates of postage.

In the parlance of the postal laws, charitable organizations are termed *philanthropic* entities. Other qualified nonprofit organizations include religious, educational, and scientific entities. Ineligible organizations include trade, business, and professional associations; certain citizens' and civic improvement associations; and social and hobby clubs. Cooperative mailings involving the mailing of any matter on behalf of or produced for an organization not authorized to mail at the special rates must be paid at the applicable regular rates.

For material that advertises, promotes, offers, or, for a fee or other consideration, recommends, describes, or announces the availability of any product or service to qualify for mailing at the special bulk third-class rates, the sale of the product or the provision of the service must be substantially

---

[21] IRC § 513(b)(2).

[22] *Sierra Club, Inc.* v. *Commissioner*, 103 T.C. 307 (1994), rev'd and rem'd, 86 F.3d 1526 (9th Cir. 1996).

[23] *Sierra Club, Inc.* v. *Commissioner*, 65 T.C.M. 2582 (1993), aff'd, 86 F.3d 1526 (9th Cir. 1996).

[24] Reg. § 1.170A-9(e)(3).

related to the exercise or performance by the organization of one or more of the purposes constituting the basis for the organization's authorization to mail at those rates. The determination as to whether a product or service is substantially related to an organization's purpose is made in accordance with the analogous federal tax law standards.[25]

The Federal Trade Commission has a role in the realm of fund raising for charitable purposes. This is primarily the case when the fund raising is in the form of telemarketing. The FTC has regulations on this subject, in amplification of the Telemarketing and Consumer Fraud and Abuse Prevention Act.[26] These rules do not apply to telemarketing conducted solely for the purpose of generating charitable gifts, unless the regulations pertain to the activities of a for-profit agent of a charitable entity.

## State Law Requirements

Much of the regulation of charitable fund raising is at the state level. This is usually accomplished by application of one or more charitable solicitation acts. There are 48 of these laws, of which 35 may be said to be comprehensive.

There are significant limitations on the extent to which fund raising for charitable, educational, scientific, religious, and like organizations can be regulated by government. Despite these constitutional law precepts, nonprofit organizations face considerable regulatory requirements at the state level when they solicit contributions for charitable purposes.

### ELEMENTS OF TYPICAL STATE *CHARITABLE SOLICITATION ACT*

These laws usually open with a set of definitions. The key terms defined are *charitable, solicitation, contribution, professional fund raiser, professional solicitor,* and *charitable sales promotion.* The ambit of these laws is basically set by the scope of the words *charitable* and *solicitation.* The word charitable in this setting includes religious, educational, arts promotion, and scientific purposes.

The term *charitable* in this context is given a much broader definition than in settings such as the federal tax law pertaining to tax-exempt organizations. Some of these state laws are applicable to fund raising by exempt social welfare organizations, business and professional associations, and other types of nonprofit organizations. State laws can differ on the point (e.g., some expressly exclude political fund raising), so it is necessary to check each one that is applicable.

---

[25] In general, 39 U.S.C. § 3626(j); Domestic Mail Manual E370, part 2.0.

[26] Federal Trade Commission Rule § 310.3. The Act is at 15 U.S.C. § 6101 *et seq.*

A key feature of these laws is *registration*. They almost always require soliciting charitable organizations to register, usually annually. There often is a registration fee. The information required by this process usually is extensive; the states have devised required registration forms. Many of the states also require the registration of professional fund raisers and/or professional solicitors. Some of these states mandate a bond for fund raisers and/or solicitors.

This registration process frequently requires charitable organizations to identify any fund raisers or solicitors they have hired. The states will use this information to determine if the fund raiser or solicitor has registered. Also, charities are often required to provide a list of other states in which they are registered. The registration form for fund raisers and solicitors usually requires them to identify the charities they are working with. The states will cross-reference this information to see if all parties are appropriately registered and bonded.

Another feature of these laws is annual *reporting*. They almost always require a report, including extensive financial reporting, by charitable organizations each year, either as an annual report or by means of annual registration. (Some states mandate both.) Annual reports are often also required of professional fund raisers and professional solicitors. A few of these laws require more frequent reports from solicitors, such as reports following each fund-raising campaign.

Many of these laws contain an extensive listing of *prohibited acts*. These are rules dictating certain fund raising practices by charitable organizations—usually in the form of practices in which they may not engage. Some of these prohibited acts go beyond the realm of fund raising and mandate certain actions (or nonactions) by charities and others generally. It is important for charities and those who assist them in the fund raising process to review each of the applicable sets of these prohibitions.

A growing practice is for these laws to mandate the contents of *contracts* between soliciting charitable organizations and their professional fund raisers and/or professional solicitors. Common requirements in this regard are a statement of the services to be provided, a summary of the financial arrangement between the parties, and a concise and accurate statement of the charitable organization's right to cancel.

*Legends* are another burgeoning requirement. These are notices required by law that must prominently appear on fund raising literature and other appeals. The typical legend must state that certain information is available about the charity from it or the state. This requirement is becoming a problem for those making charitable solicitations by mail in several states, because the differences in these legends are forcing the solicitation material to become cluttered with them, detracting from the purpose of the mailing.

Other components of these laws include record-keeping requirements, investigatory and injunctive powers by the state, and a range of civil and criminal sanctions.

## APPLICABILITY OF STATE LAWS TO ALL
## CHARITABLE SOLICITATIONS

These laws apply to all charitable solicitations, unless the solicitation is expressly exempted from the statutory requirements. Thus, these laws apply where the solicitation is by means of the mail, telephone (telemarketing), facsimile, television, video, and radio, as well as in-person fund raising. The medium used to solicit is thus not significant; the key is whether or not the activity is a solicitation. The fact that interstate commerce is involved is not per se a bar to state regulation.

For example, the law in the state of Connecticut defines the term *solicitation* to mean "any request directly or indirectly for money, credit, property, financial assistance or other thing of any kind or value on the plea or representation that such money, credit, property, financial assistance or other thing of any kind or value is to be used for a charitable purpose or benefit a charitable organization."[27] This is, obviously, a most encompassing definition of the term, yet it is typical.[28]

## APPLICABILITY OF LAWS TO
## PROFESSIONAL FUND RAISERS

These laws apply to professional fund raisers in a variety of ways. However, the basic application of these laws is dependent upon the definition of the term *professional fund raiser*. First, the states do not always use that term; the terminology instead may be *fund raising counsel, professional fund raising counsel,* or *professional fund raiser consultant.* Second, the definition of the term can vary. The most frequently used definition of the term is that employed in the state of Virginia, which is "any person who for a flat fixed fee under a written agreement plans, conducts, manages, carries on, advises or acts as a consultant, whether directly or indirectly, in connection with soliciting contributions for, or on behalf of, any charitable . . . organization, but who actually solicits no contributions as a part of such services."[29]

The states give this term broad application. Thus, those who work in collateral fields should be cautious, in that they do not inadvertently become regarded as a fund raiser and become subject to penalties for noncompliance with state law. These related fields include consulting in the areas of marketing, management, and public relations. Lawyers are usually exempted from the definition by statute. Volunteers are also not included.

---

[27] Solicitation of Charitable Funds Act § 21a-190a(3).

[28] Technically, the solicitation of charitable contributions on the Internet is embraced by these laws. See II *Fund-Raising Regulation Report* (No. 4) 3 (July/Aug. 1995).

[29] Solicitations of Contributions Law § 57-48.

It is common for a state charitable solicitation act to impose the following requirements on a professional fund raiser working for one or more charitable organizations: registration, bonding, annual reports, record-keeping, and a contract with the charity.

## APPLICABILITY OF LAWS TO PROFESSIONAL SOLICITORS

These laws apply to professional solicitors in a variety of ways. However, the basic application of these laws is, like those pertaining to professional fund raisers, dependent upon the definition of the term *professional solicitor*. First, the states do not always use that term; the terminology instead may well be *paid solicitor*. Second, the definition of the term can vary. The most frequently used definition of the term is that employed in the state of Virginia, which is any "person who, for a financial or other consideration, solicits contributions for, or on behalf of, a charitable . . . organization . . ."[30]

The states give this term broad application—even broader than the term professional fund raiser. Many individuals and firms that consider themselves professional fund raisers are regarded by the state as professional solicitors because of their (ostensible) direct involvement in the solicitation process. For example, a fund raiser who assists a charity in placing solicitation material into the mails may, for that reason alone, be regarded as a solicitor. Also, those who work in collateral fields should be cautious, so that they do not inadvertently become regarded as a solicitor and become subject to penalties for noncompliance with state law. Again, these related fields include consulting in the areas of marketing, management, and public relations. And, again, lawyers are usually exempted from the definition by statute. Volunteers are also not included.

It is common for a state charitable solicitation act to impose the following requirements on a professional solicitor working for one or more charitable organizations: registration, bonding, annual reports, postcampaign reports, the filing of solicitation notices, record keeping, and a contract with the charity.

Professional solicitors do not enjoy positive reputations, due to greedy and other abusive conduct by some of them, and are in particular disfavor with state legislators and regulators. That is one of the reasons why fund raisers are loath to be perceived as solicitors. More importantly, the states are endeavoring to drive paid solicitors for charity out of their jurisdictions, by heaping regulatory requirements on them. The laws of some states are so onerous in this regard it is unclear how the solicitor can profitably function in the gift solicitation task. Thus, it is important for those persons who can to avoid classification as a professional solicitor.

---

[30] *Id.*

## LIMITATIONS ON FEES PAID TO
## PROFESSIONAL SOLICITORS

From time to time, a state will enact a law placing a percentage limitation on the amount of compensation and other funds payable to a professional solicitor. The most recent example of this occurred in California. Nonetheless, these laws are blatantly unconstitutional.

For example, the state of Kentucky enacted a law that placed a 50 percent limit on the amount of fees a charitable organization could pay a professional solicitor. This law was struck down in 1994 as being unconstitutional.[31] The California provision was similarly nullified in 1995.[32]

## CHARITABLE SALES PROMOTIONS

The phrase *charitable sales promotion* means, as defined for example in New Hampshire law, "an advertising or sales campaign, conducted by a commercial co-venturer, which represents that the purchase or use of goods or services offered by the commercial co-venturer shall benefit, in whole or in part, a charitable trust or purpose."[33] The term *commercial co-venturer* is there defined as "a person who for profit is regularly and primarily engaged in trade or commerce other than in connection with soliciting for charitable trusts or purposes and who conducts a charitable sales promotion."[34]

The term *commercial co-venturer*, though understandable as to its derivation, is unfortunate phraseology. It suggests that the charity involved is engaged in a *commercial* undertaking, which is not favorable from the charity's standpoint. It further conveys the thought that the charity is in a joint venture, which also can have adverse legal consequences.

For the most part, state law mandates accurate disclosure of the arrangement between the charitable organization and the commercial co-venturer. Some states' laws require a formal accounting by the commercial enterprise; two states mandate annual reporting and bonding.

## PROHIBITED ACTS

This aspect of these laws can be very extensive, with a delineation of over 20 *prohibited acts*. Some of these prohibitions apply specifically in the fund raising setting. Examples of these prohibitions include the following:

- A person may not use the name of another person, as part of a charitable solicitation, without that person's consent.

---

[31] *Kentucky State Police Professional Association* v. *Gorman*, 870 F. Supp. 166 (E.D. Ky. 1994).

[32] *National Federation of Nonprofits* v. *Lungren* (N.D. Cal., Mar. 29, 1995).

[33] Revised Statutes Annotated § 7:21 I.

[34] *Id.* § 7:21 III.

- A person may not, in a charitable solicitation, use a name, symbol, or statement so similar to that used by another charitable organization or government agency that it would tend to mislead the public.
- A person may not exploit the fact of registration with a state so as to lead the public to believe that the state has endorsed the solicitation.
- A person may not misrepresent the status of an organization so as to lead the public to think that it is a charitable one, or that gifts will be used for charitable purposes, when that is not the case.
- A person may not represent that the solicitation is for a charitable organization without proper authorization from the charity,

However, these prohibitions can also apply more broadly in the realm of charitable operations generally. For example, under the law in some states:

- A charitable organization cannot expend funds for purposes not referenced in the application submitted as part of the registration process.
- There are point-of-solicitation disclosure requirements.
- There are limitations on the solicitation of tickets to be used at promotional events.
- Directors are expressly obligated to supervise the organization's fund raising activities.
- Conflicts of interest at the board level are prohibited.

These prohibited acts rules are applicable with respect to any solicitation in the state. Thus, a charitable organization or other person soliciting in more than one state can find that there are a multitude of prohibited acts with which to contend.

## EXCEPTIONS

There are many exceptions to these laws. These exceptions apply with respect to charitable organizations. Some states exempt certain types of charitable organizations from the entirety of these laws; others exempt them from only the registration and reporting requirements.

The most common exception is for religious organizations; this exception rests primarily on constitutional law grounds. Ironically, many of the abuses in the field of charitable fund raising are committed in the name of religion.

The next most common exception is for schools, colleges, and universities. Other entities that often have some form of exemption are libraries, museums, healthcare providers, membership organizations, veterans' groups, and political entities. Some states exempt small solicitations and fund raising for a named individual.

These exemptions are largely predicated on the reasonable thought that the organizations can be excused from the rigors of this regulation because those whom they solicit do not need the protections of the statute, due to their close relationship with and understanding of the charitable organization. At the same time, this approach leaves the remaining regulated charities unhappy with their burdens of compliance. This matter of exceptions from state charitable solicitation acts can be divisive in the world of public charities.

There are some traps in this area. First: These exemptions are not uniform; a charitable organization can be exempt in its home state, yet not in another state where it is also soliciting gifts. Second: The membership exclusion cannot be utilized simply by making a donor a "member"; the state laws usually forbid that practice. Third: Some universities, healthcare providers, and the like conduct their fund raising through related "foundations"; not all of the states that exempt these institutions likewise expressly exempt their affiliated foundations. Fourth: A "small" solicitation in one state is not necessarily small in another; these thresholds range from $1,500 to $25,000.

Some states exempt charitable organizations by name. These laws are of questionable constitutionality; they may be violations of the equal protection doctrine.

An exception may not be automatic. In some states, a charitable organization must make application for exemption. In some states, an otherwise-applicable exemption is not available where a charitable organization uses a professional fund raiser or a professional solicitor.

## CHARITABLE ORGANIZATION COMPLIANCE

Assuming the charitable organization is not exempt from the requirement, it must comply with a charitable solicitation act in a state when it is soliciting contributions in that state.

The applicable law almost always is that of the state in which the soliciting charitable organization is located. It is rare for a charity to solicit contributions but not in the state in which it is headquartered. Thus, a soliciting charitable organization should first endeavor to be in compliance with the fund raising regulation law in the state in which it is based.

An argument that the state's law is inapplicable because the charity is only using the U.S. mail or because the fund raising involves interstate commerce will fail. The state's police power enables it to regulate in this field as long as the forms of regulation are sufficiently narrow.

The matter of when a charitable organization must comply with more than one of these laws is a subject of some confusion and frustration. Basically, the law is that a charitable organization, unless exempted from the requirement, must comply with *each* of the charitable solicitation acts in force in the states in which it is soliciting contributions. Thus, a charitable organization fund raising in all of the states and the District of Columbia may well have to annually comply with over 40 of these laws. (This is in addition to nonprofit corporation acts and other state laws that may apply in the fund raising context.)

Soliciting charitable organizations also are supposed to be in compliance with the hundreds of county, city, and town charitable solicitation ordinances in effect throughout the country. While some charitable organizations comply with some of these ordinances, there is undoubtedly no organization that is in full compliance in this regard. State law compliance is difficult enough; the staff required to cope with all this local regulation would be extensive.

There is no lawful way to avoid this extent of multistate enforcement. These laws are based on the states's police power and have been generally upheld in the face of challenges as to their constitutionality. There is no legitimate authority—based on concepts of interstate commerce or other theory—for the proposition that these laws are inapplicable to charitable organizations raising funds on a multistate basis.

## PROFESSIONAL FUND RAISER AND PROFESSIONAL SOLICITOR COMPLIANCE

The considerations in this regard are much the same as those for charitable organizations. A fund raiser or solicitor may not be assisting a charitable organization in the state where the fund raiser or solicitor is based. Although this would be infrequent, the state law may nonetheless apply. Each state's law must be examined to see how it treats this subtlety.

The considerations in this regard are basically the same as with charitable organizations. That is, a fund raiser or solicitor must be in compliance with these laws in every state in which it is working with a charitable organization to assist it in raising funds. However, usually where the charitable organization is exempt from the requirements, so too is the professional fund raiser and/or professional solicitor.

## VIOLATIONS

The general practice—although this is not reflected in any statute—is that, when a state regulatory office discovers a violation of the state's charitable solicitation act, the office will contact the offending party and request compliance. This approach is usually taken, for example, when a person is required to register in the state but has not. Of course, where the violation is more egregious, such as the commission of fraud, the reaction of the state authorities would likely be sterner.

If the violation is willful or ongoing, and persists despite polite requests to come into compliance, most of the state regulators have the authority to obtain an injunction and enjoin the practice that is contravening the law. For example, if a charitable organization is fund raising in a state without having first registered there, the state's attorney general could enjoin the solicitation until compliance has been achieved. Likewise, a professional solicitor could find the solicitation enjoined if the solicitor's contract with the charity was not in conformity with the state's requirements.

A host of civil and criminal law penalties can come into play as well. For example, most of the states are empowered to levy fines and impose prison terms. Most of these violations are misdemeanors, with fraud being the predominant exception (a felony).

Despite the enforcement that exists—the intensity of which varies from state to state—there are many charitable organizations, professional fund raisers, and professional solicitors that are not adhering to these laws or are only in partial compliance. Just as few states have the resources necessary to fully enforce these laws, most charitable organizations lack the capacity to fully comply with them. There are more outlaws in this field of the law than any other applicable to nonprofit organizations.

## EFFECTIVENESS OF STATE LAWS

As a basic matter, these laws are ineffective. The purpose of these laws is to protect people from fake charities and unscrupulous fund raisers, by deterring unlawful activity and punishing that which does occur. These laws keep increasing in number and complexity, and yet are having little impact on abusive practices. The chief imprint these laws are placing on the charitable sector is in the form of administrative burdens (including diversions of funds from charitable programs) on legitimate charities.

The thought that these laws are effective is a myth fostered by the regulatory community. (For example, the impact of Pennsylvania law on the activities of the New Era for Philanthropy Foundation may be contemplated.[35]) On occasion, the courts will accept the rationale. In the most recent example of this, where a court upheld the constitutionality of a registration fee imposed on fund raising charitable organizations on the ground that it is a "user fee," the court wrote that the state's charitable solicitation act is a "benefit" to soliciting charities and an enhancement of "donor confidence."[36]

The truth is that no one knows the full extent of the ineffectiveness of these laws. More fundamentally, there are no respectable data as to the magnitude of the problem these laws are supposed to rectify and prevent. It is astonishing that these laws are evolving so quickly and becoming so intricate, while there are absolutely no data defining the reason for their existence. Research in these areas is long overdue.

---

[35] See, e.g., III *Fund-Raising Regulation Report* (No. 2) 10 (Mar./April 1996).
[36] *Center for Auto Safety, Incorporated* v. *Athey*, 37 F.3d 139, 144 (4th Cir. 1994).

## MANAGEMENT SYSTEM

A charitable organization that is soliciting contributions in several states and that wishes to be in full compliance with the law of those states needs to take several steps:

1.  The organization should obtain a copy of the charitable solicitation act in effect in each of the states. It should determine, with the assistance of a lawyer if necessary, what its various obligations pursuant to these laws are. At a minimum, the organization should ascertain whether any exceptions are available to it, principally with respect to registration and reporting requirements. Some of these laws are amplified by rules and regulations, and the charitable organization or its lawyer should have these sets of additional law to refer to in interpreting the statutes. There may be some court opinions that pertain to these laws as well.

2.  Once the organization has determined which states have registration requirements that are applicable to it, it should obtain the necessary registration forms, and prepare and file them. This should be done in advance of solicitation. In this connection, the organization should be certain to pay the requisite registration fee and obtain all required bonds.

3.  If the organization is using the services of a professional fund raiser and/or professional solicitor, it should make a reasonable effort to see to it that these persons are adhering to these laws as well. Although, technically, the responsibility for compliance is on these persons and not the charity, the charity does not want legal difficulties to thwart a fund raising effort.

4.  If the organization is subject to one or more reporting requirements, it should be certain that its financial records are properly maintained. Particular emphasis should be placed on fund raising costs, so that the organization knows precisely what its solicitation expenses are. If the entity has costs that are allocated between fund raising and program, it should obtain the services of an accountant who is knowledgeable as to those rules.  The due dates for the state forms will vary, so the organization should have a system for notification as to the dates, so it can be in timely compliance with those requirements.

5.  If the charitable organization is being assisted by a professional fund raiser or professional solicitor, it should be certain that there is a written contract between it and that person (or persons). Further, the organization should see to it that the contract (or contracts) has all of the provisions required by the states laws. These considerations also apply to relationships with commercial co-venturers.

6.  The organization should be certain that its solicitation materials contain any and all of the applicable legends.

7.  The organization should review the list of prohibited acts in each of these applicable laws and be certain that it is in conformity with them.

8. The organization should endeavor to be in compliance with the applicable record-keeping requirements.

There are other aspects of these laws that the charitable organization should monitor. This includes receiving copies of all materials that affiliated parties file with the states, such as the solicitation notices filed by professional solicitors and reports filed by commercial co-venturers.

## Looking Ahead

This chapter is appropriately closed with speculation about what is likely to happen in and to the world of fund raising and philanthropy, in both the short and long run, with regard to the development of law and regulation.

It is easy to predict that the nonprofit world will, in the coming months and years, be laboring under more regulation by government. This will be true at both the federal and state level. There are many reasons for this phenomenon.

Much of it is sheer extrapolation from what has already occurred. At the federal level over the past two and one-half decades, the fund raising community has seen enactment of the Tax Reform Act of 1969 (which brought most of today's statutory charitable giving rules, and the public charity and private foundation rules), growing sophistication in application of the unrelated business income rules, increasing emphasis on reporting and disclosure (including expansion of and public access to the annual information returns), more involvement of the tax law in the administration of the fund raising process, Congress' decision to make public a wider variety of IRS pronouncements (including private letter rulings, technical advice memoranda, and general counsel memoranda),[37] Congress' decision to make it easier to litigate charitable organizations' tax issues in federal court,[38] Congress' decision to become more involved in the realm of planned giving,[39] and the emergence of agencies other than the IRS in fund raising regulation, such as the Postal Service and the Federal Trade Commission.

This type of regulation is founded on the belief that too much abuse is taking place in the charitable fund raising setting. Certainly the prime illustrations in this regard are the substantiation and quid pro quo contribution rules. But other practices of charitable organizations that some are finding noxious (or at least taxable) are emerging: corporate sponsorships, special events, gambling (such as raffles and sweepstakes), tours and

---

[37] IRC § 6110.
[38] IRC § 7428.
[39] IRC § 7520.

cruises, product endorsements, affinity cards, mailing list exchanges, and valuation of property.

The IRS sees "scandal" in fund raising, being particularly annoyed at what its officials perceive as "misleading" solicitations. This largely concerns the practice of some charitable organizations of advising prospective "donors" that "gifts" are deductible as charitable contributions when they in fact are not (because they are not gifts at all) or when there is only a partial deduction (because the payments are partly a purchase of a service or product). Although the revenue implications of this are not enormous, these fund raising practices are causing unhappiness within the IRS and are tainting that agency's attitude about charitable fund raising in general, with unfavorable consequences for the future.

Another factor is the federal government's deficit. Tax laws are being written with the revenue impact the primary consideration. Good ideas about tax policy and tax law revision usually do not move very far or very fast unless they generate some tax revenue. Bad tax policy can advance in this environment where there are tax dollars to be produced.

Somewhat the same phenomenon is playing out at the state level. There is great interest in narrowing the range of the exemptions from sales, use, and property taxes. It is not that these regulators are suddenly seeing the performance of less charity in their jurisdictions; it is that they are desperate for additional tax revenue.

The role of states' attorneys general continues to be expansive, often augmented by activist secretaries of state and directors of departments of consumer protection. There has been a breathtaking increase in the number and scope of state charitable solicitation acts.

The scandal factor is more important at the state level. Recent episodes in the field of direct-mail fund raising (e.g., sweepstakes promotions) are involving new forms of government regulation. Several states are in this picture, strenuously enforcing their charitable solicitation acts and successfully procuring injunctive relief from the courts. At the same time, as the recent episode with the New Era for Philanthropy Foundation illustrates, the states are often missing the big picture and these laws cannot forestall misrepresentations in charitable fund raising.

Still another element is the perception by many in government that the distinction between nonprofit and for-profit organizations is blurring. The difference continues to be readily ascertainable as a matter of law, but is often too vague for much of the regulatory community. It is easier for lawmakers to promote new statutory law or regulators to advocate a new regulation or rule when they see the task as one of precluding charitable and other nonprofit organizations from doing what they ostensibly ought not to be doing as a matter of principle.

Obviously, this is not the best of regulatory climates for charitable organizations and those who assist them in the raising of money. Indeed, this is not the best of climates for nonprofit, tax-exempt organizations in general.

What, then, will be happening in the worlds of charity, fund raising, and law in the coming months and years? Easy answer: more law and more regulation. Much of this will be increased involvement by the IRS in the charitable fund raising process. The annual information return is being significantly revised and this will have a major impact on fund raising, including the manner in which solicitation results are presented. Other aspects of this field to watch are the possibility of intermediate sanctions, the role of the private inurement doctrine in fund raising regulation, IRS crackdown on abuses of charitable remainder trusts, revised criteria for the charitable tax exemption (such as is developing with respect to healthcare institutions), and the imposition of self-dealing rules on public charities.

Another easy prognostication is increase in state regulation of fund raising by charitable organizations and of professional fund raising consultants, by reason of expansion of the contents and enforcement of charitable solicitation acts.

In general, then, for the short term, federal and state regulation of the charitable fund raising process will continue to intensify.

Matters are far less clear for the longer term. Federal tax policy plays a critical role in determining the environment for charitable fund raising. In the past, when tax considerations have been involved, the subjects have usually been income tax rates and the like. While it remains true that the magnitude of income and capital gain taxation is important, circumstances are uniquely different as the 20th century winds to a close.

Discussion of tax policy in the mid-1990s infrequently focuses on income tax adjustments. Rather, the focus is on wholesale replacement of today's graduated income tax with a much simpler flat (or flatter) tax, a consumption tax (often termed a national sales tax), or a value-added tax. The likelihood of any of this is highly dependent on the outcome of the 1996 federal elections. If one of these courses of action is selected, there may not be any tax incentive for charitable giving. The fund raising community may want to start positioning itself for the eventuality of soliciting gifts in a climate where there is no tax advantage for giving.

The research implications in all of this are enormous. For purposes of the subject of this paper, two topics desperately need research. One is to attempt to quantify the extent of fund raising fraud and other abuse. The other is to measure the effectiveness of state law in deterring these practices.

# On the Regulation of Fund Raising

## Richard Steinberg, PhD

*IUPUI (Indiana University—Purdue University at Indianapolis)*

In this chapter, I summarize my scholarly research (and selected works of others) concerning the regulation of fund raising practices and reflect on some implications for practitioners and researchers. First, I lay the groundwork, detailing the regulatory approaches I have considered. Second, I analyze the various rationales offered in support of governmental regulation. Third, I evaluate current approaches and suggested alternatives.

I consider three types of regulations—restraints on fund raising share (the ratio of solicitation expenditures to contributions received), mandated disclosures, and "process" reforms. Direct restraints on fund raising share are clearly unconstitutional under three Supreme Court decisions (Schaumburg,[1] Munson,[2] and Riley[3]), whether posed as a ceiling on the solicitation-expenditure ratio or a floor on the service-expenditure ratio (mission-related expenditures divided by either contributions received or total available revenues). Whether the campaign is conducted using only in-house staff or in collaboration with outside contractors, for-profit or nonprofit, the Court regards share restrictions as overly broad infringements on First Amendment rights whose relevance to substantial state interests has not been shown.

However, the indirect regulation of fund raising share, accomplished through administrative denial of tax-exempt status, may prove to be permissible. To test this theory, the Internal Revenue Service defends its revocation action against a charity alleged to have spent only 4 percent of donations on a charitable program (United Cancer Council v. Commissioner, decision pending at U.S. District Tax Court, hereinafter denoted the UCC case). Perhaps awaiting a decision in this case, legislative proposals have suggested formalizing the procedure. For example, one federal bill proposed in 1987 would require certain charities that solicit contributions from the public to use at least 50 percent of gross receipts for charitable purposes or forfeit their exemption from the federal corporate income tax.

---

[1] *Village of Schaumburg* v. *Citizen for a Better Environment* (440 U.S. 620, 1980).

[2] *Maryland* v. *Joseph H. Munson Co.* (467 U.S. 947, 1984).

[3] *Riley* v. *National Federation of the Blind* (108 S. Ct. 2667, 1988).

Instead of restricting fund raising share, the state may seek to mandate various disclosures by fundseekers—the fund raising share, the use of outside or professional fund raising counsel, the method of compensating fund raising staff (internal and external), and the availability of financial statements and other documents. Some mandated disclosures are unconstitutional (point-of-solicitation disclosure of fund raising percentages), whereas other disclosures are probably permitted (lower courts have upheld the compelled point-of-solicitation disclosure of a solicitor's professional status and required statements that "financial statements are available"). The Constitution does not restrict state speech rights, so government may evaluate fund raising programs and contractors and disseminate the results.

Several "process" reforms will also be considered. Nonprofit boards of directors may be required to seek multiple competitive bids before signing with external fund raising counsel. Alternatively, the opinion of independent legal counsel may be required prior to signing. Board members may be held personally liable for fund raising excesses. This possibility mimics the current proposal for intermediate sanctions, which holds the board liable for approving excessive executive compensation.

## Should Government Regulate Fund Raising?

What is the overriding state interest in regulating fund raising practices? Some argue that the state must protect donors from fraud, inefficiency, or their own folly. Others allege that the state must protect nonprofit organizations from unscrupulous fund raising contractors. Still others argue that society is hurt when scarce resources are wasted on inefficient fund raising practices. Do these rationales provide sufficient reason for state action, and are current and proposed state regulations likely to alleviate these problems?

The fraud and inefficiency arguments are usually intertwined. A high fund raising share is thought to betray the donor's trust that his or her donation will be applied to the furtherance of the organization's asserted charitable mission. This argument has a certain surface plausibility; if, for example, solicitation expenditures are 75 percent of funds raised, a donor might reasonably believe that three-quarters of a contemplated donation would be diverted from mission. If the donor had no reason to expect such a high fund raising share, some regard the solicitation as fraudulent (at least in the passive sense of not providing information that rebuts donor presumptions); even if the high share is widely publicized, the process of converting donations into charitable services appears inefficient. However, on further reflection, I find that there is generally no relation between fund raising share and inefficiency. To look at fund raising share as a measure of inefficiency is rather like looking at a car's speedometer to ascertain the temperature: A different kind of gauge is needed.

The Court noted some of the reasons: Donors are aware that at least some fund raising expenditures are required; prospecting for new donors brings future returns that are not apparent in the fund raising cost ratio; solicitation can foster educational and advocacy missions as well as raise funds; donations of volunteer time are omitted from the denominator of this ratio; and most importantly, the lack of popularity of a cause is not the same as inefficiency or fraud. My chief contribution to the debate is to note the difference between fund raising share, which represents the average success of the whole campaign, and the marginal share, which represents the success of the last dollar donated (Steinberg, 1986a, 1989).

Suppose, for example, that a particular charity has budgeted $1,000 for solicitation and does not adjust that figure up or down as a result of the campaign's success. Then, 100 percent of donations would further the charitable mission. If nobody else donated, my marginal donation would reduce the campaign deficit dollar-for-dollar, freeing the organization from a debt burden that would preclude spending other (or future) resources on its mission. If instead, others donated $1,000, my marginal donation would still allow the campaign to supplement mission-related expenditures dollar-for-dollar. Finally, if others donated $1,000,000, my marginal donation would have the same dollar-for-dollar impact on program expenditures. In each case, 100 percent of my donation is used for services, but note the very different fund raising shares: 100,000 percent, 100 percent, and 0.1 percent, respectively. Clearly, fund raising share cannot tell the whole story.

We need not assume that the solicitation budget is unresponsive to campaign success. Some charities might view early donations as a sign that potential returns are higher than expected, increasing their campaign budget accordingly. In this case, the share of one's gift diverted to fund raising results in increased donations by others, an outcome the initial donor may applaud. If the resulting increment in net donations exceeds the share of the initial donation spent on fund raising, then the initial donor's dollar is leveraged, purchasing more than an additional dollar in mission-related services. Whether one's donation is efficient in this case depends on the response of other donors to marginal increases in fund raising expenditures, not on the fund raising share.

It is also possible that early donations lead to reductions in the campaign budget, as it becomes apparent that the campaign goal can be met with a smaller budget. In this case, the initial impact of my marginal donation would exceed a dollar, but once again I should consider the feedback effect. If other donors were especially responsive to the last dollar spent on solicitation, my donation could be partly or totally neutralized by the response of other donors. On the other hand, if the initial solicitation budget were excessive, the feedback effect works to my advantage. Once again, although with opposite sign, the response of other donors to marginal decreases in fund raising expenditures is critical, and the fund raising share is irrelevant.

There is one special case where the marginal effect is related to fund raising share (Steinberg, 1986b, 1990). If fund raisers receive a fixed share of gross (or net) returns, this compensation share is relevant. This method of recompense, known as "contingent" or "incentive" payments, is generally frowned on in the ethical codes of various societies of professional fund raisers, but is employed by some nonmember firms. To see why contingent-payment shares are relevant, suppose that a solicitor's contract provides payments equal to 25 percent of funds raised regardless of the campaign's success. Then, a given donor would need to donate roughly $1.33 for the charity to spend an additional dollar on its mission. There is no feedback effect, since the $0.33 goes into the solicitor's pocket, rather than the search for additional donors ($1.33 − .25 × 0.33 = $1). However, there is an incentive effect that complicates matters. If this sort of compensation agreement induces the solicitor to work harder, he may obtain more donations from any level of fund raising expenditure. This is largely external to the individual donor, as the $0.33 incentive payment to the solicitor is added on top of the incentive payments from other donors, so that the incremental effort resulting from this payment is vanishingly small.

Although contingent-payment shares are relevant for calculating the efficiency of individual donations, it is important to remember that it is not the realized, after-the-fact, share of donations received by solicitors that is relevant. Regardless of contract terms, one can always calculate a ratio after the fact, but this ratio is only meaningful if it forms the basis for compensation. If solicitors receive a fixed fee (or a fee based on number of mailings or other cost measures, rather than on the success of the campaign), marginal donations are not diverted into solicitor compensation and so are efficiently applied to program.

Consider now the rationale that seeks to protect nonprofit organizations from their own mistakes. Nonprofit board members, inexpert in the nuances of campaigning, might fall prey to unscrupulous fund raising counsel, signing contracts that do not protect organizational interests. Thus, it is argued, honest nonprofit boards ought to support restrictions on fund raising share. Similarly, nonprofits need to be protected from exchanging assets (such as the right to remarket mailing lists) for what appears to be a beneficial contractor concession (such as the guarantee that the contractor will absorb losses in the event the campaign is not successful). These issues arose in the UCC case (Steinberg, 1993) and could, in the future, be raised with respect to other contracting decisions.

The effort to formulate operational rules of good practice is deeply worthwhile, but exceedingly difficult. One can easily characterize efficiency by defining its opposite: a contract is inefficient if there is some alternative feasible contract that would, without compromising ethical standards or the organizational mission, produce the same gross donations at lower costs (or equivalently produce more gross donations for the same cost). To be feasible, these alternative contractual terms must be sufficiently attractive to secure a willing contractor.

Can we formulate operational rules that will protect nonprofit organizations from mistakes of commission (signing bad contracts) while not creating mistakes of omission (by prohibiting the signing of some good contracts)? I do not believe we know nearly enough at this time to do so. The costs of efficient fund raising are highly idiosyncratic, varying with organizational age, mission, press coverage, competition from other fundseekers, scale, experience, perceived levels of need, the economic wellbeing of potential donors and a variety of other factors (Steinberg, 1985, 1991b, 1994; Young & Steinberg, 1995). Charities situated in favorable fund raising environments may be highly inefficient and still secure low fund raising shares, whereas charities advocating unpopular causes or prospecting for new donors will have high fund raising shares (perhaps exceeding 100%) even if they operate at the limits of efficiency.

It seems that with current knowledge, we cannot distinguish a good contract from a bad one with regulatory precision unless we employ a vague facts-and-circumstances test. But we should not allow vague standards to form the basis for public intervention. Laws and regulations, especially those impinging on core speech interests (advocacy and public education), should have a clearly predictable application or speech will be chilled. Vague standards also allow state regulation to be subverted for private interests. For example, it has been alleged that state-level court suits against the Watson and Hughey company were brought because of pressure by large health-research charities seeking to squelch competition from smaller charities.[4] I do not know whether these allegations have merit in the present application, but the example highlights the potential for abuse.

I therefore believe process reforms provide a superior remedy. If nonprofits were required to seek competitive bids and/or the opinion of disinterested counsel before they could sign fund raising contracts, the competitive process would educate nonprofit boards and protect them from errors. State requirements concerning the bidding process provide the clarity and predictable application needed for governmental regulation while allowing contract terms to be decided on a case-by-case basis. In concert with antitrust laws that prohibit bid-rigging and proscriptions on private inurement that prohibit the paying of bribes to nonprofit decision makers, process regulations probably offer the best solution to the problem of unscrupulous fund raising counsel.

That is not to say that competitive bidding is a perfect solution. Each individual nonprofit board should probably seek competitive bids, but a state mandate that massively increased the use of bidding would alter the competitive nature and performance of the contracting industry. Those

---

[4] *The State of Texas* v. *Watson and Hughey Co. et al.*, District Court of Dallas County, Texas, 1991 (settled); *State of Hawaii* v. *Cancer Fund of America, Inc. et al.*, 1991 (settled) or *State of Ohio* v. *Watson and Hughey Co. et al.*, 1990 (settled).

bidding for a contract might be tempted to use subtly misleading or high-pressure solicitation methods in an effort to cut costs and thereby offer lower bids. Honest contractors, who would follow board directives on ethical fund raising practices even when they knew that their compliance could not be observed by the board, would have higher costs and more difficulty winning bids. If the nonprofit board were unable to distinguish whether low bids stem from ethical compromises or contractor efficiencies, it is even possible that all the honest contractors would be driven out of business (Chillemi & Gui, 1990; Kim, 1992; Steinberg & Gray, 1993; Steinberg, forthcoming). More research is needed here; I suspect that requiring competitive bids is nonetheless superior to regulating fund raising outcomes.

Is there a social interest in regulating fund raising? Proponents of regulation cite two kinds of arguments—that high-cost organizations directly waste society's scarce resources and that there is market failure in the fund raising market (Rose-Ackerman, 1982; Steinberg, 1989). The first argument has not received the careful analysis it deserves. Although similar charges have been levied against the other two sectors, do we feel the same way about advertising by for-profit firms or about state lotteries? Advertising is a costly activity that, if all goes well, induces consumers to purchase an item priced, perhaps, at 10 percent more than the cost of production. Lotteries "waste" resources on administration, advertising, and prizes. Are either worse than "wasting" resources on printing and postage in a direct-mail campaign?

Fund raising serves several purposes, so the social value of a campaign cannot be determined by looking only at the ratio of revenues to costs. First, controversial organizations play important political roles despite their necessarily high costs. The social value of, say, an organization in the antebellum South advocating an end to slavery would not be revealed by its fund raising costs. Second, solicitation provides information to potential donors, and this information has value regardless of donor response. An extreme example is provided by a recent American Civil Liberties Union mailing I received. On reading it, I learned more about the organization and decided I would no longer support them until some changes are made. I was glad for the mailing, which had social value in convincing me to *not* donate to something I would otherwise support. Third, charities that seek to compete with established "brand-name" giants (as in United Cancer Council's competition with the American Cancer Society) have social value that is not revealed by their necessarily high costs. Pluralism and innovation are fostered when competing notions of the public good can each find a home. In addition, competition provides a spur that may lead the established giant to improve its operations or to reassess its approach.

The second argument concerns a market failure due to what is known as a "commons externality." Like cattle grazing in the old Boston Commons, solicitation by some organizations thins the donor grass through which other fundseekers must graze. This argument has been used to justify the creation and protection of united fund raising organizations such as

United Way. More recently, Cliff Landesman (1995) applied this argument to donor needs and governmental regulation:

> The percent of income that donors give away has been pretty flat over that last few decades, . . . so practically speaking, it's a fixed pie. Money spent on marketing one organization can convince donors to give less to other organizations. [Thus], if a donor wishes to not just help one organization fight hunger, but help fight hunger generally, then she *should* pay attention to fund-raising ratios in an effort to limit the spending organizations' waste in competing for market share. . . . [These] externalities . . . may not only justify government regulation or coordinated campaigns, but also individual donors disciplining organizations by penalizing ones with excessive fund-raising expenditures.

The chief problem with this argument is that the wrong parties are being punished. The fund raising-cost ratio bears no necessary relationship to the size of the market failure created by the commons externality. Although we do not have solid research one way or the other on the subject, I would guess that the impact of one campaign on the difficulty of raising funds in other campaigns depends primarily on the size of the first campaign. Thus, a comparatively low-cost campaign by the giant American Cancer Society may have larger detrimental side-effects than a high-cost campaign by its smaller rivals like United Cancer Council. Imagine how much easier it would be for a new organization of any sort to raise funds if there were no United Way, no American Heart Association, no American Cancer Society. The externality argument for regulation must be used with caution if it is used at all.

Further complications arise when we consider externalities across charities of vastly different types. Political fund raising by one candidate has obvious external effects on the opposition, simultaneously depleting a portion of the donor pool, expanding the opposition donor pool (when the first candidate, by virtue of fund raising success, is viewed as a threat that must be dealt with), and expanding the urgency of fund raising for the opposition. If I, a Democrat, felt that spending by the Democratic party decreased the efficiency of Republican fund raising, I would count this as a benefit, not a cost. Much of the competition between nonprofits for funds comes from fields where ideas about the proper output are contested, so this example is not vanishingly rare.

If, nonetheless, one decides that the commons externality provides a basis for regulation, this does not imply that individual donors have a cause for action. There is a difference between private and social interests here, and individuals who follow their own interest work against the solution to the externality. To see this, suppose that I liked a particular charity because I felt that no other charity was suitably addressing a particular problem, but that this charity had high fund raising costs (presumably because others disagree with me about the importance or efficiency of this charity's work). Were I to "punish" the charity by not giving the paltry sum I typically contribute, other donors would not follow my example and the charity would not have a strong incentive to change its practices. All that would happen is that less would be spent in support of a cause I care about. If, instead, I could successfully convince every other donor to "punish" this charity, I would still care for the charity and now that they had lower costs, I would want to give myself. Cooperation breaks down without a coordinating mechanism larger than the individual—either state action, or perhaps collective action through interorganizational agreements such as those employed by United Ways.

The final argument here supporting the regulation of fund raising costs is that there is public demand for such regulation. Putnam Barber (1995) put it this way:

> The "beneficial ratio" approach to measuring the worthwhileness of organizations making appeals is a pretty weak reed. . . . Yet it is looked to with fervor by many donors, and strongly endorsed by many leaders at the intersection between politics and charity. The ratio is, of course, least likely to embarrass a large, established organization raising funds for a widely supported cause. Hence, I suppose, its appeal to those for whom the established order works pretty well. [However,] I've had no luck at all complaining about the "benefit ratio" without anything to offer as a substitute.

Similarly, Charles Heying (1995) argues:

> Steinberg's caveats. . . . do not address the need by the public for a simple measure for making choices with extremely limited information. The various "payout ratios" are probably inadequate, but they do provide a rough comparative measure. The need for such measures is not being underestimated by fund raisers who, if my mail is any indication, are increasingly citing "payout ratios" in their solicitations.

This is a problem for which I have no good solution. The public is hungry for sound-bite news stories and appeals, and a skeptical public is unlikely to pay attention to lengthy explanations that high fund raising costs are warranted in a particular instance. However, I do think there is merit in showing leadership and trying to educate the public. Too many in the nonprofit sector prefer to marginalize those whose costs are necessarily high, throwing them to the wolves as "not like us." Feeding this wolf, in my mind, will only make it hungrier, and in light of the externality argument, today's established charities may be tomorrow's high-cost sacrificial lambs. This issue deserves much more discussion and analysis.

## Harmful Side-Effects of Regulation

In this section, I consider those side-effects common to alternative government regulatory strategies that key on the fund raising cost ratio, summarizing my earlier work (see Steinberg, 1991a). Whether high-cost charities are outlawed, denied tax-exempt status, or are publicly derided through press releases, the common effect is to pressure charities to cut their costs. This creates a number of distortions that weigh against any benefits to such regulation.

First, there are compliance and regulatory costs. Mandating expenditures on an external audit, bonding of fund raising staff, and legal fees may be worthwhile, but the immediate impact is counterproductive, raising the cost ratio. The disparate and changing registration, approval, reporting, and licensing requirements of the various states and localities make interstate campaigns even more expensive, forcing the hiring of costly full-time specialists or the abandonment of interstate campaigns. Some sort of model fund raising code, if universally adopted, would ameliorate these costs, but some costs are inherent in any centralized regulatory scheme.

Second, it becomes more difficult to maintain the integrity of the campaign because misleading, high-pressure, and intrusive tactics can yield a high rate of return. Under the threat of prosecution, taxation, or concerted adverse publicity, organizations in difficult fund raising environments may compromise their integrity and utilize otherwise unacceptable techniques.

Third, attention to this false indicator of efficiency may lower the real efficiency of fund raising. Volunteers appear to be costless in an accounting sense, so that one can lower the apparent cost of fund raising by allocating all available volunteers to the campaign. However, volunteers are a scarce resource, and there is a substantial opportunity cost when using them for any particular purpose—one loses the opportunity to employ them elsewhere. If volunteers are used for fund raising when they are more efficient as service deliverers, and paid staff are used for service delivery when they are more efficient as fund raisers, the real efficiency of both the campaign and service delivery will suffer. The opportunity cost would be even greater if some of the available volunteers disliked fund raising, and quit in response to the reallocation.

The efficiency of prospecting campaigns would also be hurt. Prospecting is a very high cost activity if one ignores its investment aspect—a new donor, once located, can be induced to continue giving for many years by fairly low annual expenditures on donor retention. Even long-established organizations may require a major new prospecting effort due to changing circumstances, and it would be best to get this prospecting over with as soon as possible to secure maximal returns next year. However, in an effort to keep the overall cost ratio low, these nonprofits might spread their campaigns out over many years, inefficiently delaying their fund acquisition.

## Conclusions

There are some prima facie reasons to regulate fund raising practices and contracts, but it is difficult to relate these ends to the means most commonly chosen. Fund raising cost ratios do not provide useful information to donors, nonprofit boards, or regulators. Regulation premised on these ratios is unlikely to help, and has unintended but deleterious side-effects. Political forces and common intuitions have led to prosecution on the basis of costs because of the need to be seen to be doing something, however imperfect, to stop abuses.

To my mind, better solutions can be found through mandated reforms in the process of nonprofit board decision making. In addition, existing laws and regulations prohibiting collusion, fraud, and private inurement are more appropriate remedies. Policymakers and regulators would better serve the public by refining antitrust, fraud, and nonprofit corporation statutes and enforcement procedures. I do not think the public objects to high-cost fund raising when this cost is essential to attaining the organization's mission; they just figure that high costs are probably a sign of someone profiting excessively from something that is supposed to be altruistic. Bid-rigging, bribes, distributions of profit to those who select fund raising counsel, and the like can be directly prosecuted, and evidence on fund-raising cost ratios will not be needed for this sort of action.

Regulators object that it is costly and difficult to prosecute fraud and inurement cases. One could probably rack up more convictions if allowed to prosecute on the basis of fund raising share, but those convicted would not necessarily be guilty and many of the guilty would go free. And even if the costs of prosecution are lower under share restrictions, the costs to society of this strategy would be high. In addition to enforcement costs, the social costs of share regulation include specified compliance costs, efficiency costs, and increased use of high-pressure and misleading fund raising appeals. To paraphrase and distort Barry Goldwater, thoughtless extremism in pursuit of vice is no virtue.

## Bibliography

Barber, Putnam. 1995. Electronic mail discussion conducted via ARNOVA-L list-serve. Archived at wvnvm.wvnet.edu.

Chillemi, Ottorino, and Gui, Benedetto. *Uninformed Customers and Nonprofit Organizations: Modelling "Contract Failure Theory"* (Working Paper). Trieste, Italy: University of Trieste, Department of Economics and Statistics. 1990.

Heying, Charles. 1995. Electronic mail discussion conducted via ARNOVA-L list-serve. Archived at wvnvm.wvnet.edu

Kim, In-Gyu. *On the Use of Selective Tendering in the Procurement Market* (Working Paper). Blacksburg: VPI Dept. of Economics, 1992.

Landesman, Cliff. 1995. Electronic mail discussion conducted via the ARNOVA-L list-serve. Archived at wvnvm.wvnet.edu.

Rose-Ackerman, Susan. "Charitable Giving and 'Excessive' Fundraising." *Quarterly Journal of Economics,* 1982, 97, 195–212.

Steinberg, Richard. "Competition in Contracted Markets." In *Selling Public Services.* Ed. Perri 6. Hants (U.K.): Arena/Ashgate Publishers. Forthcoming.

Steinberg, Richard. "Economic Perspectives on Regulation of Charitable Solicitation." *Case Western Reserve Law Review,* 1989, 39(3), 775–797.

Steinberg, Richard. "Economics and Philanthropy: A Marriage of Necessity for Nonprofit Organizations." In *New Directions for Philanthropic Fundraising,* 3, Eds. Jim Greenfield and Robert Fogel. *Fund Raising Economics,* 1994.

Steinberg, Richard. "Optimal Contracts Need Not Be Contingent: The Case of Nonprofit Firms." In *Models of Health and Human Services in the Nonprofit Sector: Chapters Presented at the 1986 AVAS Conference.* Eds. Drew Hyman and Kurt Parkum. 1986b. Indianapolis: ARNOVA.

Steinberg, Richard "Optimal Fundraising by Nonprofit Firms." *Giving and Volunteering: New Frontiers of Knowledge.* Washington, DC: INDEPENDENT SECTOR and United Way of America, 1985.

Steinberg, Richard. "Profits and Incentive Compensation in Nonprofit Firms." *Nonprofit Management and Leadership,* 1990, 1(2), 137–152.

Steinberg, Richard. *Regulation of Charity Fundraising: Unintended Consequences* (Working Paper). Indianapolis: Indiana University Center on Philanthropy, 1991a.

Steinberg, Richard. "Should Donors Care about Fundraising?" In *The Economics of Nonprofit Institutions: Studies in Structure and Policy.* Ed. Susan Rose-Ackerman. New York: Oxford University Press, 1986a.

Steinberg, Richard. "The Economics of Fundraising." In *Taking Fund Raising Seriously.* Eds. Dwight Burlingame and Monty Hulse. San Francisco: Jossey-Bass, 1991b.

Steinberg, Richard. *United Cancer Council v. Commissioner of the IRS and the Indirect Regulation of Fundraising* (Working Paper). Indianapolis: Indiana University Center on Philanthropy, 1993.

Steinberg, Richard, and Gray, Bradford H. "The Role of Nonprofit Enterprise in 1992: Hansmann Revisited." *Nonprofit and Voluntary Sector Quarterly,* 1993, 22, 4, 297–316.

Young, Dennis R., and Steinberg, Richard. *Economics for Nonprofit Managers.* New York: Foundation Center Press, 1995.

# PART VI

# What's Next

# Bowling Together

## Fund Raising Practices and Civic Engagement

JON PRATT

*Minnesota Council of Nonprofits*

*I am trying to imagine under what novel features despotism may appear in the world. In the first place, I see an innumerable multitude of men, alike and equal, constantly circling around in pursuit of the petty and banal pleasures with which they glut their souls. Each one of them, withdrawn into himself, is almost unaware of the fate of the rest. Mankind, for him, consists in his children and his personal friends. As for the rest of his fellow citizens, they are near enough, but he does not notice them. He touches them but feels nothing. He exists in and for himself, and though he may have a family, one can at least say that he does not have a [community].*

—Alexis de Tocqueville on "What sort of despotism democratic nations have to fear," *Democracy in America* (1988, p. 690)

Tocqueville was right to be pessimistic about the future of democracy. Modern economies provide thousands of alternatives and distractions. The good news, to the extent that Tocqueville found it, was that America has two institutions capable of countering the tendency toward isolation: local government and voluntary associations.

The hope for voluntary associations to build the vitality of democracy is often promoted in the United States, and is especially keen in the new democracies of Europe. From the Czech Republic and Russia to Romania, local organizers have hailed developing the "civil society" as an essential ingredient in successful democracies.

If Tocqueville was right, then it is important to analyze the civic condition of the nonprofit sector. While nonprofit expenditures and employment have grown at four times the rate of the overall U.S. economy since 1970, a new analysis argues that Americans are substantially less involved and more isolated than 30 years ago, and that direct participation in a wide range of nonprofits has been on a steady decline.

## Declining Participation in Public Life

In an essay titled "Bowling Alone," Robert Putnam begins by making a strong case for the importance of individual involvement:

> [He cites] a wide range of empirical evidence that the quality of public life and the performance of social institutions are indeed powerfully influenced by norms and networks of civic engagement. Researchers in such fields as education, urban poverty, unemployment, the control of crime and drug abuse, and even health have discovered that successful outcomes are more likely in civically engaged communities. (Putnam, 1995, p. 66)

Putnam goes on to document a decline in U.S. civic engagement, from voter turnout (down 25% since the 1960s) to attending public meetings on town or school affairs (down 33%). Fewer Americans report that they trust the government, churchgoing is down, union membership has dropped by half, and even though more people are bowling than ever before, league bowling decreased by 40 percent between 1980 and 1993(!). According to Putnam, "Similar reductions are apparent in the number of volunteers for mainline civic organizations, such as Boy Scouts (off by 26% since 1970) and the Red Cross (off by 61% since 1970)" (Putnam, 1995, p. 69). While some organizations have added millions of dues-paying members (NOW, AARP, and the Sierra Club), Putnam describes these as "tertiary" organizations in which the members seldom meet or greet one another, but simply write a check.

The possible reasons cited by Putnam include the movement of women into the labor force, increased mobility, fewer children, more divorces, and the "technological transformation of leisure" (e.g., the TV and VCR replacing the PTA; Putnam, 1995).

## Nonprofits' Role in Civic Life

Putnam is only one of many that have remarked on the decline in public life, though the National Civic League (a Denver-based organization formed in 1884 to promote good government and citizen participation) is less pessimistic and has the beginning of an action plan. Last November the Civic League and its chair, John W. Gardner, announced the start of the "Alliance for National Renewal," a project to mobilize Americans to become involved in their communities. The Alliance includes 100 national "stakeholder" organizations, a veritable Who's who of national U.S. coalitions ranging from the AARP and Habitat for Humanity to the National Urban League and the Center for Community Change.

The relationship between organizations and the people they serve is a key difference between nonprofits and for-profits. Given the size and history of the nonprofit sector, one would assume that the differences in service effectiveness between nonprofits, for-profits, and government would be well documented, but they are not. Studies have shown, however, that:

- Nonprofit child care tends to be of higher quality than for-profit child-care chains (Wittbrook, 1989).
- Nonprofit nursing homes use less behavior control drugs than for-profit nursing homes (Weisbrod, 1988).
- Nonprofit vocational training has lower loan default rates than for-profit vocational training (U.S. Department of Education, 1983).
- Nonprofit housing experiences fewer tenant-caused damages than private or government rental housing (Morse, 1990).
- Clients of nonprofit service agencies report that they feel better treated than clients of government agencies.

While nonprofits provide many valuable services, and are efficient and effective service providers, the essence of the nonprofit sector is not simply service provision. Every service delivered by a nonprofit could be delivered by a private enterprise. A key reason nonprofits are needed is their role in engaging the individual citizen.

Bob Johnson made this point in *The First Charity* (1988), in which he reported on community organizations in Baltimore, Denver, and Chicago. *The First Charity* set out five expectations for participation in a democracy:

1. Protection from tyranny.
2. Reconciliation of private individual concerns with public community concerns.
3. Invigoration of the individual citizen.
4. Inclusion of everyone in public life.
5. Maintenance of a satisfying representative government.

According to Johnson, an effective nonprofit is not simply one that has a positive cash flow, but one that has an inclusive, diverse community board, collaborates with others in the community, is involved in public policy issues that affect its clientele, brings people together, and invigorates the community.

As organizations explore how to promote civic engagement, we need to ask whether any of the following changes in the nonprofit sector may have decreased its function as a source of civic involvement:

- Increased reliance on paid staff.
- Importation of standard business management techniques through management schools and corporate consultants.
- Recruitment of board members to maximize revenues, not participation (often failing the "zip code" test, according to John McKnight—do the decision makers have the same zip codes as the intended beneficiaries?).
- Lack of attention to benefits of participation.

- Adopting a service model that sees citizens as customers, clients, or donors (the financial relationship) rather than constituents.

To his credit, business guru Peter Drucker says he resisted using the customer terminology in nonprofit settings because he saw it as foreign to the charitable sector (1993). In the end, he decided to use the word anyway because of its shock value: to jar organizations into thinking about how to be accountable to the people they serve. In Jane Smiley's new book, *Moo* (1995), about power politics and misuse of grant funds on a university campus, the arch villain is an economics professor who refers to students as "customers" and champions a market philosophy the author implies is antithetical to the schools' mission. Consultants now crowd around nonprofits offering to conduct "customer assessments" in focus groups or surveys. For some organizations, the biggest meeting that discusses the organization's direction is held at a board or staff meeting, facilitated by a consultant.

In a follow-up Minnesota Nonprofit Assistance Fund study on the financial health of nonprofits, Susan Stevens found that organizations' 1994 budgets were more solid than four years ago, but that the organizations more detached from the communities they served. In a report named after one of the key recommendations, "Refocusing on Community," Stevens was surprised to learn that only 9 percent of nonprofit managers saw their clients as an important catalyst for change, while 86 percent saw themselves, their staff, or their boards in this role.

## Fund Raising and the Decline in Participation

The nonprofit sector represents only 5 percent of the U.S. Gross Domestic Product, and has historically been characterized by low wages, lack of access to capital, and constant worrying about income. It is understandable that an industry under chronic financial stress would embrace technologies that dramatically improve cash flow, and would seek to justify the side effects by the funds they raise. As a result, nonprofits have gone to the bank with direct mail, telephone solicitation, payroll deduction, cause related marketing, prospect research and planned giving without a great deal of worry about levels of direct participation.

U.S. nonprofits have long employed a variety of techniques, from simple direct solicitation to a wide range of special events, dues and membership systems, bingo, paddle wheels, tip boards, lotteries, and other games of chance, many of which cannot be said to enhance democracy. However, these fund raising modes at least involved personal contact.

For most organizations, the use of modern marketing techniques in fund raising is a prudent response to a changing society. The modern nonprofit sector's use of these methods to raise funds often disassociates the donor from direct involvement in the organization's day-to-day activities. These impersonal fund raising techniques, using direct mail, prospect research, and telemarketing firms to locate and recruit members and donors, have helped organizations increase their donations without increasing other types of participation.

As Putnam points out, there is a cost to society of the decreased participation opportunities of "tertiary" associations, and by extension a cost to the nonprofit sector. Public perceptions of nonprofit organizations are changing as involvement is increasingly remote, and there is a risk that historic justifications for property tax exemptions, low postal rates, and deductibility of contributions will strike the public as antique.

Much of the growth in fund raising is in methods that generate income yet have little or no impact on direct participation. These effective but impersonal fund raising approaches are seen as practical responses to a busy and changing society, but create little stake in the organization or social connectedness for the individual.

## DIRECT MAIL AND TELEMARKETING

Direct-mail solicitation is the most frequent contact many Americans have with charitable organizations. Direct mail and telemarketing are used because they are relatively inexpensive ways to prospect for and resolicit contributors. Each year, Congress allocates about $450 million to support nonprofit postal rates in the broadest direct subsidy for charitable activity.

Over the past five years, Congress has been concerned about excessive commercialism in nonprofit mailings and has placed content restrictions on the use of postal subsidies by limiting nonprofit marketing of travel and insurance. A large but unmeasured portion of federal mail subsidy is expended for "mega mailers," organizations that owe their size to large-scale direct mail with narrow margins of net income. For these organizations, the vast majority of donors' contributions are eaten up by mailing costs. The mailing organizations allocate much of these costs as program expenditures, generally citing the educational content of the letter or brochure.

Some organizations are so dependent on direct-mail contributions that without the postal subsidy their direct mail would generate a loss. Taking this use of the mail to its illogical extreme, the Mays Mission for the Handicapped in Arkansas has defined its direct-mail operation as the mission of the organization. "Handicapped" persons are hired to assemble ballpoint pens used in direct-mail solicitation, and are given "job training" to "run printing presses, run an assembly line and run inserter equipment and perform data processing" (House Committee, 1991). Mays Mission sends out mail to raise funds to hire handicapped persons to send out mail, so all of the mail expenses could be considered program. Mays Mission was a featured organization in the testimony of the Nonprofit Mailers Federation, serving as an exemplary use of subsidized mail, at a hearing November 19, 1991, before the House Committee on Post Office and Civil Service.

What is the public benefit received from this expenditure, and what is the relationship of the donors to the organization? In two recent cases of direct-mail hyperbole, the World Wildlife Fund and the National Rifle Association both justified widely criticized appeals as being above average in raising resources for their organizations. In direct mail, like daytime talk shows, shock value may attract a bigger audience and donor base, by involving people as spectators and distant supporters instead of direct participants.

## COMMERCIALISM

In its 1987–1988 production of *The Nutcracker*, the Boston Ballet offered corporate sponsors a $20,000 opportunity to sponsor a performance, and in exchange be allowed to promote its products or services to the ballet's audience. During the performance sponsored by BMW, the automobile manufacturer's newest car model was parked in the lobby of the Wang Center.

Another sponsor paid for a dancing bear to be added to the performance, an animal not usually associated with *The Nutcracker*. The bear's floppy red nightcap bore a striking resemblance to those worn by the two bear mascots of Filene's, the Boston retailer, that were outside in the lobby mingling with ballet patrons. A number of the play's characters, including the bear, toured Filene's stores as the "Nutcracker Players" to help promote the play.

The McDonald's corporation has organized Ronald McDonald Children's Charities to provide temporary housing for children and their families during a serious illness of the child. The charity is named after the restaurant chain's mascot, effectively promoting the public image and visibility of the for-profit and is actively promoted by the corporation.

Both cases represent successful cross-promotion, but blur the distinction between nonprofit and for-profit activity. Both cases represent technical compliance with the law yet stretch the definition of an organization sworn to be *organized* exclusively for charitable purposes.

There is a serious question about what the long-term effect is on public perceptions of joint promotions, product tie-ins, official corporate sponsors. At some point, the dissonance of combining a charitable and a commercial message will change the perception of the charitable cause, somewhat like the adverse public reaction to Aramony's limousines or the Points of Light Foundation paying celebrities to lecture the rest of us about the rewards of volunteering.

## PLANNED GIVING

In this area, there is face-to-face contact between the organization and the public. At death, people have the potential to make the largest gifts of their lives. As a result, many nonprofit organizations have hired staff and consultants to conduct "Planned Giving" campaigns (perhaps more accurately described as "planned receiving") to seek contributions from Americans with substantial estates at death. Closed probate case files in Minnesota (Minnesota Charitable, 1992, p. 17) and a recent article in the *Chronicle of Philanthropy* (1995, p. 1) reveal a growing number of contested wills, where family members are charging that representatives of organizations have exercised undue influence over vulnerable persons.

Practices include multiple visits by representatives of organizations to the homes and hospital rooms of elderly people, befriending of potential donors through social calls, performing of personal favors such as driving elderly people to the doctor or picking up prescriptions, drafting of wills by attorneys for an organization, referrals to lawyers selected by the organizations, and other actions that involve organizational representatives in the personal lives of people identified as having substantial estates. Some workshops term this practice "friendraising," suggesting a boundary-straddling role for the planned giving professional, or argue that the true "client" of the planned giving officer is not their institutional sponsor but the charitable intent of the prospective donor.

California has restricted bequests and lifetime gifts to home healthcare aides, and several states have investigated hearing aid sales firms for exploiting lonely elderly persons. A recent news story told of a Dennis Vaughn who expects to inherit $250,000 from an elderly women he has cared for over several years. A lawyer for a local charity thinks otherwise. (*Minneapolis Star Tribune*, 1993, p. 4D) "The lawyer wrote the will, and he says I'm not in it. I have a copy and I am," Vaughn said.

A growing number of surprised relatives are learning late in the process of the number and personal nature of planned giving visits, and the prospect over the media's field day over "charitable gigolos," "ghouling for dollars," or "night of the giving dead" is frightening. Some of the planned giving donors are involved in the causes to which they will bequeath, but many are in a closed loop of solicitous attention of development departments, insulated from the operations or governance of the organizations.

The Shriners' Hospitals for Crippled Children and related organizations recently stated their position that they will go to court to fight any family members contesting the charitable bequests (*Chronicle of Philanthropy*, 1995, p. 23). The Shriners have suffered one of the most dramatic declines in membership among the groups cited by Putnam, and appear not to fear alienating current young members.

## Commodotizing Donors

The cost of fund raising, personal preference, and practical limits on people's available time mean that a limited number of people will become frequent direct participants. There are financial and management incentives to generate income without complicating governance.

There is a connection between giving and volunteering, and a large part of the active volunteers and donors are eligible for AARP membership. We need to know more about the relationship between giving and participation, and to pay attention to generational aspects of involvement.

In many ways, we are now reaping the generosity of a generation that has been very involved in their communities, and who believes in devoting a portion of their private wealth to our common interest. It is hard to argue with success, and depersonalized fund raising is succeeding, even among people actively engaged in their communities. The danger is somewhat like the successes of clear-cutting old growth forests or overfishing the Grand Banks—using modern fund raising technology to achieve economic success over the short run at the expense of the future.

What will characterize future donors and citizens, and how involved do they expect to be? Amid the discussion of donor motivation, we should also look at other aspects of human behavior and at the quality of involvement in our organizations. It is worth thinking about a sustainable ecology of citizens directly involved in and financially supporting the organizations they care about.

## Enhancing Nonprofit's Civic Capacity

For nonprofits to take their role in a democracy seriously, they need to create civic values, practices, and expectations within their own institutions. Though the community organizing role has received too little attention or funding in the past decade, engaging people is what nonprofits are good at. The organizing role is not just for neighborhood groups or issue coalitions, however, but should be a part of what every nonprofit does. Some of the steps nonprofits can take:

- Strategically organize and recruit for public meetings, promoting face-to-face involvement in discussion, not just customer surveys.
- Put more resources into organizing and less into direct mail and telemarketing.
- Post board meeting times and locations and open the meetings to the public, and select board members from nearby zip codes.
- Reduce the barriers between neighborhood groups, human services, and the arts, and promote one another's events.
- Encourage voter participation by educating, cajoling, and driving people to the polls.
- Be intentional about staff and board development that increases the civic capacity of their own organization.
- Challenge members to contribute solutions to problems they have defined.

The nonprofit sector's best "customer" is an engaged citizen. Those are the people that volunteer, donate, come to board meetings, prevent crime, nurture their children, know their neighbors, and vote. Nonprofits and their fund raising techniques are not the cause of increased social isolation, but can be an important part of the cure. Changes in society have made that job both harder and more important.

"Bowling Alone" deserves a careful reading by anyone interested in the nonprofit sector. Civic engagement is one of the most important defining features of organizations—that which distinguishes nonprofits from ATT and McDonald's. Nonprofit boards and managers need to make certain that the means of obtaining funds does not undermine one of the principal reasons the nonprofit sector exists.

## Bibliography

"Charities Lawsuit Dilemma: Groups Are Hesitant to Sue Donors Who Renege on Pledges, but Reluctance May Cost Millions." *Chronicle of Philanthropy,* March 9, 1995, 7(10), pp. 1, 23.

Drucker, Peter. *Videorecording.* New York: The Peter F. Drucker Foundation, 1993.

House Committee on Post Office and Civil Service, November 19, 1991.

Johnson, Robert M. *The First Charity.* Cabin John, MD: Seven Locks Press, 1988.

Minnesota Council of Nonprofits. *Minnesota Charitable Bequest Study.* 1992.

Morse, A. Conversation on October 23, 1990, with the Consumer Insurance Cooperative Agency, Minneapolis, MN.

Putnam, Robert D. "Bowling Alone." *Journal of Democracy,* Jan. 1995, 6, 1, pp. 65–78.

Smiley, Jane. *Moo.* New York: Knopf, 1995.

Stevens, Susan. *Refocusing on Community.* Minneapolis: Minnesota Nonprofit Assistance Fund, 1994.

Tocqueville, Alexis de. *Democracy in America.* Ed. J. P. Mayer. New York: Harper & Row, 1988.

U.S. Department of Education. *Status of National Direct Student Loan Defaults as of June 30, 1982.* Washington, DC: Office of Student Financial Assistance, 1983.

Weisbrod, B. A. *The Nonprofit Economy.* Cambridge, MA: Harvard University Press, 1988.

"Will Easy St. Be the Next Stop? It Depends on the Beneficiary." *Minneapolis Star Tribune,* June 27, 1993, p. 4D.

Wittbrook, M. *National Child Care Staffing Study.* Oakland, CA: Child Care Employee Project, 1989.

# 16 ▼ Critical Issues for Research

## Dwight F. Burlingame, PhD, CFRE
*Indiana University Center on Philanthropy*

The "Think Tank on Fund-Raising Research" participants included an unusual array of 14 scholars, 20 senior fund raising practitioners and 4 association executives (all of whom had conducted or fostered research), who discussed and debated 21 papers presented in advance. The conference was devoted to seven theme areas, each of which was represented by a major paper and one to three supporting commentaries. Under each theme area, I have included the key research questions that emerged from the presentations and discussions. Many of the research interests have been integrated into the new Research Agenda distributed by NSFRE. It is anticipated that other professional associations in the field will also encourage work on these issues.

The practicality of a good theory based on sound research and tested in the field is self-evident. This observation applies well to the current state of fund raising research. Much of the research is in flux and in fact our thinking about what is needed can also be characterized as in flux. As a result, the development of the fund raising profession is in need of better information and analyses of the critical issues facing it.

The framework used to categorize the following questions is not necessarily the right way. It is however, the way the Think Tank participants responded and reacted to the issues in the field. For consistency, I have included them in the order that they were presented at the conference.

### Demographics of Giving or the Community Determinants of Giving

- In what ways should research tracking national patterns of giving be expanded?
- What are the various forms in which giving takes place in diverse communities and how do they inform our understanding of philanthropy and fund raising?
- How can research be developed further on the impact of giving on local communities?
- How can research be expanded to increase our understanding of donors over time?
- What social policy research on philanthropy responds critically to political thinking?

256

- How and when can comparable international databases be developed?
- What defines philanthropy in the various indigenous traditions around the world?
- How do cultural contexts affect fund raising activity?
- How can additional comparative studies on issues of fund raising practices be developed that will aid to understanding what fund raising professionals do or might do better?
- What, if any, are the characteristics distinguishing small or grassroots or ethnic not-for-profit organizations from majority-orientated not-for-profit organizations in operations and fund raising?

## Financial and Management Issues

- How does fund raising relate to overall resource issues in charitable organizations?
- How can the effectiveness of fund raising be measured other than by just dollars; how should it be measured?
- What are the effects of not-for-profit organizations' reliance on market-based revenues on their charitable missions?
- What policies should guide not-for-profit agencies in maintaining, growing, or spending down their endowments?
- What variables in fund raising should be utilized in evaluating the cost of fund raising?
- When do traditional fund raising models not work, and why?
- How is fund raising management affected by ethnic and/or cultural traditions?

## Motivation of Donors

- In addition to the current emphasis on motivation, should other mobilizing factors be examined?
- How can population studies on giving be improved to assist in distinguishing between the more important and less important determinants of charitable giving?
- What additional segmented analyses of giving for different parts of our population (including ethnic and racial groups) are needed?
- What additional analyses of sectoral giving should be undertaken to aid understanding of the determinants of nonreligious giving in general and in particular?
- What can causal path analyses add to the understanding of giving as the outcome of a series of influences and forces?
- What effect do changes in tax law have on giving?
- What micro- and macromeasures of the capacity to give might be developed that focus on a combination of discretionary wealth and discretionary income?

- What are the connections between giving and volunteering in traditions across the globe?

## Impact of Government and Public Policy

- How can the social value of fund raising programs be measured and translated to policymakers?
- What is the scope of the problem that fund raising regulation is attempting to control?
- What are affects of different legal frameworks on fund raising?
- How should a fund raiser be defined and differentiated in the context of regulation?
- What fund raising practices foster philanthropy and promote public trust?
- What is needed to understand others who work in similar fields within the broader context of philanthropy?

## Equity and Ethical Issues

- How can fund raising balance the perceived conflicts between diversity and equity?
- What ethical decisions do fund raisers face? What ethical standards do they see as relevant to their work?
- How do demographic variables affect ethical perception and conduct among fund raisers?
- What are the donor perceptions of fund raising ethics? What responsibility does the fund raising profession/professional have to shape those perceptions?
- What are the ethical dimensions of "potential donor" research?
- What has been the history of attention to fund raising ethics?
- Why are people participating less in not-for-profit organizations today, what are the generational aspects of involvement and giving, and what are the moral issues we must address in these trends?

## The Fund Raising Profession

- How has fund raising evolved, and what are the historical implications for the practice?
- In what ways do the social, political and economic contexts in which fund raisers work influence how they practice and what they accomplish?
- How does the organizational environment (subcommunities of a larger moral community) affect the profession of fund raising?
- What does or should the professional fund raising community look like in its makeup, its standards, and its practices?

- How do comparative studies of fund raising practice in other localities add to our understanding of what fund raising professionals do or might do better?
- What does or should the professional fund raising community look like in its makeup, its standards, and its practices?
- What is the impact of organizational mission and dynamics on the character of the fund raising profession?

# Appendix

## Participant List

*Think Tank on Fund Raising Research*

Dianne A. Brehmer, PhD
Santa Fe Chamber Music Festival

Marianne G. Briscoe, PhD, ACFRE
Hayes/Briscoe Associates

Dwight F. Burlingame, PhD, CFRE
Indiana University Center on
    Philanthropy

Stephen L. Calvert, PhD
Carnegie Mellon University

Paul Chewning, EdD
Council for Advancement and
    Support of Education

Sandra C. Danforth, PhD, CFRE
Consultant

Margaret A. Duronio, PhD
University of Pittsburgh

Marilyn Fischer, PhD
University of Dayton

Robert Fogal, PhD, CFRE
OPRS Foundation

Susan L. Golden, PhD, CFRE
The Golden Group

James Greenfield, CFRE, FAHP
Hoag Memorial Hospital
    Presbyterian

Bruce Hopkins, JD, LLM
Powers, Pyles, & Sutter, PC

Warren F. Ilchman, PhD
Indiana University Center on
    Philanthropy

Robert R. Jennings, PhD
Albany State College

Ann Kaplan
American Association of Fund
    Raising Council

Kathleen S. Kelly, PhD, CFRE,
    APR
University of Southwestern
    Louisiana

Patricia F. Lewis, CFRE
National Society of Fund Raising
    Executives

Joseph Mixer, PhD, CFRE
Consultant

George J. Mongon, CFRE
Consultant

Jack R. Ohle
Drake University

Michael O'Neill, PhD
University of San Francisco

Barbara Owens
Tuskegee University

Jon Pratt
Minnesota Council of Nonprofits

Paul Pribbenow, PhD, CFRE
School of the Art Institute of
   Chicago

Paul Schervish, PhD
Boston College

Richard Steinberg, PhD
Indiana University—Purdue
   University at Indianapolis

Charles Stephens, CFRE
Indiana University Center on
   Philanthropy

Eugene R. Tempel, EdD, CFRE
Indiana University—Purdue
   University at Indianapolis

Stefan Toepler
Johns Hopkins University

Lilya Wagner, PhD, CFRE
National Association for
   Community Leadership

Cathlene Williams, PhD
National Society of Fund Raising
   Executives

Marjorie A. Winkler, ACFRE
Neighborhood Reinvestment
   Corporation

Julian Wolpert, PhD
Woodrow Wilson School-Princeton
   University

Ernest W. Wood, EdD, CFRE
Ernest W. Wood & Associates

Dennis Young, PhD
Case Western Reserve University

# Index